Dinner Roles

Dinner Roles

AMERICAN WOMEN
AND CULINARY CULTURE

Sherrie A. Inness

University of Iowa Press ℩ Iowa City

University of Iowa Press, Iowa City 52242
Copyright © 2001 by the University of Iowa Press
Printed in the United States of America

Design by Erin Kirk New

www.uiowapress.org

The publication of this book was generously supported by the
University of Iowa Foundation.

I wish to acknowledge the University of Pennsylvania Press for
permission to include a revised version of a previously published
work: Sherrie A. Inness, "'The Enchantment of Mixing-Spoons':
Cooking Lessons for Boys and Girls," in Kitchen Culture in
America: Popular Representations of Food, Gender, and Race,
ed. Sherrie A. Inness (Philadelphia: University of Pennsylvania
Press, 2001).

Printed on acid-free paper

Library of Congress Cataloging-in-Publication Data
Inness, Sherrie A.
Dinner roles: American women and culinary culture / Sherrie A.
Inness.
    p.   cm.
Includes bibliographical references and index.
ISBN 0-87745-762-X (cloth), ISBN 0-87745-763-8 (pbk.)
I. Cookery, American.   2. Cookery, American—History.
I. Title.
TX715.I545   2001
641.5973'082'0904—dc21   00-053637

FOR JULIE M. HUCKE

No life is blessed that is not graced with love.
—Ben Jonson

Contents

Acknowledgments

My first words of gratitude are for Julie M. Hucke. She is a rare person, and she makes my life better in an infinite variety of ways. As a writer, she shares her passion for her work with me. As a critic, she gives me the advice that any author needs. As a teacher, she shows me the importance of being kind and considerate. As a friend, she shares with me her tremendous zest for life. For everything that she gives to me, this book is dedicated to her.

My work has benefited from the input of many friends and colleagues. I would like to thank the people who have read drafts of my entire book or chapters of it, including Faye Parker Flavin, Stephanie Levine, Michele Lloyd, Robi Malone, Diana Royer, and Whitney Womack.

I want to thank my friends and family members: Hallie Bourne, Cathy Ebelke, Stephanie Levine, Michele Lloyd, Debra Mandel, Heather Schell, Shannon Simonsen, Lisa Somer, and Liz Wilson. I especially am thankful for the wit and friendship of Liz, Heather, Hallie, Michele, and Lisa. My Miami University colleagues provided invaluable support and encouragement during the process of writing this book. Thanks to Kathryn Burton, John Krafft, Sharon Krafft, Pete Martin, Diana Royer, Dianne Sadoff, Heather Schell, and Whitney Womack. The University of Iowa Press and its staff, especially Holly Carver, deserve praise for their wonderful work. My copy editor, Kathy Lewis, did a meticulous job.

I also appreciate the work of past food scholars who have made my work possible. I am especially grateful for the warmth and kindness of Warren Belasco, Jane Dusselier, and Janet Theophano. Arlene Voski Avakian, Amy

Bentley, Anne L. Bower, Carole Counihan, Barbara Haber, Lisa Heldke, and Lucy M. Long all deserve my thanks, too.

I wish to thank the numerous librarians and libraries that have helped make this book possible. In particular, I want to thank the Miami University library staff, especially Christa Branson and Rebecca Zartner. I also appreciate the efforts of the librarians at Smith College. Members of the interlibrary loan staff of the Strong Museum Library were particularly helpful in locating some of the more arcane sources I required.

My final words of appreciation I reserve for my father, mother, and twin sister. My dear mother, Ruth Ebelke Inness (1920–98), in particular, receives my deepest gratitude and love. I can never express how much she has given to me.

Dinner Roles

Introduction

Who cooks dinner in most American homes? It is difficult to escape noticing that cooking in the United States is very much considered to be mom's responsibility, not dad's. Food and its preparation are strongly gender-coded as feminine. How has this gendered relationship to food developed over the twentieth century, and why has it proven so enduring? The purpose of this book is to provide readers with a better understanding of how cooking was gendered throughout the first half of the twentieth century and how the gendered relationship of people, food, and cooking in this period did a great deal to keep women in the kitchen, performing the cooking-related duties. Women's relationship to food and its preparation has been a significant form of gender socialization throughout the twentieth century (and earlier centuries), helping to ensure the subordination of women and a gender role division of labor that exists to the present day. Women remain the individuals in the household mainly associated with preparing a meal, including grocery shopping, devising menus, cooking and serving the food, and maintaining the kitchen with all its accouterments. The American kitchen continues to be strongly gendered as female.[1]

My interest in food and gender stems from my lifelong relationship to shopping, cooking, and other food-related tasks; food and its preparation have been strongly gender-coded in my own life, with a distinct line drawn between men's and women's roles. When I was a child, I (along with the majority of young children growing up in America during the 1960s and 1970s) primarily associated my mother with cooking. She planned the meals, prepared and cooked them, and dealt with the leftovers — whether that meant making chicken stock out of the carcass of the fowl we had consumed or storing away the uneaten spoonful or two of spinach, which would later go into a stew or some other concoction. (As a child of the Depression, my mother was a careful and thrifty cook. I don't ever remember seeing a morsel of food spoil in her well-ordered refrigerator.) Day in and day out, despite her grumbles, my mother was responsible for the bulk of the food preparation in our home.

My father had a different relationship to food and cooking. He never played even a minor part in meal planning; my mother devoted hours to planning and organizing meals so that they would be aesthetically pleasing as well as nutritious. He seldom performed any of the actual cooking — I cannot remember him ever making a complete dinner, and I remember going to the grocery store with him only a few times when my mother was ill. If he did cook a main dish, it was usually because he had taken a trip to the beach, where he had gathered a bucketful of rock crabs or eels. Sometimes, when I was very young, he brought home a duck that he had shot at the local salt marshes. When he brought home seafood or game, he was responsible for preparing and cooking it. My father also occasionally baked a loaf of bread, usually sourdough. Once, I remember, he made wine and stored it in a dozen ten-gallon bottles that filled the garage. For a long time after that, the room reeked of fermenting grapes, a pungent odor that permeated everything, attracting hordes of hungry hornets. These few forays into food preparation failed to conceal that my father was not much of a cook (although he might beg to differ). When he was forced to fend for himself and make something to eat, he would concoct a hearty, manly mixture — salt cod and potatoes or beef stew, full of hunks of sinewy meat and chunks of onions. Father prepared dishes that smelled so strongly of mussels, haddock, or salt cod that all my mother and I could do was to vanish out the doorway, where we would wait on the porch until the fumes dissipated. Only my dad delighted in his masculine concoctions.

In many ways, my mother and father's relationship with food and its preparation is what mainstream American society has long accepted as "normal." Typically, women are responsible for food and its preparation and serving, with men being responsible for making an occasional dinner or two. Men are expected to assume responsibility for food preparation if the food happens to be a "manly" one, such as barbecue or grilled steak. In addition, like my dad, men are supposed to prepare the game or seafood that they hunt, taking a dim interest in making lighter, more "feminine" foods. But women are expected to prepare the family's food on a daily basis, no matter how tedious they might find this chore. When it came to food preparation, my mother and father fit neatly into this traditional division between men and women.

Growing up in a more liberal era than either my mother or father did, I find that I, too, have adopted a traditional gendered relationship to food and cooking, at least in some ways. Having been taught to cook at an early age (my brother was never involved in such cooking lessons), I have long been comfortable in the kitchen and can prepare a meal with ease. Grocery stores hold few surprises for me, and I typically cook the evening meal in my home. I have been socialized to adopt a certain relationship to food, one coded as womanly or feminine. But how and where did this relationship to food preparation evolve? In this book, I examine how millions of American women develop into what are viewed as correctly socialized females in regard to cooking. Where do we pick up the ideology that women "naturally" belong in the kitchen and men "naturally" do not?

Some people might argue that such a belief is old-fashioned, no longer applicable to our contemporary society, since men and women share the burden of buying, cooking, and serving food. But is this really true? How far-reaching are men's activities in food-related areas? True, more American men cook, but they seldom do 50 percent of the cooking, even if they have a wife or girlfriend who works full-time outside of the home. Men might prepare a special meal for a family (father cooks brunch on Sundays or makes a barbecue on Friday nights), but they are much less likely to be responsible for the day-to-day cooking than women. Divorced men who live by themselves and men who have no girlfriends or wives sometimes perform the majority of the cooking. In these households, however, the presumption frequently exists that this should be a temporary state of affairs, lasting only until a woman comes along to take over the daily cooking duties.

One of the reasons for the scarcity of men in the kitchen is that our society makes it clear that a man's place is *not* in the kitchen unless he is a chef. Women's magazines consistently devote many pages to food and its preparation. Men are seldom featured in these recipes and articles, which are directed at an audience of women. Men's magazines, in contrast, contain few articles about food; those that exist are apt to discuss gourmet foodstuffs and wines, with which, these magazines assume, men might occasionally dally. We have a society in which food preparation, especially in the private home, is considered feminine and inappropriate for men and boys. Since its beginnings, American culture has been structured around a division between the private realm of the home and the public sphere of the workplace. This division continues to hold sway in the United States: women are still associated with the "unimportant" domestic sphere, including cooking, while men are associated with the "important" world of the public workplace.

There are many reasons why women are charged with the majority of kitchen tasks. This book explores just one: how U.S. food culture was gendered throughout the first half of the twentieth century in a wide range of media sources, including cookbooks, women's magazines, and advertisements, which helped spread the message that cooking was primarily an activity for women, not men. By examining these sources, we shall discover the vast network of texts that perpetuate the myth that the kitchen is a woman's realm and cooking is women's work. Analyzing the gendered ideology that surrounds cooking, I argue, is essential to understanding how men and women have been constituted as gendered subjects in twentieth-century America.

But why study food and cooking in the first place? Food is basic to all human life, so ubiquitous that it, paradoxically, disappears from our attention entirely. "We do not see our own food or, worse, we assume that it is insignificant," observes French cultural theorist Roland Barthes ("Psychosociology," 167). He wrote these words decades ago, but they remain germane to the relationship between people and food. Although people must eat on a daily basis and spend a great deal of time, effort, and money to obtain food, they frequently pay scant attention to what they consume, just as they give little attention to other rituals of their daily life: bathing, getting dressed, driving to work, going to bed. If anything, we more completely ignore the rituals associated with food and eating than other domestic routines, because food always carries with it the guilt associated with sensual pleasure.

In the past, scholars have also suffered from this cultural amnesia about food, paying little or no attention to food and domestic cooking and considering such issues insignificant. Even encyclopedic works about America frequently exclude food and its preparation. This is a curious absence. People wage wars, conquer countries, explore unfamiliar lands and oceans, build empires — all accomplished, apparently, without stopping for a bite of lunch.

Food has been elided from much past scholarship about American society because it has been associated with women and the domestic sphere, which were rarely studied in earlier decades. "History almost never records the struggles of anxious middle-class cooks," historian Laura Shapiro notes (*Perfection*, 3). For decades, scholars (many of them influenced by the feminist movement) have stated that it is essential to address women and their concerns, but cooking and food continue to be overlooked today, sometimes by the very feminist scholars who would seem to be the first defenders of the importance of studying food and its past and present relationship to gender. Barbara Haber, curator of books at Harvard's Schlesinger Library, notes that "most contemporary feminist writers have shied away from the subject of kitchens and cooking. . . . Typically, when feminist scholars have looked at food, their investigations have focused on eating disorders and the victimization of females, especially young girls, reflecting an intellectual framework that sees food and its preparation as fraught with conflict, coercion, and frustration" ("Follow the Food," 68).[2] Although many women have discussed the troubled relationship between women and food, frequently bringing up personal stories about anorexia and bulimia, such research has sometimes drowned out other scholarly work on gender and food that does not focus on eating problems.[3] To some feminist scholars, food might seem of little importance when women confront countless other issues that imperil their lives: violence, lack of child-care facilities, lack of equal legal rights around the world, and inferior pay in many jobs.

But food is intimately and irrevocably entangled with everything we do on our planet.[4] We need to remember Virginia Woolf's famous words in *A Room of One's Own* (1929): "The human frame being what it is, heart, body and brain all mixed together, and not contained in separate compartments as they will be no doubt in another million years, a good dinner is of great importance to good talk. One cannot think well, love well, sleep well, if one has not dined well" (18). Her words apply to everyone. Eating is intertwined with all our other human activities; it is difficult (or impossible) to think clearly if you are ravenous. On a daily basis, people are subject to the demands of their stomachs. How these demands are met — by whom and with what — reveals a great deal about a society and its values.

Despite some scholars' reluctance to study food and cooking, a number of researchers from an eclectic variety of backgrounds have contributed to food studies. Anthropologists (Margaret Mead, Claude Lévi-Strauss, Mary Douglas, among others) have had a long-standing interest in food research, but the field of scholars includes many others: sociologists, folklorists, economists, geographers, historians, home economists, nutritionists, and psychologists. Knowledgeable writers not associated with a particular academic discipline, including M. F. K. Fisher, Jane and Michael Stern, and Calvin Trillin, have approached American food habits from the standpoint of the amateur or professional gourmet.[5] Despite this long tradition, much food research mentions little or nothing about women and gender issues. Scholars have sometimes overlooked the crucial role of women in the production and consumption of food.

A number of historians have written about food and cooking, but gender has not always been one of their major concerns.[6] Some scholars have focused primarily on the objects involved in cooking. For instance, in her edited collection *Dining in America, 1850–1900* (1987), Kathryn Grover brings together a number of essays that explore the connections between food culture and the material culture of the second part of the nineteenth century, but gender is a minor issue.[7] Similarly, Louise Conway Belden's *The Festive Tradition: Table Decoration and Desserts in America, 1650–1900* (1983) is chiefly concerned with changing service styles, addressing gender in passing. Like Grover and Belden, Eric Quayle gives more attention to the material culture of cooking than to the people who actually used the objects he discusses. In *Old Cook Books: An Illustrated History* (1978), a survey of cookbooks from their beginnings through the 1800s, he mentions women only briefly. Quayle describes changes in cooking and in recipes rather than charting the influence cookbooks have had on gender role expectations.

Other historians have written epic accounts about the development of food and drink in the United States. No matter how definitive they are, these works generally pay little attention to women and gender-related issues.[8] Waverley Root and Richard de Rochemont's monumental *Eating in America: A History* (1976) addresses women in a cursory fashion, a curious oversight in a book that sets out to be a comprehensive study of American food habits. Anyone interested in the study of America and food is indebted to Richard J. Hooker's *Food and Drink in America: A History* (1981), a thoughtful, detailed account. Hooker, however, is more concerned with charting changing food habits than with reflecting on gender issues. He focuses so rarely on the involvement of women in the production of food that the clam chowder, apple pie, strawberry shortcake, turtle soup, and other delicacies that he describes seem to have appeared on the dinner table by magic. Even some of the most exciting and insightful historical research on food culture does not always address women's connections with food in great depth. For instance, in his books *Revolution at the Table: The Transformation of the American Diet* (1988) and *Paradox of Plenty: A Social History of Eating in Modern America* (1993), Harvey A. Levenstein creates a thorough and carefully documented record of America's changing eating patterns, but he discusses the connections between women and food relatively briefly.

Not all food scholars slight gender. In recent decades, a number have shared my interest in studying cooking culture and its relationship to women. For example, Ruth Schwartz Cowan focuses on women and kitchen technology in *More Work for Mother: The Ironies of Household Technology from the Open Hearth to the Microwave* (1983). Mary Anna DuSablon describes the important role that women have played in creating American cookbooks in *America's Collectible Cookbooks: The History, the Politics, the Recipes* (1994). Other scholars make gender and women even more central to their research. Gender is the focal issue for Laura Shapiro in her book *Perfection Salad: Women and Cooking at the Turn of the Century* (1986).[9] In *Women, Food, and Families* (1988), Nickie Charles and Marion Kerr analyze women's relationship to food by studying two hundred contemporary British families.[10] A number of scholars have examined gender questions related to cooking and food. Nonetheless, the field of food studies tends to be belittled as trivial and has no true "home" in academe. Research on women, cooking, and food remains skimpier than research on many other social issues.[11]

Women must not be overlooked when researching food, since cooking has been considered women's responsibility for centuries. As food scholars Stephen Mennell, Anne Murcott, and Anneke H. van Otterloo note in *The Sociology of Food: Eating, Diet and Culture* (1992), "Cooking at home . . . has always been women's business" (88). Robert B. Schafer and Elisabeth Schafer echo this thought: "Traditionally, women in Western culture have performed most of the housework roles, including food-related activities. There has been a profound sex-typing and gender segregation" (119). American society (like the majority of societies around the world) structures itself around the assumption that women perform the cooking in the home and the majority of associated food-related tasks, from shopping for groceries to setting the table. The wisdom seems to be that *all* women, whatever their economic or ethnic background may be, should "naturally" be the ones responsible for cooking. This belief has had profound reverberations throughout all levels of U.S. society and has been a powerful influence in shaping gender roles and expectations for men and women.

The traditional connection between women and food preparation has proven to be remarkably durable over the decades. Even in today's "liberated times" when many women work outside the home, they are the ones most likely to be responsible for domestic cooking tasks, as numerous scholars have demonstrated. In their late 1980s study of the relationship between women and household food preparation, Charles and Kerr discovered that most women were responsible for the majority of food-related jobs, with men and children offering only occasional assistance (227). In *American Foodways: What, When, Why and How We Eat in America* (1989), food scholar Charles Camp concurs:

> With the exception of large restaurant kitchens, most American cooks are women. . . . [E]ven in a society whose career and social demands on men and women are changing rapidly, today's men of marriageable age have usually received no more training in the culinary arts at home than their fathers did in theirs. A given household situation — parents with two jobs or night classes, single working parents, and so on — may require a boy's learning to cook, but the association of gender and cookery appears to remain consistent.[12] (97)

In her study *Feeding the Family: The Social Organization of Caring as Gendered Work* (1991), sociologist Marjorie L. DeVault discovered that equality in kitchen chores between a husband and wife was the exception, not the rule. She found that the majority of kitchen work was performed by women, even in many households that strove to achieve an equitable division of domestic duties between husband and wife. Mennell, Murcott, and van Otterloo also found that women performed the majority of the domestic cooking. They affirm that "the convention dies hard that in wage economies men are the breadwinners and women the homemakers" (99). The link between women and cooking was omnipresent: "There is a pervasive assumption that cooking at home, along with housework generally, is women's work. . . . It is one that can be detected in all kinds of quarters — in cross-cultural surveys . . . , in magazines, cookbooks and advertising . . . , toy pots and pans provided for little girls . . . , in studies of newly married couples" (95). When women work for pay outside the home, the domestic work arrangement changes little, they determined; women remain the ones responsible for preparing meals (98). The research overwhelmingly demonstrates that women today perform the majority of kitchen-related work in the United States and Great Britain.

The issue of women's predominant responsibility for food preparation and associated kitchen work involves more than a concern about who will whip together the Hamburger Helper for Tuesday's dinner. When women are in charge of the majority of cooking tasks, they are not only making a school lunch or cooking a Saturday morning breakfast, but also demonstrating and affirming their gendered identity.[13] As men and women perform their allotted household chores, they simultaneously demonstrate what it means to be a man or woman in society. "It is not just that women do more of the work of feeding, but also that feeding work has become one of the primary ways that women 'do' gender. . . . By feeding the family, a woman conducts herself as recognizably womanly," DeVault points out (118). She continues:

> Activities such as feeding, which members of the society have learned to associate strongly with one gender, come to seem like "natural" expressions of gender. This observation does not imply that all women engage in such activity. . . . but as long as feeding is understood, collectively, as somehow more "womanly" than "manly," the work stands as one kind of activity in which "womanliness" may be at issue. (118–19)

In other words, cooking becomes an important way to identify whether a female is sufficiently womanly, and her entire image as a "correctly" socialized woman might be imperiled or strengthened by her relationship to food and cooking: "responsibility for domestic 'feeding work' is deeply embedded within the core of the whole concept of femininity, through the socialization of women into the acceptance of such obligations as natural and through the sanctioning of women who fail or refuse to fulfil these obligations" (Beardsworth and Keil, 86). It is crucial to study food culture to understand the role that cooking-related tasks play in shaping women's roles in America and the cultural expectations about what it means to be a woman.

The popular media have played a significant role in shaping the way American society perceives the complex relationship between women and food. The influence of the popular media is not surprising. Food culture has been shaped and created for centuries through a vast network of popular texts, ranging from cookbooks to articles in women's magazines.

Among the media that have shaped cooking culture, surely the most influential have been cookbooks. In 1742, William Parks reprinted E. Smith's *The Compleat Housewife*, the first cookbook printed in the United States. In 1796, Amelia Simmons published the first cookbook by an American, *American Cookery*. Since then, cookbooks of all varieties have been a part of the American landscape, instructing generations of women about cooking norms. The cookbook genre has long been associated primarily with women. According to a 1987 Gallup survey, 5 percent of book sales were cookbooks, and more than two-thirds of the buyers were women (Wood, "Who's Buying the Cookbooks?" 29). Due to this association with women, as well as other factors, cookbooks have been disregarded by many scholars, leaving Anne Murcott to call them a "severely neglected source" in 1983 ("Women's Place," 34). Her words remain germane, although this situation has been changing in the last few decades.[14]

Cookbooks (and other cooking-related texts) need to be studied because they are barometers of changing gender roles. As culinary historian Barbara Wheaton writes, "[Cookbooks] are like a magician's hat: one can get more out of them than they seem to contain. When they are read carefully, with due effort in understanding them as cultural artifacts, they are rewarding, surprising, and illuminating" (2).[15] They are treasure troves for determining how women (and men) were and are expected to behave in any given historical epoch. Anne L. Bower discusses the important role that nonliterary texts, such as cookbooks, played for women in the nineteenth century and earlier. Many women lacked access to journalism or fiction writing, but they could communicate with one another through different print materials, such as the cookbook (5–6). Thus, cookbooks are a crucial source to analyze to understand women's lives.

To determine how the media depicted cooking culture in earlier periods, we need to study more than cookbooks alone, since they were only part of a much larger community of texts (ranging from advertisements to articles in women's magazines) that focused on cooking. DeVault describes the boundaries of this cooking discourse:

> Much expert advice in this area is still disseminated through clinics and workshops aimed at wives and mothers, in books and magazines written mostly for women and in the traditional . . . "women's sections" of newspapers. The discourse is differentiated, so that women of different class groups tend to use it differently (attending to different sources of information, for instance), but much of it appears in the mass media; it is not only accessible, but to some degree unavoidable. (221)

Although DeVault is describing today's cooking discourse, her words are equally applicable to past decades, when a wide range of sources in the discourse about cooking were directed primarily at women. Thus, this book explores a broad variety of popular texts — including magazine articles, advertisements, and cookbooks — and teases out the messages such works conveyed to women about more than just cooking.[16] We shall find that cooking literature taught women lessons about how they were expected to behave and also conveyed to them that their "proper" place was in the kitchen.

Some scholars might argue that the popular texts I examine in this book do not provide a "real" image of American women and their relationship to cooking. My focus is not on living women and what they thought about cooking. Instead, I analyze texts that might or might not have influenced living women. Although it is difficult to know how women reacted to the texts I study, such works still provide valuable lessons about gender norms from different eras, as DeVault observes:

> Textual representations of everyday life — in advertising and the media — have proliferated in the twentieth century, and texts have become increasingly important in organizing contemporary life. Representations of household practice provide public, ideal images of family life — images that are influential even if they are not accurate reflections of actual household life or achievable by any more than a small fraction of the population. (215)

Advertisements, women's magazines, and cookbooks did not necessarily re-lay an image of "real" women and their individual reactions to cooking, but such sources provide valuable information about the gender norms that American society held as an ideal, even if that ideal was not obtainable by the majority of men and women due to their race, ethnicity, or class back-ground. This popular literature can reveal the dreams of an era as well as demonstrate some of the disturbing side effects of such fantasies. Studying the media's representation of cooking and women illuminates a great deal about mainstream American society and its assumptions about women's so-cietally desirable roles.

This book argues that such popular cooking literature provided a recipe for women's (and men's) behavior.[17] In particular, the popular press depicted kitchen work as "naturally" rewarding to a woman both emotionally (she nourished the ones she loved) and aesthetically (she was encouraged to de-light in the artistic pleasure of building a quivering molded tower out of Jell-O and canned fruit or decorating a seven-layer cake to look like a fairy-tale palace). If encouraging a woman to find emotional and artistic fulfill-ment in cooking was not sufficient to keep her in the kitchen, there was another highly successful tactic: guilt. The popular media cast doubt on the femininity of a woman who showed little interest in cooking-related respon-sibilities. In such ways, the media played a significant part in a larger cultural discourse, ensuring that the majority of domestic food-related work re-mained women's responsibility.

This exploration of how the media depicted women and cooking needs to begin not with women, but with men — the individuals who seldom made an appearance in most popular cooking literature, except as the presumed consumers of the recipes. Where were they? The first chapter locates the missing men, who actually were not missing at all, but existing in an odd alternative universe — a place filled with articles about cooking and cook-books written by manly men, for other equally manly men. The first chapter explores this universe, examining what messages men learned about cook-ing from men's cooking literature in the first half of the twentieth century. This male-oriented literature reveals how dad was taught that the kitchen was *not* his lair.

Chapter 2 focuses on another group of individuals who rarely appear in women's cooking literature: children. At an early age, boys and girls learn what their socially dictated roles are expected to be. Juvenile cookbooks are important because they were one of the first ways that girls and boys learned about cooking and what was considered to be gender-appropriate behavior. As we shall discover, girls learned that their place was "naturally" in the kitchen, while boys learned the opposite.

This idea that the kitchen is a realm for females, not males pervades popular cooking literature, but such literature teaches women many other lessons about how to be feminine and womanly. Our exploration of these messages to women begins in the first decades of the twentieth century, a time of great social upheaval, when Victorian ways were replaced by more modern ways — best characterized by the gin-guzzling, cigarette-smoking flapper. During this period, many cookbooks and cooking articles harked back nostalgically to images of daintiness and delicacy. Chapter 3 explores how this cooking literature perpetuated the notion that "true" ladies should be dainty and refined. Early twentieth-century cooking literature attempted to inculcate its readers with upper- and middle-class ideals of womanhood. In this fashion, women learned as much about being ladies through reading a cookbook as they learned about how to decorate tea sandwiches.

Ideals of delicacy and daintiness were not the only messages in such works about how women should act. Like any form of popular literature (romance novels or mysteries, for instance), cookbooks and cooking articles conveyed a myriad of ideas about gender roles. While some works about cooking harked back to earlier beliefs about the inherent daintiness of middle-class women, other works looked forward to a much more up-to-date image of middle-class womanhood — a modern housewife working in a squeaky-clean kitchen filled with the latest electric gadgets. In this era, technology revolutionized the kitchen, which would never be the same after the invention of the electric stove, electric refrigerator, and dozens of small electric kitchen appliances. Chapter 4 focuses on how the media encouraged women to buy and use electrical appliances by assuring consumers that electricity would not usurp their place in the kitchen. The appliances would take care of the drudgery associated with cooking, the media asserted, while women would be free to be more creative. Advertisements and cooking literature claimed that such exciting new inventions would make cooking as simple as the flip of a switch. Why would a woman want to be anywhere but the kitchen?

Chapters 3 and 4 focus on ideals that were achievable by a minority of American women. The genteel emphasis on daintiness reflected upper- and middle-class notions about women's lives; most women could not afford the ladylike lifestyle that cookbooks and cooking articles promoted. Similarly, most women could not afford the scores of expensive electric devices that would be necessary to fill their lives with luxury and ease. Cooking literature provided a fantasy about how women should live, but it was not always an obtainable one, especially for women of different races or ethnic backgrounds, who were given very different roles to play than Anglo women. Chapter 5 focuses on ethnic foods as they were depicted in American cooking literature published between World War I and World War II, revealing that such literature frequently depicted women from different racial backgrounds as inferior to whites. Popular cooking literature helped promulgate the notion that the "correct" American housewife was white and middle class; thus, cooking literature not only encouraged women to stay in the kitchen, but also suggested the desirable race, ethnicity, and class for these idealized American housewives.

Chapters 6 and 7 focus on crises in America's history: the Depression and World War II, when women experienced dramatic changes in their domestic lives. During the Depression, many men could no longer adequately fulfill the role of breadwinner, forcing countless families to scrutinize traditional domestic gender roles. During World War II, millions of families coped with domestic lives turned topsy-turvy by the war. Dad was apt to be thousands of miles away, fighting in the war, while mom might be working fifty-hour weekly shifts in the local munitions or airplane factory. During these periods of epic change, cooking literature played an important part in suggesting what gender roles women and men should adopt. Such popular literature was a venue for emphasizing that, even in times of turmoil and mass displacement, mom's place was still in the kitchen. Chapter 6 argues that cooking literature played a role in perpetuating traditional gender roles and norms during the Depression by encouraging women to return to the home. Chapter 7 shows that women were taught that their role as cooks was all-important during the war; after all, the soldiers were fighting for mom and apple pie. As the wartime popular media affirmed, women had to do their part for the war effort, even if that meant working in jobs outside the home. This state of affairs, however, did not suggest that women should forget their domestic responsibilities; their families, the popular rhetoric declared, always came first.

The final chapter turns to the 1950s, analyzing how cooking literature encouraged women to return to their kitchens after the war, transforming Rosie the Riveter to Rosie the Housewife and leaving jobs open for men returning from the war. In discussing the creative ways that a woman could prepare meals with canned foods and casseroles, 1950s cooking literature affirmed that any woman should want to return to the kitchen because cooking was pleasurable and aesthetically rewarding. Some of the same messages that circulated about food preparation in the early decades of the twentieth century were renewed with vigor after the war, as cooking literature played a role in ensuring that millions of women spent the decade as domestic goddesses for their returning soldiers.

I hope that reading this book will encourage readers to think more closely about the role that food plays in our society. We need to acknowledge that analyzing food and its rituals is a valuable way to understand how society is constituted. "The rules of the menu are not in themselves more or less trivial than the rules of verse to which a poet submits," wrote Mary Douglas in her essay "Deciphering a Meal" (80). Figuring out the rules that guide food consumption is one strategy to understand how a society is structured. Studying the gender roles that govern food preparation is also a way to understand how gender is constituted in a particular culture; food plays a crucial role in this gender indoctrination.

As I have noted, women in particular are affected by this relationship to food because for centuries cooking and its associated tasks have been considered women's responsibility. Advertisements, cooking articles, and cookbooks have played an influential role in shaping America's understanding of the "natural" connection between women and cooking. I hope this book will show how the media have shaped women's (and men's) culinary experiences.

Finally, I hope readers recognize that the topics discussed in the following pages are not isolated to the first fifty years of the twentieth century. Many of the questions about food and gender that this book raises remain relevant today. How is food represented in the popular media? Why do women still do the majority of the cooking? What roles does food play in constructing our identities as men and women? These questions remain as important now as they were a century ago. If we are to understand our daily lives and how we constitute gender in our domestic duties, we must study the messages conveyed by food and its preparation. I hope this book will play a role in helping to articulate how food culture has shaped and continues to shape our lives on a regular basis, making it one of the dominant influences in all of our lives.

Chapter 1

"Bachelor Bait"

Men's Cookbooks and the Male Cooking Mystique

"As far as I'm concerned, Men and Cooking is an oxymoron. Oh sure, lots of guys cook *something*. But if your life depended on someone to cook for you, who you gonna call? A man? I doubt it," wrote Suzanne O'Malley in a 1990s *Cosmopolitan* article (166). Even in our liberated times when a woman is supposed to be free to give up a housewife's saucepan in favor of a doctor's scalpel, the idea of a man regularly cooking for a family (or for anyone) makes many women incredulous. Although her words are tongue-in-cheek, O'Malley describes a remarkably durable stereotype: a man who is so inept in the kitchen that he needs to phone his mother to find out how to scramble an egg. Like any stereotype, this one is only partially valid; some men are perfectly at ease with cooking. Superstar chefs, the majority of them male, have dominated American fine dining for well over a century. On a less lofty level, many men today cook for families and friends, sometimes enjoying such cooking and occasionally doing it because no one else is available to take over the responsibility. Nonetheless, cooking remains the domestic task most commonly associated with women, and it is widely perceived as "feminine" (except for certain cooking endeavors like grilling a steak). Men cook for many reasons, but women continue to be in charge of the majority of food preparation and cooking in the United States (and around the globe).[1] As folklorist Thomas A. Adler writes, "In the American nuclear family, Mom is nearly always in the culinary foreground; typically it is she who cooks, serves, cleans up, and informally instructs children—especially female children—in the particulars of her realized culinary competence" (45).[2] Why do many modern Americans still perceive cooking as women's responsibility?[3] Why do numerous men feel uncomfortable and unfamiliar with cooking responsibilities, even those that are no more complex than tossing a frozen dinner into the microwave? Why is it that men are an endangered species in most general cookbooks and popular literature about cooking? A reader may browse through dozens of cookbooks and women's magazines without encountering any mention of a man in connection with cookery or seeing one picture of a man assembling a meal. This chapter addresses that invisibility and analyzes why men have been and continue to be distanced from domestic cooking in the media and in real life, a distancing that has broad ramifications for men and women and how gender is constituted in American culture.

To locate these seemingly invisible men, this chapter turns to men's cookbooks and cooking articles from the first half of the twentieth century (and beyond), revealing how the media have consistently reinforced the idea that daily domestic cooking should be women's responsibility, while men should have a different relationship to cooking.

I argue that a male cooking mystique has emerged in the United States that is evident in men's cooking literature.[4] This mystique, like Betty Friedan's feminine mystique, has helped to perpetuate traditional gender roles, particularly the long-lasting idea that women are the "natural" cooks, not men. The male cooking mystique in men's cooking literature can be broken down into several different assumptions about the relationship of men to food and cooking:

1. If men *choose* to cook, they must make sure that their masculinity is not diminished. Men's cooking literature plays a role in reassuring men that a trip into the kitchen won't feminize them.
2. Men's and women's tastes in food are antithetical: women are always inclined to feed a man some fluffy frippery such as marshmallow-and-maraschino Jell-O salad instead of steak and potatoes, his heart's true de-

sire. Men must constantly guard against women who wish to feed males food that would be more appropriate for ladies attending a tea party.

3. It is perfectly acceptable and even desirable for men to cook *some* foods that are associated with masculinity and manliness—most importantly, meat. A man should take charge of outdoor cookery. He should also be the chef when wild game needs to be prepared. Grilling a steak, it goes without saying, is a man's responsibility. If a woman attempts any of these manly tasks, she will end up failing, burning the deer, turning the steak into a charcoal briquette, or making the barbecue a mockery by tossing in "lady-like" additions such as pineapple chunks or coconut. (Men fret constantly about women destroying a perfectly good steak or other piece of meat, since, at least in men's cookbooks, women have no idea how to cook meat correctly. Presumably, men acquire this skill while still in the cradle.)

4. Men may sometimes cook meals other than steak and barbecue, but this should be a rare event. When men do cook, no matter how simple a meal, it is cause for applause. If men desire to learn how to cook, they will inevitably be better cooks than any woman can be.[5]

5. If a woman wishes to attract a man or keep the one she has, she should always strive to please his taste in food. He need not pay attention to her tastes.

By espousing these five elements of the male cooking mystique, men's cookbooks and cooking articles have helped formulate an image of men's cooking as being antithetical to women's. Men and women "naturally" have different attitudes and relationships toward food and cooking. Male cooking literature convinces men to do some kinds of cooking, but only on rare occasions.

How Cookbooks Assure Men of Their Masculinity, Even If They Cook

Although women have been and continue to be the ones primarily associated with cooking in the popular media, writers have published a number of cookbooks and articles that address the specific needs of the man who dares to venture into the kitchen.[6] Although these works are dwarfed by the overwhelming number of books and articles directed at women, they are a useful source for anyone interested in examining how the media helped promulgate the male cooking mystique. The media played a role in assuring males that cooking can be masculine, albeit only in certain situations.

Of course, men have been cooking since America's earliest years. Whether working as trappers on the Western frontier or serving in the American Revolution, men have not always had women available to prepare and cook meals. Sometimes men have had to tend the campfire or rustle up chow in a chuck wagon on their own. These forms of cooking, however, were coded as far more masculine than daily domestic meals, which were, for the most part, women's responsibility. Nonetheless, some men in earlier decades dared to cook in their own homes and ventured to write about their experiences.[7] For example, in the 1930s Leo Nejelski wrote about men's cooking for *Good Housekeeping*. "Not a week passes without discovering among my friends and acquaintances more and more men who enjoy cooking," he claimed (120). Other men in the first half of the twentieth century also wrote about their experiences as cooks and chefs, producing an eclectic assortment of cookbooks and cooking articles that promised to unravel cooking's mysteries for men. One men's cookbook from 1944 observed: "Within these covers is food for thought. . . . Here will be found fearless exposure of the most intimate household secrets. . . . The forbidden realm of the culinary arts has at last been penetrated, its mysteries laid bare for the hungry male" (Keating, ix).

Men required careful guidance with the mystery of cooking, since they were portrayed as entirely ignorant or even fearful about it. Addressing this manly fear, Robert H. Loeb, Jr.'s cookbook *Wolf in Chef's Clothing* (1950) was composed entirely of pictures because the author assumed that men would need the simplest of recipes; he used only tablespoons for measurements because he thought that men would not be able to tell the difference between tablespoons and teaspoons. This belief in men's absolute ignorance of kitchen matters was deeply engrained in American society. Men's cookbooks described cooking as a secret art that the bold man had to conquer; women's cookbooks presented cooking as a practical, mundane experience, with which most women were assumed to be already familiar.[8]

Men's cookbooks from the first half of the twentieth century are of interest not so much for the practical tips about cooking that they offered to fearful men but because they reveal a great deal about how the male cooking mystique gave cooking a more masculine aura, making it more palatable to men. Even today, men's cookbooks must be careful to reaffirm the connection between cooking and masculinity, assuring male readers that cooking is not an endeavor that will make them effeminate. Food scholar Barbara Haber writes that "men who chose to write about food [have] feelings of self-consciousness, of not wanting to be mistaken for being effeminate or sissies" ("Food, Sex and Gender," 30). As George L. Mosse points out in *The Image of Man: The Creation of Modern Masculinity* (1996), in a society where presenting a masculine image and, thus, asserting one's manhood has been an "all pervasive" concern, the connection between femininity and cooking has assured that many men continue to look at the kitchen as women's territory (3).⁹ Frederic A. Birmingham rushed to reassure his readers that they would not become "sissies" if they cooked. He noted in *The Complete Cook Book for Men* (1961): "When he cooks [a man] is not a housewife in trousers. He is not larking away at what is essentially a woman's task. He is actually asserting his claim to an art which is his masculine birthright" (3). Birmingham urged his readers to "reverse the feminine trend in cooking" and to "recognize that cooking is a man's prerogative" (3). Achmed Abdullah and John Kenny's *For Men Only: A Cook Book* (1937) asserted that cooking was "most eminently a man's artistic province, a masculine craft and accomplishment" (xi). Even in 1995, Steven Bauer (writing for *Glamour*) felt a need to address the perceived femininity of cooking: "Like playing the flute or doing needlepoint, cooking has long been seen as something that feminizes men" (236). All these masculine protestations assured men that cooking was a suitably masculine endeavor, no matter what they might previously have assumed.

In the first half of the twentieth century, men's cookbooks went to any length to assure readers of their masculine focus, including addressing an exclusively male audience in their titles: C. Mac Sheridan's *The Stag Cook Book, Written for Men, by Men* (1922), Abdullah and Kenny's *For Men Only*, and Brick Gordon's *The Groom Boils and Stews: A Man's Cook Book for Men* (1947). Cookbooks continue to be published with titles directed specifically at men, such as Caroline Kriz's *Cooking for Men Only* (1984) and Cici Williamson and John A. Kelly's *For Men Only: Mastering the Microwave* (1986). If labeling a book as "for men only" did not suffice to mark it as masculine, authors resorted to assuring readers that the book was "entirely masculine" (Birmingham, 6). The writer of *Tough Guys Don't Dice: A Cookbook for Men*

Who Can't Cook (1989) cautioned: "Now, this book is not intended to be a manifesto for the androgynous male, and I don't have a subscription to *Ms*" (Thorson, 12). For these authors and others, cooking was a dangerous terrain to navigate. Men had to worry that cooking moved them too close to femininity; thus, men's cooking literature constantly had to affirm that cooking was masculine, not feminine.

Men's cooking literature further reinforced the linkage between manliness and cooking by identifying many recipes with men's names. For instance, Williamson and Kelly's book contained recipes for Ronald Reagan's Onion Wine Soup (20–21), Senator Lloyd Bentsen's Texas Seafood Dinner (38–39), Bob Hope's Favorite Chicken Hash (60–61), George Bush's Pecan Pralines (128), and Billy Graham's Missionary Chicken (58–59).[10] Men's cookbooks had a vested interest in assuring males that cooking was a task for men. Although they asserted that men could be masculine and still be cooks, they were careful to distance men from the daily cooking that was perceived as women's work. According to the wisdom of these cookbooks, cooking was men's work when men wanted it to be; cooking for women, however, was not optional but was something they all had to do. This was an important distinction. It established men's cooking as an optional hobby. Thus, men had a different relationship with the kitchen than women did. Men could come and go at will, while women never had this choice. A hierarchy of cooking was created in which men's cooking was raised to the level of an art, while women's cooking was much lower on the scale of prestige.

Another method that men's cookbooks adopted to assure male readers that their masculinity was not threatened by perusing their pages was sexualizing men's cooking. For instance, *Esquire's Handbook for Hosts* (1949) contained numerous cartoons of older men gallivanting with curvaceous young beauties. Paul K. Tibbens's *Cookin' for the Helluvit* (1950) featured sketches of skimpily clad beauties to adorn his collection of recipes, which had names like "hot dish" (59) and "luscious tomato" (134). Loeb's *Wolf in Chef's Clothing* referred to "gastronomic foreplay" (36). Another cookbook suggested serving what it called sweater girl salad to the men at a stag dinner, but only after tying "the ladies outside to a stout hickory post" (Gordon, *The Groom*, 18). This salad was composed of two whole peach halves filled with cottage cheese and decorated with maraschino cherries and mayonnaise to resemble a woman's breasts (19). Men's cookbooks did more than record recipes; they helped to differentiate the genders and established that cooking was an act that men performed only under special circumstances. Cooking literature suggested that men's masculinity was not diminished by cooking when food was sexualized because males were still portrayed in a stereotypical aggressive, masculine relationship to the food they prepared. After all, engaging in "gastronomic foreplay" was worlds away from mom's baking biscuits. By sexualizing cooking, men's cooking literature took it out of the kitchen and into the bedroom, a sphere where men have traditionally demonstrated and affirmed their masculinity.

Guy Food

In order to demonstrate to men that their masculinity would not be diminished if they cooked, men's cooking literature had to do far more than teach males a recipe for sweater girl salad. Such texts carefully spelled out which foods were appropriate for women and which were appropriate for men. Thus, men's cooking literature played a role in separating male and female food tastes and establishing male tastes as "naturally" superior. By carefully distinguishing between women and men's tastes in food, men's cooking literature also distanced itself from the suspect world of the feminine.

One way in which men's cookbooks distanced themselves from femininity was by emphasizing that their pages contained real he-man food. *Esquire's Handbook for Hosts* reassured its readers: "You won't find doily tearoom fare here: no radish roses, no menus designed for their calorie content. [The book] has concentrated on food of, for and by MEN" (11). "This book . . . is for men," the handbook continued. "There is, I promise you, no tarty stuff about rolling pastry and baking cakes or upside-down, inside-out, back-to-front puddings. There are no abominations along the lines of 'glazed gooseberry chicken with fried eggs and ice-cream' to titillate our already punch-drunk taste buds" (1). Another cookbook writer proclaimed to his male readers: "We have not sullied your confidence by instructing you as to how to make a Brown Betty or an Apple Pandowdy. We can't picture you humming your way around the kitchen, either, preparing hot cereals, putting up jams or jellies, cutting out cookies, or making sherbet" (Birmingham, 7). Men's tastes were glorified; women's tastes were disparaged. By extolling the pleasures of men's foods, the cookbooks asserted the superiority of male tastes.

Men's cookbooks and articles articulated a clear vision about foods that were suitable for a man to prepare, cook, and eat. Such cooking literature made it equally clear that women were unprepared to cook "men's food" and possessed little or no understanding of what men enjoyed. One male writer from the 1930s lamented:

> You can't appease a man's appetite with a fruit salad or a bit of fluff like marsh-mallow-date whip, and yet women continue to overlook this fact and go right on serving dishes that have no relation to muscle and brawn. . . . Keep your dainties for women's luncheons but remember that where such delicacies as squab leave a man cold, the very mention of corned beef hash with a poached egg on top will bring a gleam into his eye. (Moats, 33)

Cookbook authors Abdullah and Kenny wrote about similar terrors: "The deathly marshmallow and the bloody Maraschino cherry lurk in the hidden corners of too many feminine kitchens, waiting to stick a dirty dagger into the honest masculine palate" (xv). Worried that women would try to feed men "sissy food," Byron MacFadyen encouraged women to cook dishes that men could "sink their teeth into" ("Give a Man," 106). If women wished to attract men, he suggested, they should prepare dishes like boiled beef with horseradish sauce, braised oxtails, or boiled tongue. This societal obsession with women feeding men "sissy foods" was an indicator of a general mascu-line uneasiness with the kitchen, a space widely perceived as the focal point of women's power in the home. Men needed to be constantly vigilant that women did not de-masculinize them by serving the wrong foods or insisting that men should perform kitchen duties.

"Men's food" was more than a matter of preference; it served as a way for a man to emphasize his masculinity. Ideally, according to the male cooking mystique, men's foods should be hearty and substantial as well as greasy, coarse, and highly spiced, a belief promulgated by magazines and cookbooks. Abdullah and Kenny's *For Men Only* contained recipes for sausages in ale, corned beef hash with mustard sauce, spaghetti with chili con carne, boiled dinner, stuffed cabbage, English mutton chops, broiled pork chops, Bruns-wick stew, German fried potatoes, campfire stew, and a mysterious concoc-tion called hunter's delight composed of dried beef, cooked oatmeal, onions, and a pound of American cheese (171). Arthur H. Deute's *200 Dishes for Men to Cook* (1944) included recipes for marinated herring, cooked sardines, baked haddock with onions, creamed cod, roasted oysters, roast duck, "man-made" beef stew, barbecued spareribs, and roast pork. An article from a 1950s edition of *Good Housekeeping* suggested a number of hearty dishes for the aspiring male cook, such as barbecued steak, spaghetti with meatballs, barbecued franks and beans, and "Tom, Dick, and Harry's Corned-Beef Hash" ("A Little Summer Cook Book," 95, 98, 100).[11] All these hearty dishes did not just satisfy a man's appetite; they also helped confirm his masculinity when he consumed them.

Another way for the male cook to affirm his manliness, according to many cookbooks, was to cook with alcohol, particularly beer, whiskey, or rum. For instance, *Esquire's Handbook for Hosts* included recipes for beer cabbage slaw, beer dressing, beer soup, and even beer cheesecake. Cookbooks also stressed their masculine identification by including numerous drink recipes. Tibbens's *Cookin' for the Helluvit* contained recipes for a silver gin fizz, golden gin fizz, royal gin fizz, gin rickey, gin pick-up, scotch and soda, dry martini, brandy bulldog, sloe gin cocktail, and an odd drink referred to as Jeff's "h" bomb that included a jigger of gin, a jigger of brandy, and half a jigger of Log Cabin syrup (48).

Men's interest in cooking hearty foods that contain alcohol has not vanished from American society. One commentator in the early 1990s described men's cooking tastes with words that would have been equally applicable much earlier in the twentieth century:

> Even when cooking for the family, men may more readily attempt preparation of those foods and beverages which stereotypically are thought to be preferred by men: meat and potatoes, pie, coffee, and alcoholic beverages, and to some extent, breads made with corn, rye, or whole wheat. Moreover, many urban and suburban men seem primarily attracted as both eaters and cooks to those foods which are especially hearty, large, spicy, and complex. (Anderson, "Imperative Cooking," 42)

The assumption that men "naturally" prefer hearty foods and foods that contain alcohol (beer bread, steak marinated in bourbon, chicken in red wine) is so engrained in mainstream American society that men and boys today are apt to be belittled if they do not enjoy such foods. Although this situation has been changing in recent decades, millions of people continue to assume that men should eat heavy, spicy foods or risk being considered "sissies." It comes as little surprise that men's cooking contests today often feature foods like chili or barbecued ribs, not light, delicate foods like chiffon cake or meringues. These choices are far from insignificant; they are part of a much larger system of ways in which females and males continue to be constituted as feminine or masculine.

Grilling Out

Men might sometimes prepare sole in dill béchamel sauce or a similar complex recipe, but men's cookbooks make it clear that they should not get carried away with preparing such fancy dishes. The "real" guy food is meat. This is still a deeply held belief in America and other cultures around the world. Writing about French society, sociologist Pierre Bourdieu observes: "Meat, the nourishing food par excellence, strong and strong-making, giving vigour, blood, and health, is the dish for . . . men" (192). Men and meat are so closely linked in the American imagination that it is almost impossible to separate the two. The connection between men and meat is not merely about personal food preferences—it is about power.[12] Whether a man eats a hamburger or steak, meat consumption symbolizes power over animals and other humans. Meat carries with it a complex iconography; it is linked in our imagination with prehistoric times when man (not woman) had to hunt for his meal. In Western culture, meat has long been associated with wealth, power, and masculinity. American assumptions about these "natural" connections are so deeply ingrained that we rarely question them. The idea that real men should like meat has been changing in recent decades as the general populace has become more aware of the health problems associated with a diet heavy in red meat, but the belief in a connection between masculinity and meat is still strongly held today across classes, age groups, ethnic and racial groups, and genders. To many people (although not all), a man seems less of a man if he orders a tofu cutlet for lunch instead of a steak.

Meat is perceived as intrinsically male in American culture, and men's cookbooks affirmed that connection in many ways, including stressing meat recipes. *Meats for Men: Eighteen Favorite Meat Dishes for Men* (1954) includes recipes for barbecued hamburgers, beef stroganoff, beef stew, pot roast, roast leg of lamb, and roast veal. Jim Hayes's *How to Cook a Deer—and Other Critters: A Game Cookbook for Men* (1991) is perhaps the quintessential male cookbook, with recipes for roast haunch of venison, elk steaks in beer, venison steak, chicken-fried deer meat, venison chili, baked bear chops with sauerkraut, curry of bighorn sheep, fried rabbit, roast curried duck, and braised venison kidney. No recipes were included for nonessentials—desserts or vegetables, for instance. Such cookbooks affirmed that the *only* food for men was meat.

If there is one meat that stands out in American society as the ultimate male food, it is steak—preferably a huge slab of blood-red meat cooked over an outside grill by a man. Men's cookbooks assumed that women would be incapable of cooking this king of foods. *The Life Picture Cook Book* (1958) expressed the belief held by many similar books: "Whenever the menu calls for a delicate dish or a fancy pie, most men are more than happy to let their wives take care of the cooking. When it's a matter of steak, the tolerant attitude is replaced by an unassailable belief in masculine know-how. Steak is a man's job" (8).

This "natural" connection between men and steak is one way that assumptions about foods shape our culture and our expectations about gender roles. Red meat has the highest status of foods, and steak has the highest status of meats (Charles and Kerr, 77). Thus, the association between men and steak helps to reaffirm their high status. Eating a steak (or any piece of meat) becomes a potent signifier of manliness.[13] Consuming steak is a way to gain the virility and power associated with the meat. Roland Barthes writes in his short essay "Steak and Chips" in *Mythologies* (1957): "Steak is a part of the same sanguine mythology as wine. It is the heart of meat, it is meat in its pure state; and whoever partakes of it assimilates a bull-like strength" (62). Thus, consuming steak makes men seem more powerful, more potent because of what they eat.

If steak is considered to be the ultimate male food, the ultimate method of cooking the steak (or other foods) is outdoor cookery.[14] "Primarily, outdoor cooking is man's work and man-sized menus and portions should be the rule," wrote James Beard (vii). Another cookbook echoed his words: "The main role [in outdoor cookery] is masculine, as it should be. No woman looks her best leaning over a bed of glowing charcoal, and she knows it. The fact that the man of the house has taken up outdoor cookery is something she hears with unalloyed joy" (Botsford, *What's Cookin' Men?* n. pag.).[15] Similarly, *Esquire's Handbook for Hosts* observed: "Game can be cooked in a spick-and-span tiled kitchen, of course, and even exceptionally by some women. . . . But a log cabin or an open grill is the logical place—and a man's the proper cook" (45). Journalist Russell Baker wrote about a similar cooking-out craze in his essay "Grilled Macho" (1986). He discussed the perceived connection between being macho and cooking out, an issue that was highlighted for him when he moved into a new neighborhood "where men cooked out three times a week. It was apparently an obligation of good citizenship, like doing jury duty" (10).

Like the connection between men and meat, the connection between men and outdoor cooking established a cooking hierarchy. Men were expected to perform the "important" special cooking associated with grilling food out doors; women were expected to do the "unimportant" daily cooking, which almost always happened indoors and lacked the status of cooking outside. Although a man was doing the grilling, he might not be doing much of the cooking labor. A woman probably performed the more feminine work of food preparation, chopping vegetables, fixing a salad, and making any necessary side dishes for the meal. Mrs. Raymond Hargrove commented in a 1956 article from *Parents' Magazine* about outdoor cooking: "When a man works all day to support his family, it seems only proper that his home should be as much of a castle as his wife can make it. So when Raymond becomes an outdoor chef I do whatever advance preparation is required" (63). Cooking out distanced men from the kitchen and its association with women, as food historian Harvey A. Levenstein points out in discussing the barbecuing craze of the 1950s and 1960s:

> To assuage any fears that Dad might really be serious about moving into the kitchen, he was encouraged to wear large aprons with macho slogans, which were the opposite of [Mom's] frilly ones, and wield oversize utensils, which were clearly inappropriate for the kitchen. The idea that cooking over an open fire was itself a particularly masculine pursuit also helped, reflecting American images of cowboys on the range or fishermen in the woods rather than the fact that it is women's daily task throughout much of the world. (*Paradox*, 132)

Levenstein makes it clear that cooking outside is an activity that men were allowed to pursue without social stigma because it was strongly identified with masculinity. Outdoor cooking, unlike cooking in a kitchen (mom's realm), could affirm a male's manliness. Grilling out became more than merely a pleasurable activity for pop and the kids on a summer weekend. It became a carefully choreographed display of the gender divisions that structured society.

Men's Cooking—"Extra Special, No Matter How Simple"

Along with carefully distinguishing between women's foods and men's foods, men's cooking literature helped to perpetuate the belief that when men did have to take the responsibility for cooking, they would be naturally superior to women: only men could raise cooking to an art form.

A time came in a man's life when he could not take responsibility for only the outdoor grill; he needed to venture into taboo territory: the kitchen. Perhaps his wife was ill. Perhaps she needed to visit her relatives for the weekend. For one reason or another, the regular cooking routine of the household ground to a halt. Usually, cooking literature suggested, the good wife prepared for such exigencies. She made meticulous plans to prepare for her absence since her menfolk were often depicted as incapable in the kitchen. The essay "Caring for the Summer Bachelor" (1957) in *Sunset* magazine suggested that the "attentive wife will leave a larder well stocked," but she should do far more (154). The absent housewife should make elaborate box dinners, with each item stored in its own compartment, before leaving. One dinner consisted of "jellied consommé, fried chicken, sweet potato and pineapple casserole, baking powder biscuits, butter, celery, ripe olives, [and] frozen cream puffs" (154). Another elaborate box dinner was composed of "clam chowder, [a] miniature bread loaf, tomato aspic salad, mayonnaise, [and] waffles with boysenberries and whipped cream" (156). This meal, however, was not as fancy as box dinner number seven: "scalloped seafood in shells, shoestring potatoes, peas, roll and butter, raspberry sherbet, sliced peaches, [and] cookies" (158). (Reading these menus, it becomes clear why many American women perceived the advent of frozen meals as a great blessing.)

But maybe one weekend the wife did not leave the scalloped seafood and tomato aspic salad neatly tucked away in the freezer. The husband was forced to fend for himself—not even one frozen dinner in the freezer and no friendly female available to bail him out.[16] As Richard Blake observed in "Pop's in the Kitchen!" (1947), there is "a time in every husband's life when he has to mix with the pots and pans and baking powder in kitchen. A new arrival, a temporary indisposition—and the routine of meal-getting jars to an abrupt stop. That puts it up to the man" (51). He did not suggest that men should cook for more than a brief time, however. An article from *Ladies' Home Journal* affirmed that the male visit to the kitchen should be an unusual event: "A husbandly talent that comes in handy, and is to be encouraged, is cooking. Because it is not an everyday affair, a meal prepared by the man of the house becomes extra special, no matter how simple" (Wood, "Papa," 166). Similarly, Carl Malmberg in "Dad and Daughter Cook" (1941) encouraged dad to visit the kitchen to bond with his daughter by sharing a cooking experience, but the article did not assume that dad should become a permanent fixture in the kitchen: "Many situations are made to order for a paternal invasion of the kitchen. For example, there is the maid's night off. There are Sunday and holiday suppers, and those occasions when mother is away or not feeling well. There are times when father may want to try his hand at a new dish for no other reason than the fun of it" (44). Mother, of course, did not have the option of whether or not to try a dish for the sheer pleasure of it, and she could not assume that her meals would be "extra special" merely because she prepared them. These examples show how cookbooks and cooking discourse in general affirmed that men could cook, but this was always a special event that should not be taken for granted—by no means should women become accustomed to men taking more than rare responsibility in the kitchen.

No matter what a man cooked when he bravely made a foray into the kitchen, he was "naturally" superior to a female as a cook.[17] In the popular magazine *Century*, a 1920s writer commented: "As women were born without any real taste for food—they, when alone, absorb anything at hand, chocolate éclairs and barbaric salads by preference,—they must learn, now that they are legally declared to be the equals of man, to discover why he has always been superior in that art which for centuries they have unrighteously proclaimed as entirely their own" (Egan 203).[18] Ted Trueblood's opinions about women cooks in *Field and Stream* in 1961 were little different from those of his predecessor of forty years earlier: "There are some things women can't cook. I call them man dishes. They are the ones that require a dash of boldness, as well as a dash of seasoning, and most women are too cautious by nature to treat them as they must be treated if they are to be superb rather than merely edible" (12). It is not surprising to find steak—the "greatest of all foods" according to him—first on the list (12). More surprising is that salad was next on his list, but it was a salad with a difference: "Another man dish is salad, fresh and crisp, the kind of salad that sets off a good steak as nothing else can. The typical female salad is limp and flabby, with a dressing that is never exactly right" (24). Trueblood also was scornful of women's abilities when it came to pancakes: "Very few women know how to make good hotcakes. Most have two faults: They never quit stirring the batter, and they don't keep the griddle hot enough" (24).[19]

It was not only in flipping pancakes that men excelled. Men's cooking literature also showed that men prepared with ease gourmet specialties that were so complex that would (presumably) stymie a woman chef.[20] One cookbook wrote about male cooks who were "deadly serious about their cooking. They may joke about their methods and their mistakes, but they accept only perfection in the final product. These are men who scour a city in search of an obscure herb, type of flour, or other fillip needed to complete a culinary triumph" (*Men Cooking*, n. pag.). The book contained recipes for sole in dill béchamel sauce (34), fish en papiotte (37), lobster Naranjal (50), broiled quail (66), scaloppini of veal with prosciutto and cheese (111), and veal Arturo (113). Although such dishes lacked the masculine aura of steak or chili, it was still acceptable for a man to cook such complex dishes because they demonstrated his mastery of cooking. He was raised to a lofty level of expertise that few women could ever achieve, according to the male cooking mystique. In fact, the assumption was that whenever men *did* cook, they raised it to an art form.

According to the cooking discourse that dominated much of the last hundred years, women lack the drive and talent to be bold and experimental cooks; it was assumed that men, not women, would be the great chefs. In the first half of the twentieth century, cookbooks and cooking articles frequently emphasized that women lacked the special knack of male cooks, and men were always better cooks than women. Jack Dempsey wrote in the 1930s: "When a man really sets himself to cooking, . . . he can outdo a woman any day. . . . Generally speaking, men are more original and individual cooks than women. They have a knack for putting unexpected uppercuts in ordinary dishes and making them really knockout fare" (16). Similarly, a male cook wrote in a 1933 article in *American Home* magazine: "Once a man has the knack of the kitchen he can do things in a culinary way that a woman either never dreamed of doing or would consider revolutionary" (Brown, "Men," 288). In the 1940s, another writer shared similar thoughts about women as cooks, observing that "with the average American female, I have a bone to pick. Bluntly, I find she lacks imagination in her cooking" (Fontaine, 8). What explains the repeated stress in men's cookbooks on women's lack of ability in the kitchen? This emphasis assured men that women's cooking responsibilities were not nearly so onerous as women made them out to be since any man could easily turn out a masterful meal. Also, men's absence from the kitchen stemmed from having more challenging tasks to accomplish elsewhere, not from an innate lack of ability. Overall, the emphasis on male competence assured men that kitchen duties were simple tasks, not "real" work at all, privileging the world of the workplace outside the home and trivializing the domestic realm of the kitchen.

Not all women who wrote cooking literature accepted man's claim to culinary superiority. Some scoffed at male pretensions. The "average male is a bankrupt when it comes to cookery," wrote one woman in the 1930s (Dunham, "Men," 17).[21] She sneered: "In all probability there is not one man in ten thousand, despite his eloquence to the contrary, who can go into a kitchen and produce a dinner for two people that has balance and flavor and attractiveness" (17). Another woman wrote in an article for *Good Housekeeping* entitled "Men Are Dopes as Cooks" (1949): "You've all met him. One-dish Harry, who, if the wind is right and everything else equal, can prepare an entrée, a salad, or a dessert quite well. . . . The fact that most women prepare entire meals not only on grand occasions, but night after night he considers not at all" (Pollock, 38). Writing for *House Beautiful* in the 1950s, Evelyn Humphreys was equally critical about men's cooking abilities when she discussed her husband's talents: "He is a kind of culinary straw boss. It is I who scrape carrots, cube beef, weep over onions, and peel potatoes. It is my husband who, with the preoccupation of a florist at work on an orchid corsage, compiles the bouquet of herbs and tosses it into the pot" (189). At least in popular literature, men viewed their forays into the kitchen very differently than did women. What was at stake was far more than who was going to scrape carrots or dice the potatoes; the issue being addressed was how women's kitchen work was made invisible and insignificant compared to the more glamorous cooking that a man did. Even today, it is common to hear that women do all the preparation work for a meal while a man might toss the salad at the table or grill the pork chops, the more visible cooking tasks that are apt to draw applause from family and friends. Who stops to applaud the person who cuts up the salad ingredients or marinates the pork chops?

Man Bait

Another important element of the male cooking mystique that men's cooking literature helped to promulgate is the belief that women should always cook foods that men will appreciate—even if that mandates Herculean effort—since good cooking is a way to win a man's heart. This is such a widely held belief that many people do not pause to question it. Mom, it is assumed, will cook foods that dad enjoys, not vice versa. This belief is far from benign, because it solidifies the notion that men's tastes are of more importance than women's. It also helps to ensure a patriarchal order in which women are supposed to cook in order to please men.

In the first half of the twentieth century, men's cooking literature emphasized that women should be primarily concerned with cooking dishes that men (particularly future husbands) would savor.[22] One of the most important tenets of the male cooking mystique is that a woman's food tastes should always be less important than a man's, helping to ensure that her tastes will be subordinate in other areas as well. Early-twentieth-century cookbooks rarely suggested that men should cater to women's tastes or notice their tastes at all, but commonly asserted that men's tastes were critically important to women. For example, Louise Bennett Weaver and Helen Cowles LeCron's book *A Thousand Ways to Please a Husband with Bettina's Best Recipes* (1917) was crammed with recipes for the wife who wished to impress and delight her husband. A woman was expected always to bear in mind the man's pleasure. One 1928 article from *Delineator* magazine advised the June bride to "find out what his mother cooked" and "train yourself to like his dishes" ("Dishes to Tempt," 49). In *How to Appeal to a Man's Appetites* (1962), Toby Stein cautioned his women readers: "If your husband really and truly and profoundly . . . wants steak for dinner every night, serve it to him.

Make fancy lunches for your girl friends. That way you will be sure to keep yourself in friends. And with a husband" (185). Cookbooks and cooking articles assumed that women would find it much more interesting to cater to men's desires than to women's. One article from *American Home* pronounced: "If you are one of those who cook for men—and to be honest, what woman would not prefer hearty applause from the men than from women guests—I hope that some of these tried and true recipes, pleasantly inexpensive and good enough to please the most exacting male of your acquaintance, may be of help" (Head, 89). Cooking literature suggested that only men's tastes mattered, regardless of who was doing the cooking.

According to the male cooking mystique, the primary reason for women to cook food is to please men, who presumably will reward them for their endeavors. In the first half of the 1900s, cookbooks and popular magazine articles were filled with indications that good cooking directly translated into material rewards for women, whether that meant matrimony or a mink coat. One article from *Delineator* magazine suggested making man-favorites, such as spaghetti West Texas, chili en casserole, or pork and apple surprise, if a woman wished to receive a new fur coat from her husband ("Food," 53). The same article also provided a recipe for a chocolate cake called "Bachelor Bait," promised to "get its man" (53). Another article from a 1960 issue of *McCall's* made it clear that good cooking was the best bait for men. The text that accompanied a group of "man-tested recipes" proclaimed that they were "designed specifically with your man in mind. We can almost guarantee that, with . . . *McCall's* at hand, you can cook your way into his heart—and live happily ever afterward" ("Cook Your Way into His Heart," 74). Today the popular media still present having "man" food around as a way for women to attract men. For instance, a 1990 issue of *Mademoiselle* magazine described a strategy for women who wished to attract and keep men: "Hungry men are not unlike tropical fish or small house pets: Feed them regularly and well and you'll at least get a positive reaction when they see you, if not undying love" (Brody, 74). The author suggested that women should stock their refrigerators with "guy food" such as nuts, pasta, salsas, hot sauces, pickles, mashed-bean dip, and cold pizza (74). The media continue to teach the message that has been perpetuated throughout the twentieth century: the best way to get a man is through his stomach.

But cooking for a man was only a small part of the show. As a 1950s article about Italian actress Gina Lollobrigida warned, "When cooking for a man, employ feminine psychology, recommends the international beauty. . . . No matter how long you have toiled in the kitchen, don't look it. Remember, *you* should be delectable, too" ("Cook Your Way," 70). In *Cooking as Men Like It* (1930), J. George Frederick made grander claims for the importance of women's cooking, asserting that "woman without a background of a real home, in which she personally cooks and serves food—occasionally even if not habitually—is robbing herself of her most subtle, instinctive attraction to man, is depriving herself of her most deep-rooted basis of appeal and charm, and is tampering with the very foundations of human happiness, both for herself, her family, and society as a whole" (5). According to Frederick and other writers, women's cooking skills were more than merely a way to fulfill men's hunger. Cooking skills were essential for the woman who wished to be alluring to a man. Men could cook or not cook—presumably, this would make no difference to prospective mates—but women, whether they wished to or not, had to think of cooking as a central element in their emotional and even sexual appeal.

The Male Cooking Mystique Today

Men's cooking literature is part of a much larger cooking discourse throughout the last hundred years (and earlier) that has helped to establish domestic cooking as an activity that is regarded as primarily women's responsibility. Although men do cook today more than in the past, their kitchen roles and responsibilities are far fewer than those of women, and the food-related tasks that men perform are delineated with great care: "Men's everyday participation in feeding the family is . . . usually limited to a few carefully chosen and bounded activities: running the barbecue, carving the roast, making alcoholic drinks, . . . and . . . cooking pancakes for Sunday breakfast" (Bell and Valentine, 73). Even now, men are more likely to be the star cooks than the ones who do the daily cooking that is essential to maintaining a family.

This division of cooking labor remains an important element in how we separate our society by gender roles, which often offer more power and status to men than to women. The male cooking mystique, with its assumption that the regular daily cooking is women's job, has far-reaching ramifications. Women are the ones responsible for a double shift, working a full-time job and then rushing home to cook a meal for the family. Since cooking in our society remains deeply linked to gender, if a wife decides *not* to cook, this frequently is perceived as a sign that she is "abnormal" and "bad." Society polices how women (and men) relate to cooking-related responsibilities because this is an effective way to maintain traditional gender roles. Every time a woman goes to a grocery store, cooks a meal for a family, or prepares a menu for the week, she reassures society that cooking and other nurturing activities are women's "natural" activities.

Chapter 2

"The Enchantment of Mixing-Spoons"

Cooking Lessons for Girls and Boys

The Betty Betz Teen-Age Cookbook (1953) informed its readers: "If a girl is reasonably attractive and a good cook as well, she has better odds for marriage than her playgirl friend who boasts that she 'can't even boil water'" (Betz, 1). "Remember that the good-looking girl who's also a 'good-cooking girl' stands more of a chance of sniffing orange blossoms!" Betz cautioned (1). She was teaching a great deal more than how to cook; she was also teaching girls lessons about gender behavior that were expected to last a lifetime. The juvenile cookbook, a popular subgenre, has existed for over a century. Despite their prevalence, juvenile cookbooks have been largely overlooked by scholars. Since boys and girls are regarded as less significant than adults in Western culture, they are often left out of the picture in discussing cooking and its ideology. To understand how adults come to hold very definite ideas about cooking and its relationship to gender, we must turn to the lessons that boys and girls learn about food and cooking while still young. Like men's cookbooks, juvenile cookbooks do more than teach how to grill a steak or bake a cake; they demonstrate to boys and girls the attitudes that society expects them to adopt toward cooking and cooking-related tasks. In the first half of the century, juvenile cookbooks charted the culinary path for boys and girls from the undifferentiated years of early childhood, when both genders were sometimes encouraged to help with small cooking tasks, to later years, when boys were warned to stay out of the kitchen and girls were encouraged to remain there. Juvenile cookbooks are an intriguing genre because they teach not only cookery but also sex roles.

The practical necessity of teaching girls (and sometimes boys) about cooking has always existed in human society, and juvenile cookbooks serve as one method of conveying cooking knowledge. In the nineteenth century, juvenile cookbooks such as Elizabeth Stansbury Kirkland's *Six Little Cooks, or, Aunt Jane's Cooking Class* (1877) were a way to pass down recipes and cooking lessons, primarily to little girls. These books became more prevalent in the twentieth century, when the rising importance of the juvenile book business helped ensure that children's cookbooks were broadly published and distributed. Late-nineteenth- and early-twentieth-century manufacturers of foods also discovered that juvenile cooking literature was an effective way to hook consumers at an early age, since such literature often featured brand-name foods from a variety of companies.[1] For many reasons, juvenile cookbooks have become a staple product of both large and small book publishing companies. It is impossible to discuss all these books, but the ones examined here are representative of the others. Although these books were published between the 1910s and 1950s, many of my observations are applicable to more recent cookbooks as well.[2]

This chapter does not focus exclusively on cookbooks, since these books were involved in a much larger discourse about juvenile cooking. Unfortunately, I cannot adequately explore the countless intersections between juvenile cookbooks and girls' (and boys') material culture, which includes dolls, toys, books, and numerous other items.[3] I hope another scholar will study the intriguing issue of how the material culture of cooking influences young people.[4] This chapter discusses cooking culture primarily in cookbooks and magazines from the first half of the twentieth century, which display many of the same messages about cooking and gender that we discover in cookbooks for adults.

Every Boy and Girl?

Whether directed at an audience of children or adults, cookbooks are one of the most strongly gendered forms of popular literature (along with romance novels). It is important to understand the process through which a cookbook becomes identified as reading material "for women only," because this strong identification is one reason that domestic cooking remains women's work even today. From their earliest years, children in the first half of the century were indoctrinated to assume that cooking was women's responsibility. Juvenile cookbooks promulgated this belief in many ways, most obviously by targeting girls, not boys, as their "natural" audience; this message was strongly emphasized by titles and cover art. Thus, boys learned that cooking was not an acceptable male activity before they cracked open a single volume.

Although most cookbooks from the first half of the twentieth century did not address both boys and girls in their titles, there were exceptions, including Henrietta Fleck's *A First Cook Book for Boys and Girls* (1953); Julia Kiene's *The Step-by-Step Cook Book for Girls and Boys* (1956), and Betty Crocker's *Cook Book for Boys and Girls* (1957). Other cookbooks adopted different approaches to acknowledge a co-ed audience, such as one 1920s cookbook dedicated "to every girl and boy who enjoys cooking" (Judson, *Child Life*, n. pag.). Books that mentioned both girls and boys, however, were largely outnumbered by those that addressed only girls: Caroline French Benton's *A Little Cook Book for a Little Girl* (1905); Olive Hyde Foster's *Housekeeping, Cookery and Sewing for Little Girls* (1925); and Maud Murdoch's *The Girls' Book of Cooking* (1961). A book might also be dedicated to a girl, such as Marie P. Hill and Frances H. Gaines's *Fun in the Kitchen* (1927), "dedicated to all little girls who love to play house and to make things" (n. pag.).[5] Often boys were disregarded completely when cooking was discussed, as in Kate Douglas Wiggin's *Good Housekeeping* article "A Little Talk to Girls on Cookery" (1912). The large number of cookbooks (and other forms of cooking literature) that addressed girls, not boys, supported a culture in which cooking was supposed to be girls' "natural" employment. Boys were taught to view cooking with uneasiness and were instructed at a young age that their masculinity was imperiled in the most feminine home environment: the kitchen.

Juvenile cooking literature also referred to an implied audience of girls in more subtle ways. For example, Helen Powell Schauffler's article "The Five-Year-Old Cook" (1926) discussed only a girl's cooking efforts. The article also relied on feminine pronouns to describe young cooks. Similarly, the generic title of Mae Blacker Freeman's juvenile cookbook *Fun with Cooking* (1947) suggested that the book could address both boys and girls. The book's introduction, however, told a different story, informing readers: "A girl who makes the things in this book . . . gains enough experience to go on to more complicated dishes" (5). Clearly, boys were not part of the intended audience. The majority of juvenile cooking literature considered the girl to be the cook. In Mrs. S. T. Rorer's article "Cakes and Candies Children Can Make" (1910), she warned mothers to make sure that "each little girl ha[d] an apron, sleevelets, a blank book and a pencil" if she was going to try making candy, even though the article's title referred to children, not just girls (40).[6] Peggy Hoffmann's *Miss B.'s First Cookbook: Twenty Family-Sized Recipes for the Youngest Cook* (1950) prepared young girls to follow in their mothers' footsteps. Hoffmann wrote that the book would give the beginning cook "a fine chance to help in her own way and will prepare her to be a good cook when she grows up" (n. pag.). As these examples demonstrate, juvenile cookbooks often addressed a female audience, even if the books' titles did not address *only* girls. In such a fashion, the books indicated that girls were "naturally" the ones who should cook.

Juvenile cookbooks also suggested the "correct" audience by including photographs only of girls. Hill and Gaines's *Fun in the Kitchen* was decorated with pictures of little girls cooking, not boys.[7] Betz's book could more accurately be entitled *The Betty Betz Teen-Age Girl Cookbook*, because the heavily illustrated book pictured only girls cooking. When the rare boy was depicted in a juvenile cookbook, he was typically not a cook but a consumer. Fleck's *A First Cook Book for Boys and Girls* included numerous pictures of girls cooking and boys eating the delicacies they dished up. Alice D. Morton's *Cooking Is Fun* (1962) had a number of pictures of girls making and serving food, but just two pictures of a boy cooking. Mary Blake's *Fun to Cook Book* (1955) featured a cover illustration of a small girl cooking. The dominance of illustrations of girls cooking, not boys, conveyed one underlying message of these books: girls were the cooks and boys were the consumers. Girls and boys carried these messages into adulthood, assuring that the majority of women prepared and served food to men.

"Sugar and Spice and All Things Nice": *Girls' and Boys' Food Preferences*

Juvenile cookbooks were a small cog in the much larger machine that instructed children about the complex world of food and cooking and the "correct" gendered relationship they should adopt to food preparation and eating. Even the choice of foods, boys and girls quickly learned, was not an innocent matter of personal preference but was instead an opportunity to display their adherence to what society regarded as "proper" masculine or feminine behavior. Thus, when juvenile cookbooks mentioned boys' and girls' food preferences, they also affirmed what was considered desirable behavior for the genders.

According to juvenile cookbooks, boys and girls were supposed to have distinctly different food preferences. Boys, like men, were expected to prefer hearty foods; girls, like women, were supposed to enjoy sweet, delicate foods. As Kiene observed in *The Step-by-Step Cook Book for Girls and Boys*, "Girls may like to excel in pastries, and so forth, but boys want food that sticks to the ribs" (34). Boys were also expected to have little or no interest in food's appearance as long as it appealed to their taste buds; girls, however, were supposed to be concerned about the presentation of food. This different approach was emphasized repeatedly in juvenile cookbooks; appearance was an issue with even the most plebeian of foods: potatoes. One 1920s cookbook observed about creamed potatoes: "Most boys like them because they taste good, and girls choose them because they look pretty" (Harris, *Patty Pans*, 18). The simplest food (whether steak, potatoes, or Jell-O) carried symbolic weight. When picking a food, a girl was taught that aesthetics was more important than taste. This belief went beyond creamed potatoes: women were supposed to be concerned about attractiveness in all areas of their lives from home to personal appearance. This concern is one of the main signifiers of femininity. Thus, cookbooks were not just teaching a lesson about how to concoct a Jell-O salad; they were also giving an additional subtle lesson on how femininity was constituted.

Girls were taught to think of creaminess and sweetness as feminine. Creamy and sweet dishes appeared everywhere in juvenile cookbooks; it was implied that girls would take special delight in making and consuming them. Dad and brother might enjoy a slice of coconut cream pie or some other dessert, but it was clear that such treats were primarily for girls and women. Creamed dishes were particularly prevalent in cookbooks from the early decades of the twentieth century. Caroline French Benton's *A Little Cook Book for a Little Girl* (1905) contained recipes for creamed eggs, creamed eggs on toast, creamed codfish, creamed fish, creamed lobster, creamed salmon, creamed oysters, creamed turkey, creamed potatoes, creamed sweet potatoes, and creamed cabbage.[8] Sweet dishes were also given a star role in juvenile cookbooks. Benton assured her readers that many sweet sandwich combinations were tasty: "All jams and jellies make good sandwiches, and fresh dates, chopped figs, and preserved ginger are also nice" (*A Little Cook Book*, 168).[9] *The Teenage Cook Book* (1958) emphasized both creaminess and sweetness in a recipe for "pineapple fluff," combining a can of crushed pineapple with eight chopped marshmallows and a cup of whipped cream (Rider and Taylor, 68). The same book had a recipe for "frosted lovers' pie": thirty-two marshmallows melted in hot milk, a can of crushed pineapple, whipped cream, and nuts—all poured into a pie crust (92). Such recipes conveyed to young readers the food tastes that they were expected to adopt. Girls were supposed to prefer rich, sweet dishes; boys were supposed to prefer plainer recipes. These gendered tastes continue to serve as one of the many ways that boys and girls (and men and women) display their gender identification today. When a woman orders salad for lunch at a restaurant and a man orders pork chops and potatoes, they are sometimes doing much more than satisfying their hunger; they are also expressing their gender.

Juvenile cookbooks also gave girls other culinary advice. They learned that they should enjoy imaginative food and should fret over making it attractive and decorative. A recipe could always be made more exotic. A fanciful name helped: Louise Price Bell's *Kitchen Fun: Teaches Children to Cook Successfully* (1932) included recipes for fairy gingerbread (9), Cinderella cake (10), and rainbow dessert (13). Girls had to think about the aesthetics of food preparation, especially if they aspired to be the hostess of the month featured in *Good Housekeeping*. Even the camping cookbook *Kettles and*

Campfires: The Girl Scout Camp and Trail Cook Book (1928) urged girls to consider the appearance of food: "Camp cooking affords an opportunity to become interested in the esthetics of food combinations and table arrangements and demonstrates that an attractive meal served in an attractive place is eaten with increased relish" (Girl Scouts, 6). Even on a camping trip, cooking was more than serving food; it was an opportunity for a girl to show her artistic talents. Cooking let girls demonstrate that they were learning the "correct" feminine habits that they would require as adult women.

And there were so many ways for the aspiring young hostess to decorate meals! For example, a 1938 recipe for Gelatin Sailboats suggested creating a peach boat using a peach slice, a toothpick, and a paper sail to decorate a serving of gelatin (Maltby, 258). The same cookbook urged girls to decorate pudding with a "flower" made of a snipped-up marshmallow and chocolate shavings (261). If these recipes posed insufficient artistic challenges, a girl could try her hand at composing a candlestick salad, a recipe popular in the 1950s and included in many of the period's cookbooks, like *My First Cookbook* (1959). The cook stuck a banana half into a ring of canned pineapple, with a maraschino cherry balanced on top of the banana to imitate the flame and a bit of red-dyed mayonnaise for the candle's wax (25). Candlestick salad, however, paled in intricacy compared to some of the more complicated recipes for girl cooks. *Better Homes and Gardens Junior Cook Book for the Hostess and Host of Tomorrow* (1963) was chock-full of decorative recipes that would especially appeal to young girls. Party-surprise sandwiches were "frosted" with cream cheese to look like a cake and decorated with olive "flowers" (26). Dressed-up doughnuts had rims spread "with marshmallow cream and roll[ed] in chopped maraschino cherries" (29). Glittery sugar mallows were marshmallows dipped in cream then rolled in colored sugar (38). Fancy recipes like these demonstrated that girls were supposed to think of food as a way to highlight their aesthetic talents. They learned that their creative abilities were best focused in the home, as good homemakers.

Boys and girls also received messages from these cookbooks about why, when, and what they were expected to cook, creating two different codes of behavior. These codes had broad ramifications that went far beyond the kitchen, teaching girls and boys about the gender roles they were supposed to adopt in society at large.

"The Supreme Key to the Greatest of Womanly Arts": Girls' Cooking

The message that is most often conveyed to girls by juvenile cooking literature is that they should have a "natural" affinity for cooking, as Louisa Price Bell points out in a 1943 *American Home* article: "Any sand pile shows what little girls like to do. Witness the long rows of soggy little mud cakes with rock salt icing! The desire to cook is almost as natural to little girls as the desire to play" (80). Girls were supposed to grow up with this "natural" love of cooking passed down from mother to daughter. Daughters modeled themselves after mothers, as one 1941 article from *Parents' Magazine* described: "When you get out your mixing bowl and spoon, have you not smiled when your small daughter did the same going through the make-believe process of beating and stirring just as you did?" (Bell, "Children," 54). Through such rhetoric, girls learned that they had no option about whether or not to pursue cooking. If they did not cook, they endangered much more than their individual family's health; they threatened to unbalance a culture based on women performing their "natural" duties, whether cooking dinner or taking care of children, while men performed their "natural" activities, including working for money and being responsible for law and discipline in families.

Girls also learned that cooking was, as one writer observed, "the supreme key to the greatest of womanly arts: keeping house and family happy" (Craig, 166). For girls, cooking became a semisacred experience, because they would grow up to be homemakers. Learning how to cook, juvenile cooking literature suggested, was important not just to a girl's family, but to all humanity. It was never too early for girls to learn how to cook, as one article explained: "So many mothers think cooking is for adults only, or at least should be postponed until their small daughters enter Home Economics class at school. . . . Yet these same mothers will admit that their small daughters are embryo homemakers, that an important part of homemaking is to know how to cook and like it" (Bell, "Some Rainy Afternoon," 80). Alice Bradley wrote in 1926 about the importance of learning how to cook so that girls would mature into good cooks: "Mothers often do not realize what a handicap it is to their daughters to get married without ever having had charge of the housekeeping in their own homes for even a limited time. It would be wise for every mother to give her 'teen age' daughter at least one week of housekeeping responsibility this summer" ("When the Children Cook," 98). The lesson that cooking is a girl's sacred responsibility has not died out completely even today. Many wives and mothers—whether or not they have full-time employment outside the home—still feel that it is their responsibility to cook; this belief is hard to shake because it has been woven into the cultural fabric of American society since its earliest years.

Juvenile cookbooks promised that cooking was not just hard work; it was also fun. Constance Cassady's book *Kitchen Magic* (1932) referred to cooking as "a sort of magic" (3); young Ann was invited by her mother to "learn the enchantment of mixing-spoons and pans and things like that" (3).[10] Some writers were even more ebullient when it came to describing the pleasures of cooking. *The Seventeen Cookbook* (1964) informed teen-aged girls: "Cooking is more than a means to an end: in its most exciting, satisfying form it becomes an end in itself—an expression of one's personality" (v). The most honest comment about the role of cooking in a woman's life came from the book flap of Maud Murdoch's *The Girls' Book of Cooking*: "For every girl who wants to be a good cook, this book is an absolute 'must.' Written by a housewife who herself finds cooking eternally interesting in spite of having to do it all the time, it presents the 'how,' 'why,' and 'what' of cooking in an original and exciting way" (n. pag.). Cooking might be fun and interesting, but it was also a chore that girls were expected to perform almost every day for the rest of their lives. These cookbooks were insistent about the delights of cooking, luring girls into performing a task that might be drudgery, not fun.

Finally, girls learned that good cooking skills were essential because they were the best means to attract boys (aka future husbands). Cookbooks taught about cooking, but they also taught how girls should make themselves appeal to boys. The cook who could whip together a stellar banana cream pie or the lightest, moistest chocolate cake was promised more men than she could squeeze into the kitchen. Robert H. Loeb, Jr.'s *Date Bait: The Younger Set's Picture Cookbook* (1952) promised to give its female readers "more dates than [they] can handle" (n. pag.). *Date Bait* queried: "Does Suzy have all the boys hanging around her place like a school of fish around a worm, just because of a certain cake she bakes? Nothing to it—you can hook those fish in a jiffy" (13). The book urged readers to try its cookie and candy recipes, guaranteed to "hook a whale" (13). *The Seventeen Cookbook* was equally insistent that food served as the best bait for boys: "To many men (and most teen-age boys) cooking is one of the feminine mysteries, one they can heartily appreciate. With an ever-hungry young man, few things enhance a girl's stock as a girl as swiftly, as surely, as something really good to eat that she made herself" (v). It described a party menu containing "the foods which have proved, survey after survey, to be most popular with boys" (266). "Most of the popular girls we know have one thing in common. In the kitchen, there's a cookie jar—and there's always something in it," the author wrote (342). Cooking was repeatedly held up as the best way to get a boy; never did these books suggest that boys should use good cooking skills to "hook a girl." Girls learned early that they should cook for boys but not expect boys to cook for them. Boys rarely or never crossed this gender division, and girls were taught that they should not seek to change it because it was society's "natural" order.

Girls learned a host of lessons from juvenile cooking literature that prepared them for their adult roles as the primary domestic preparers and servers of food. Throughout the first half of the twentieth century, juvenile cookbooks remained remarkably consistent about the messages that they conveyed to young girls. Girls should cook for the family since it was their "natural" responsibility. They should enjoy cooking. And, finally, cooking was the best way to catch boys. All of these lessons instructed girls about the domestic roles they should have as adults. But what lessons did boys learn?

"Making Cake Is Not a Man's Job"

The first and most important lesson for boys was that cooking was *not* their responsibility. This fact was conveyed to them in many ways, including the dearth of books addressed to boys. Only a few juvenile cookbooks were directed solely at boys, compared to the hundreds of juvenile cookbooks addressed to girls. These boys' cookbooks were careful to build up a different image of cooking than the one found in most juvenile cookbooks directed at girls. Boys' cookbooks needed to stress that cooking was not too feminine. Jerrold Beim's *The First Book of Boys' Cooking* (1957) emphasized that its recipes were "for the kinds of things that boys like to eat most. No frills or fuss—just down-to-earth cooking with some fun ideas for good measure" (n. pag.). He referred to the kitchen as a boy's "workshop," more closely aligning it with traditional masculine environments such as garages and tool shops. Beim drew the gender lines: "The day-to-day cooking for the family is usually done by a woman. But in many families the man is considered the expert when it comes to mixing a salad" (45). Outdoor cooking was also a masculine activity, according to Beim: "Outdoors is where a man can really shine as a cook! When you cook inside, you have usually borrowed the use of the kitchen from your mother. But with outside cooking, boys or men take over completely. The world around you is your kitchen" (63). Like Beim's book, Helen Evans Brown and Philip S. Brown's *The Boys' Cook Book* (1959) carefully demonstrated its masculine allegiance by including many "manly" recipes: chili cheeseburgers, steak sandwiches, roast wild duck, fried rabbit, rabbit paprika, buck stew, cannibal steak, broiled pork chops, beef stew, chile con carne, and garlic spareribs. Clearly, the few boys' cookbooks that did exist conveyed to young men that cooking was an acceptable pursuit only in the right situation (an outdoor barbecue) or when "manly" foods (stew or spareribs, for instance) were being prepared. Primarily, however, the lack of boys' cookbooks suggested that cooking was not a duty that should concern boys, an attitude that has proven remarkably durable for the last century (and much longer).

Although few juvenile cookbooks were targeted solely at boys, a number of cookbooks mentioned both girls and boys. Alma S. Lach addressed both in *A Child's First Cook Book* (1950). Julia Kiene was helped by a panel of girls and boys when she tested her recipes for *The Step-by-Step Cook Book for Girls and Boys*. Although these children's books might have appeared egalitarian, they usually held different messages for boys and girls. For instance, *Young America's Cook Book: A Cook Book for Boys and Girls Who Like Good Food* (1938) pictured both boys and girls preparing food. But girls were shown frosting a cake (189) and canning fruits (207), while boys were depicted carving a roast (231), filleting a fish (257), and serving a rabbit casserole for a stag dinner (237). Similarly, a dozen girls and boys served as helpers in creating *Betty Crocker's New Boys and Girls Cook Book* (1965), which addressed both girls and boys. But even a book such as this featured the boys cooking out over a campfire and grilling steaks, while girls were pictured frosting a cake and making candy. If boys were included in juvenile cookbooks, their presence mandated careful explanation. One book defended its inclusion of boys: "You notice I said boy just as surely as I said girl. For how in the world is a boy going to manage a camping trip or even a one-day picnic in the woods if he doesn't know how to cook?" (Judson, *Child Life*, 1). The book later described why one small boy wanted to learn how to cook: "he was a very, very bright boy and he knew perfectly well that if he wanted to go camping and have house parties and all such fun, he'd better learn how to cook a meal by himself" (36). Cookbooks might have included both boys and girls, but they taught children about the "correct" gender division of cooking tasks. Boys learned that they were able (and expected) to perform only certain tasks. Thus, even when juvenile cookbooks might have appeared to be most egalitarian, they still conveyed rigid rules about gender divisions in cooking, which probably carried over to other arenas both inside and outside the kitchen.

Although the majority of juvenile cooking literature left out all mention of boys or carefully delineated what jobs they should perform, a few writers in the first half of the twentieth century supported the idea of boys cooking, even if they would not be grilling a steak. Cookbooks and popular magazines often promoted the idea that both very young boys and girls should learn how to cook.[11] Bertha Gagos wrote in her article "Children Love to Cook" (1949) in *Parents' Magazine*: "There is a time in every child's life when he or she wants to help in the kitchen" (43). Cooking for the youngest boys was acceptable because their gender was relatively undifferentiated, but some early-twentieth-century writers promoted the idea that even older boys should learn how to cook.[12] Bob Davis, for example, wrote in a 1936 article for *Delineator* magazine: "The public schools, and all institutions where learning is to be acquired and the younger generation enlightened to take up the responsibilities of living, should include in the curriculum plain cooking for boys. The lad who cannot assemble an edible breakfast in fifteen minutes . . . is unfitted for the responsibilities of matrimony or to pose as the head of a household" (21). An author writing in 1956 for *House Beautiful* magazine said that boys should "learn that . . . most human of all arts, which is cooking. Certainly if boys grow up, as they have in the past, with a growing contempt for girls' activities and interests, that contempt will abide in some form in adulthood. And if they themselves are not inspired in some way to know, *really* know . . . the womanly art of homemaking (which is nothing less than the art of life itself), then the future of the family is in a state of extreme danger" (Craig, 194). For these writers, cooking played such a crucial role in the family that both boys and girls should be prepared to cook; such writers, however, were rare compared to the vast majority of observers, who argued that young boys did not belong in the kitchen.

More commonly, writers suggested that boys, like men, should be prepared to cook only in an emergency. For instance, in "Boys and Cookery" (1917), Ladd Plumley urged that boys be taught how to cook because it would help prepare them for future wartime conditions, when women might be missing altogether (178). He also went a step farther by suggesting that *all* boys needed to learn how to cook so they would be prepared for the exigencies of daily life: "There is no man anywhere who would not be a more efficient citizen if, in emergencies, he could broil a beefsteak, cook chops, make coffee, bake a pan of biscuit, conjure an omelet, and, yes,—mix, knead, and bake a loaf of palatable bread" (179). Plumley, however, made it clear that boys needed to be trained for "emergencies," not the daily cooking that was part of any household's ritual. This idea that boys should cook only for special occasions was reiterated in many early-twentieth-century cookbooks.[13] For instance, in Caroline French Benton's *The Fun of Cooking: A Story for Boys and Girls* (1915) Jack Blair keeps on insisting that cooking is for girls, not boys. His attitude begins to change when he goes camping with his father and recognizes that men and boys need to know how to cook. By the end of the book, Jack concludes: "Emergency cooking is all right; men ought to know how to do that. . . . I'm perfectly willing to cook bacon for breakfast, or scramble eggs, or cook fish for supper, or make a stew" (206). Note that Jack by no means is offering to take over a larger share of the cooking. He also insists that he will not cook desserts and pies, observing that "making cake is not a man's job" (223). Inez N. McFee's *Young People's Cook Book* (1925) also suggested that both boys and girls should learn how to cook. Boys and men would need the ability to cook when "the kitchen goddesses are absent or when they go on long camping trips" (vii). Like *The Fun of Cooking*, McFee's book failed to suggest that boys needed to cook except in an emergency or when they were camping. Lucy Mary Maltby's *It's Fun to Cook* (1938) is a long narrative about two twins, Eleanor Ann and Elsie Jane, who make a variety of recipes and learn correct etiquette. The book contains menus for a tea party, a bridge luncheon, and similar activities for women and girls. The only chapter in which boys cook is "Week End at the Lake," when some boys decide they want to do the cooking for a weekend, making one woman comment, "I feel very queer about the food arrangements for this trip" (130). In Maltby's book, the boys are not expected to cook except for a special occasion. When they do cook, they prepare "manly" meals such as hamburgers, steak, and broiled steak kabobs. The girls, in contrast, make recipes like creamed shrimps and eggs on toast, watercress and cream cheese sandwiches, candied sweet potatoes, Canadian bacon, and candied apple pie.

Cooking literature sometimes instructed boys that they should select one specialty meal to prepare, but no more. Boys did not need to claim the broad expertise in cooking that girls had to possess. Louise Price Bell wrote in a 1943 *American Home* article: "Let your children cook as often as they want to; encourage them all you can. This applies to boys as well as girls. There is nothing a man is prouder of than his skill over the kitchen range. One little boy I know can make a mean waffle, another is an expert at a secret hamburger concoction, a third at baking powder biscuits" ("Some Rainy Afternoon," 80). Thus, boys were trained to become specialists at a limited task (the baking powder biscuit, for instance), but girls were not given the choice to possess such limited skills; they were being trained to be the central cooks in families. Boys were taught to be what one book called "happy amateurs in the kitchen" (Gossett and Elting, n. pag.). Armed with his single specialty, a man transforms himself into an expert. Equipped with hundreds of recipes that she must use night after night, a woman becomes a drudge, perceived as possessing no true sense of the Epicurean heights that may be reached with food (something males, presumably, understand).

The final message that boys learned from cooking literature was that cooking was so easy that any boy could do it if he so desired. One 1948 article in *House Beautiful* informed readers: "Take our word for it—any boy who can read can cook. What's more, he'll love to" ("Making a Cook," 225). The attitude that good cooking requires nothing more complicated than following a recipe is the same attitude that has defined women's domestic responsibilities (no matter what they might be) as easier than men's. A long-lasting American stereotype is that women complain too much about their "easy" household tasks, including cooking. Juvenile cookbooks support the belief that cooking is much easier than women make it out to be—and it is enjoyable. Thus, they have no right to complain about their burden of household tasks.

Of Easy-Bake Ovens . . .

Juvenile cookbooks and cooking articles in the first half of the twentieth century taught different messages about cooking to girls and boys. Boys were instructed that—if they learned to cook at all—they should become knowledgeable about only a few items. For them, cooking was an optional pursuit; no juvenile cookbook suggested that boys should take over the majority of household cooking responsibilities. In cotrast, girls were taught that cooking was one of the most joyous tasks they would perform in their households; they should perceive it as a pleasure. Girls should also remember at all times that cooking was a sacred responsibility to the family. These ideas about the gendered nature of cooking are still active today. More girls than boys participate in regular daily cooking in a household. Although a larger number of boys cook today than in earlier decades, many boys still perform relatively limited cooking chores in comparison to the responsibilities of the majority of girls.

Today girls and boys learn at an early age what their "proper" domestic responsibilities are in areas ranging from cooking to taking out the trash. They learn at an early age that cooking is "girls' work." Studying how children learn the gendered nature of cooking (and many other responsibilities) is a task that mandates going farther afield than cookbooks. The whole culture of childhood cooking, from cookbooks to toys, needs more in-depth exploration. Thus far, scholars have skimmed the top of a huge field. Even the simplest toy plays a more important role than we might first assume. What does it mean that the one toy I craved most when I was a child was a Betty Crocker Easy-Bake oven? (My mom never bought me one, which is probably why I became a professor.) I now recognize that something as "simple" as an Easy-Bake oven is more complex than it first might appear. The history of toys modeled after kitchen appliances and how such toys have been marketed to girls and countless other items that form juvenile cooking culture deserve scholarly attention.

Chapter 3

Paradise Pudding, Peach Fluff, and Prune Perfection

Dainty Dishes and the Construction of Femininity

In the popular magazine *Delineator*, Betsy Standish wrote about an up-to-date party for the modern hostess. Her article "Two Dainty February Festivals" (1915) emphasized the importance of serving delicate dishes: "The time-honored tradition of a groaning table . . . has been abandoned. The most modern and successful of hostesses in New York have learned to save time, labor and expense and their guests' health through simplicity in their modes of entertaining. A simple luncheon . . . is 'smart,' as well as sensible. The sort of simplicity which includes the most daintiness and perfection of detail is what is meant" (24). Standish described a dainty menu for a Martha Washington party that included grapefruit with cherries, egg soufflé with tomato sauce, asparagus salad with red peppers, strawberry tarts, and pink bonbons (24). She was not alone in emphasizing the importance of dainty dining for women. An article in the *Pictorial Review* by Phyllis Pulliam Jervey entitled "Novel Bridge Teas and Suppers" (1928) mentioned that "daintiness and simplicity are the key notes of . . . after-bridge refreshments" (32). Despite Standish's and Jervey's emphasis on simplicity, the hostess most likely would have been forced to labor long hours over a hot stove to provide the "daintiness and perfection of detail" that the writers suggested was the sine qua non of party-giving for the fashionable lady. Giving a formal tea party or a bridge party could require many courses, some of them ornate and fanciful—dishes difficult to prepare, especially in the early 1900s when reliable servants were becoming increasingly scarce. But women's magazines did not stop to consider the labor shortage when they described complex menus for ladies' parties. *Woman's Home Companion* in 1923 suggested one menu for a bridge luncheon that no doubt tasted and appeared dainty. It was also elaborate and expensive:

> *Chicken Soup Garnished with Hearts and Diamonds of*
> *Pimiento, Spades and Clubs of Truffle*
> *Ham Hearts with Spinach*
> *Stuffed Celery*
> *Bridge Biscuits*
> *Ginger Ale Jelly Salad*
> *Chocolate Ice Cream and Raspberry Sherbet*
> *Heart and Diamond Cookies Spread with Red Confectioner's Frosting*
> *Spade and Club Cookies Spread with Sweet Chocolate*
> *Salted Nuts*
> *Bonbons*
> *Coffee*
> (Bradley, "For Your Bridge Party," 104)

Such dainty bridge party or tea party menus appeared frequently in women's magazines and cookbooks in the first decades of the twentieth century, a period when the popular press stressed delicacy and femininity in the recipes they published for desserts, soups, and other foods that were judged to be "proper" for a woman to serve when her lady friends visited for a tea party or luncheon.[1] (A hostess presumably would understand that such meals should not be served to her husband, boyfriend, or other males, who required more substantial fare.) Foods for women were also supposed to appear fanciful and ornamental, even if such recipes mandated that women spend hours on decorating and garnishing.

Cooking literature in the early 1900s taught women not only the right way to make tea sandwiches or decorate teacakes but also how to be feminine and ladylike. A woman proved herself to be a lady by preparing dainty, genteel foods for everything from bridge gatherings to tea parties. Popular cooking literature taught women lessons about the desirability of daintiness and femininity. Since tea parties and Jell-O were important elements in the dainty food fad, analyzing how the media described these food experiences reveals much about cultural expectations.

In discussing such decorative recipes and menus, I focus on representation, not reality. Magazines and cookbooks published elaborate recipes and menus, but this does not mean that women necessarily used them frequently. Today, for instance, women might read recipes in *Ladies' Home Journal* or *Woman's Day* but not cook the meals at home, or perhaps try a recipe only after adapting it. In many ways, it does not matter how often women in the early 1900s followed such recipes in their homes; the recipes suggested an idealized upper-middle-class vision of what women were expected to achieve in the kitchen. The plethora of recipes that emphasized that ladies' food should be dainty and delicate also implicitly suggested that women should share the same attributes.

Daintiness and Conspicuous Consumption

In the first few decades of the twentieth century, a woman could hardly flip through a women's magazine or cookbook without encountering scores of articles about dainty foods, including appetizers, salads, main dishes, and desserts. One such article, "Midsummer Dainties" (1911), included recipes for tomato and cucumber jelly salad, tomato and crab salad, and fruit in cantaloupes (267). A similar article, "Dainty Fillings for Small Tarts" (1912), contained recipes for lemon honey tarts, Welsh cheesecakes, Lent tartlets, and coconut tartlets (Hodgson, 388). Yet another described the delicacies—including crystallized strawberries, frozen coffee cream, peanut sweethearts, and rosebuds (pink frosted cakes decorated with coconut)— that a mother could prepare to celebrate her "girl graduates" (Brewer, 50). Daintiness seemed omnipresent. It was one of the most popular words in the media to describe everything from women's food to women's clothing— even women's underarm deodorant.

But what did "daintiness" actually mean, since the word was attached to so many disparate things in the nineteenth and early twentieth centuries? It referred to delicate recipes, but it could also refer to rich ones, filled with whipped cream and other calorie-laden ingredients. The word "daintiness" was also used to describe items that were considered particularly feminine,

like lace or lingerie. Foods that were ornamental and ladylike—tea sandwiches, small decorated cakes, and gelatin desserts—were frequently called
"dainty." "Daintiness" suggested a whole feminine ethos about how women
should look and act. It was also a way for women to distinguish themselves
from men—who, at least according to the media, possessed an uneasy relationship to daintiness at best.

In cooking literature, dainty foods for ladies appeared everywhere, particularly in the dessert sections of cookbooks. As Sylvia Lovegren writes in
Fashionable Food: Seven Decades of Food Fads (1995), desserts in this period
were "frothy, cloudlike, and very feminine. Whipped gelatin, whipped cream,
whipped egg whites, and marshmallows were all incorporated into desserts
to make them delicate, ethereal, and devastatingly rich" (17). The recipes
in cookbooks from the period support her claim. *Sea Foam's Collection of
Dainty Receipts* (1907), a pamphlet of recipes supplied to consumers by the
Sea Foam Baking Powder Company, included numerous treats so light and
airy that they almost seemed ready to drift away to be eaten by fairies; in-
deed, one cake was called fairy cake (13). A recipe named delicate cake contained eight egg whites (3). But angel food cake was even lighter and more
ethereal, containing the whites of eleven eggs (9). *Dainty Receipts* also included recipes for delicacies such as fruited whipped cream (24), charlotte
russe (24), strawberry cream (25), floating island (26), and vanilla cream, a
dessert molded in a jelly mold and then "masked with a thin layer of jelly
and decorated with glacé cherries and angelica" (27). Mary M. Wright's
cookbook *Dainty Desserts* (1922) also contained numerous delicate recipes:
gooseberry dainty, lemon jelly dessert, lemon jelly with marshmallows, strawberries in gelatin, peach fluff, tapioca fluff with fruit, strawberry marshmallow whip, and ginger sponge, among many others. Desserts combined
daintiness and sweetness—two of the food attributes that most people considered quintessentially feminine. Eating such a dessert was more than a way
to sate a woman's hunger; it was also a chance for her to display her femininity by being associated with such ladylike desserts. (In a similar way,
men emphasize their masculinity by eating steak, a food associated with
masculinity.)

The ideal that women's food should be feminine and delicate, already well
established in the nineteenth century, became a craze in the twentieth century. The popular media were filled with dainty recipes.[2] In *Paradox of*

Plenty: A Social History of Eating in Modern America (1993), food historian Harvey A. Levenstein writes about how the cult of daintiness worked to define women as distinct from men:

> Women . . . were expected to like "dainty" foods. These were normally prepared for women's luncheons and other functions where hearty-eating men were not present. . . . Women's food . . . reflected the persistence of the nineteenth-century double standard and the Victorian ideal of womanhood. It was dainty in taste as well as quantity, for to have lusty tastes in foods seemed to betray a weakness for other pleasures of the flesh as well. It was also expected to display a certain degree of complexity—the "frills" that men disdained or did not notice and women, with their higher aesthetic sense, appreciated. (35)[3]

Women displayed their femininity (among other ways) by cooking and consuming dainty foods. The more ornate and decorative the food, the better it demonstrated the distinction between women and men, who were associated with much less refined foods. Thus, the craze for daintiness that Levenstein describes was not only about gustatory pleasure, but also about the elevation of mere women to ladies.

The cult of daintiness was popular in the early 1900s in part because it had the backing and support of the new home economics movement, which sought to remove food from its humble roots. In *Perfection Salad*, Laura Shapiro argues that the women involved in domestic science (later to be called home economics) at the turn of the century sought to conceal food: "Their goal as a group was to transubstantiate food, and it didn't matter a great deal whether the preferred method was to reduce a dish to its simplest components or to blanket it with whipped cream and candied violets" (6). In other words, the domestic scientists wished to transform food into something more ethereal—something suitable for women to consume. In a similar fashion, the dainty food fad also sought to remove food from its plebeian beginnings and transform it into something more suitable for ladies. During a time of social upheaval, when Progressive Era middle-class women were demanding something more out of life than an eternal spot in front of the stove, dainty cooking assured people that women were still ladies.[4]

Daintiness was not a concept confined to the United States; it was also popular in many other Anglo countries where the media suggested that upper- and middle-class women should be delicate and ladylike. For in-

stance, Michael Symons discusses the influence of daintiness in Australia in
One Continuous Picnic: A History of Eating in Australia (1982). Australian
cooking literature in the early decades of the twentieth century emphasized
delicacy as a key feature of feminine food (138–39). Symons argues that a
major reason for the popularity of daintiness was that it helped businesses
increase consumption:

> Not surprisingly, the great promoters of daintiness . . . were the modern food
> companies. . . . They could persuade shoppers to ask for highly advertised em-
> bellishments like chocolate, desiccated coconut, custard powder and jelly. They
> could convince women to accept a new role as consumers. Daintiness—which
> embodied feminine qualities like lightness, prettiness, and gentility—was part
> of a long campaign to pervert the traditional caring concerns of women into
> petty materialistic concerns. (139)

Symons is correct in pointing out the monetary side of daintiness. Lobster
for tea sandwiches was not cheap, after all. But daintiness also had larger
cultural reverberations. It encouraged women to stay in their kitchens because it was such an elusive goal to achieve—one that required thought and
much effort in order to produce a splendid feast for an afternoon tea or to
compose a "simple" Jell-O mold that required five flavors of Jell-O and everything from chopped marshmallows to canned pineapple chunks to Manda-
rin orange slices in syrup. Thus, promoting daintiness was a method to keep
women more securely in the kitchen, especially since the public believed
that creating dainty dishes was difficult or impossible for men (unless they
were chefs creating fancy desserts or other dishes at upscale restaurants).

In *The Theory of the Leisure Class* (1899), Thorstein Veblen explained another reason for the daintiness fetish. Veblen noted that the wife and her
possessions gave status and prestige to the husband with wealth enough to
purchase all the expensive items (from jewelry to clothing to cosmetics) necessary to create an upper-class woman. Even the leisure of the wife, Veblen
argued, served as a sign of the man's ability to afford such activity. "The
leisure rendered by the wife . . . is, of course, not a simple manifestation of
idleness or indolence," he stated. "It almost invariably occurs disguised under some form of work or household duties or social amenities, which prove
on analysis to serve little or no ulterior end beyond showing that she does
not occupy herself with anything that is gainful or that is of substantial use"

(68). Daintiness fit perfectly into Veblen's theories about a woman's role as a conspicuous consumer of the goods that her husband bought. Daintiness in women and their food served as a visible sign of the invisible wealth that was necessary to pursue a distinctly upper-middle-class concept; after all, daintiness was not available to poor women, who could not afford to worry about such frivolity.

"Dainty Bits of Delectability": Ladies' Tea Parties

At a time when daintiness represented the ideal for upper- and middle-class women, the tea party was all the rage. Tea parties served as a perfect activity to display the feminine talents of the hostess to others in the same social class. Dozens of articles in women's magazines encouraged her to make her tea as dainty and delicate as possible.[5] In a 1915 *Ladies' Home Journal* article, Ida Cogswell Bailey-Allen described tea as "a delightful custom, dear to the heart of every woman and well worth fostering." She emphasized that tea should be served in a "dainty and immaculate way" (37). Florence Spring, in a 1922 *Good Housekeeping* article, wrote about a hostess whose teas were "dainty and different" ("When You Serve," 66). She urged: "Let us, then, bring out our tea wagons and tables, see that we have on hand always a few simple dainties, and resolve habitually to offer our callers at this hour the refreshment of a hot, perfectly-made cup of tea" (66). The tea party was represented in the media as not only a social engagement but also a ritualized display of femininity; through tea parties (and preparing for tea parties) women were constituted by society as "properly" feminine ladies.

The custom of afternoon tea flourished in the early decades of the twentieth century, and this interest was not confined to the private home. Scores of small restaurants across America offered afternoon tea to hungry wayfarers. Women operated many of these tearooms, because this was judged a suitably ladylike business endeavor for anyone from the college girl seeking to earn money to pay for her school expenses to the maiden aunt in need of extra funds to keep her in groceries.[6] In an article in *Harper's Bazar* in 1909, E. B. Cutting heaped accolades on the roadside tearoom as an ideal business for women, calling it "one of the promising industries for women" (494). She noted that "farm tea-rooms for automobilists offer an admirable opportunity to establish a successful industry for women" (497). As in the domestic home, daintiness served as an essential feature of the tearoom. Cutting remarked that one woman found success with her tearoom because the food was "served with just the touch of daintiness that is always found when it is the work of a gentlewoman" (497). In a 1911 *Good Housekeeping* article, Sarah Leyburn Coe emphasized that a successful tearoom should be "daintily appointed": the "secret of a successful tea room is daintiness, first in the service, and then in the quality of the food served" (699). Writing in 1923 for *Ladies' Home Journal*, Caroline B. King stressed the importance of serving dainty food at a successful teashop.[7] She particularly recommended one delicacy, the maraschino sandwich: "Daintily made, they are a delight to the eye and a wonderful accompaniment to afternoon tea or a real addition to any luncheon" ("Hostess Dishes," 129). With dainty environments and dainty foods, tearooms were an ideal place for women to visit, either alone or with friends. At a time before the massive growth of fast food restaurants, tearooms offered women a safe environment in which to eat and converse.

Dainty foods were equally essential to the tea party at home, where serving delicate edibles served as a sign of a woman's ability to be a lady. Even for the woman who might rarely (or never) have prepared a tea party for her female friends, the constant emphasis on dainty foods for tea parties (the quintessential ladies' event) indicated how women were expected to behave and eat in order to be considered genteel and feminine. Women's magazines repeatedly elaborated on the ladylike foods a hostess should prepare for her gathering. In "Gay Garden-Parties and Porch-Teas" (1928), one writer suggested serving garden teacakes, jellied chicken, and raspberry cream meringues at a garden gathering (Jervey, 29).[8] Yet another article noted that a tea hostess could prepare delicacies such as lobster club sandwiches, chicken and almond mousse, tiny lemon tarts, ham and chicken tartlets, macaroon cream in molds, Boston cream cake, and maple parfait (Batchelder, "Bridge Party," 43).

The ability to provide a wide selection of dainty and delectable dishes also served as a marker of a family's class background, as a sign of middle-class tastes, since only well-off people can afford to think about the taste and appearance of foods. The French cultural critic Pierre Bourdieu asserts that the idea of taste itself is typically middle-class "since it presupposes absolute freedom of choice" (177). He distinguishes between "the tastes of luxury (or freedom) and the tastes of necessity" (177). In other words, the affluent can consume food simply for its gustatory pleasure; the poor cannot afford this luxury because they are hungry and forced to eat something inexpensive that will fill their empty stomachs in the most economic fashion. In terms of Bourdieu's theory, a tea party functioned as a sign of eating as luxury, when guests possessed the freedom to eat any of the expensive, elegant items presented with no consideration other than taste. The numerous dainty dishes described for tea-party entertaining suggested the elite status of the woman giving the party (and the people attending it), because many items could be served, with no sense that a guest needed to worry about eating for mere sustenance. Thus, a tea party (and the dainty food craze in general) affirmed not only a woman's feminine tastes but her social status as well.

A woman could also display her aesthetic sensibilities by preparing foods for tea. For a successful party, women's magazines urged, she was not only supposed to serve foods that tasted delicate and refined, but also to present them in unique ways. One 1930 article reminded readers, "To the modern hostess the serving of food to one's guests is not only a science, it is an art as well, and all the accessories must be chosen as carefully and with as much thought and foresight to the artistic effect as is expended upon the viands themselves" (Brandom, 683). The article described "dainty baskets, boxes and cases" to hold nuts, bonbons, or ice cream at a party (683). The creative hostess who wished to make her own containers would "derive a great deal of pleasure from seeing the dainty receptacles grow into works of art under her skillful fingers" and would enjoy decorating cups to look like a Halloween pumpkin, a bunny or chicken for Easter, or perhaps a potato for St. Patrick's Day (684). "The ingenious hostess need never lack for new and original ideas if she but keeps her eyes and mind open to the suggestions all about her," the article enthused (685). Desserts were a particularly useful menu item for a woman striving to show off her artistic talent, since they were often highly decorated. One 1928 article provided recipes for a wide range of desserts, including ginger ale salad, date bars, candied grapefruit, and "surprize [sic] pear salad" (canned pear halves filled with hot cheese balls) (Jervey, "Novel Bridge Teas," 32). Teacakes could be decorated in all kinds of ways, some simple, some fancy. For instance, in *Woman's Home*

Companion in 1923, Alice Bradley described a recipe for small cakes cut into cubes and then decorated:

> Cover the four sides with a thin layer of frosting. Then sprinkle thickly with finely chopped coconut colored pink, green, yellow, or lavender. Cover the top of the cakes with the same frosting. From the frosting stiffened with more confectioner's sugar, model tiny roses, daisies, sweet peas, and other simple flowers, and place on each cake. . . . Make the stems and leaves of the flowers with a paintbrush dipped in green vegetable coloring. ("For a Club Hostess," 41)

No doubt many women quailed at the thought of preparing Bradley's elaborate decorated cakes. But this recipe serves as an apt example of how cooking literature established lofty goals for the woman wishing to make her tea party into a dainty festivity. Such goals were difficult to achieve for the average middle-class housewife, but they represented culinary ideals that the media encouraged her to follow. If she wished to be considered feminine and ladylike, the media assumed, she would not regret the hours in the kitchen that such recipes demanded.

One of the most malleable food items to display the hostess's sense of refinement and her aesthetic ability was the tea sandwich—what one *Good Housekeeping* author described as "dainty bits of delectability"—which could be created and re-created using a wide variety of different breads, fillings, and shapes (Spring, "The Afternoon-Tea Sandwich," 64). An author writing for the *Ladies' Home Journal* in 1927 assured her readers that decorative tea sandwiches "may seem fussy to make, but once your artistic fervor is aroused, you are intrigued to see what you can accomplish with even a few ingredients" (Willson, 173). Cookbook writer Helena Judson wrote in *Light Entertaining: A Book of Dainty Recipes for Special Occasions* (1910): "Nowadays sandwich-making is a veritable art, and admits of much originality. Not only is the modern sandwich more pleasing to look upon than the old-time affair, but the dainty arrangement of chopped meat or fowl, fish paste or minced vegetables is much more easily eaten" (1). Judson informed her readers that they could change anything about a sandwich, including its shape. "Dainty squares and triangles are the shapes most used for sandwiches, but there is always the fancy cooky cutter to resort to when more unusual effects are desired for any particular occasion," she observed (3). If shapes could be

elaborate, fillings could be even more fanciful. Judson listed the most delicate and exotic sandwiches, including ones filled with caviar, lobster, shad
roe ("among the daintiest and most palatable of fish sandwiches" [6]), watercress, and ginger and orange. Her daintiest sandwiches were called simply
"scented sandwiches"—bread and butter sandwiches scented with the odor
of nasturtium, rose, violet, or another aromatic flower.[9]

Judson was not alone in suggesting that the tea sandwich should be used
as a palette for demonstrating a woman's artistic sensibilities. In a *Woman's
Home Companion* article, "For a Club Hostess" (1923), Alice Bradley described
an elaborate recipe for Valentine sandwiches: heart-shaped sandwiches filled
with creamed butter and cream cheese, with a border of chopped maraschino
cherries or pimiento strips. Marion H. Neil's *Salads, Sandwiches and Chafing
Dish Recipes* (1916) included recipes for daisy sandwiches, round pieces
of bread topped with grated cheese and eggs arranged to look like a daisy
(94–95), and ginger and nut sandwiches, whole-wheat bread spread with a
mixture of chopped preserved ginger, chopped nut meats, and candied orange peel, "cut into fancy shapes and serve[d] at afternoon tea" (99). A variation of this recipe called for putting two cups of preserved ginger into a food
chopper along with half a cup of preserved cherries, the juice of an orange,
and whipped cream (99). Lady Mary sandwiches were ladyfingers spread
with a mixture of chopped dates, pecans, and honey then tied into small
bundles (103). Perhaps the daintiest item in Neil's book was the rose petal
sandwich, composed of thinly sliced bread spread with fresh butter scented
with rose petals (111).[10] Janet McKenzie Hill's book *Salads, Sandwiches
and Chafing-Dish Dainties* (1922) also contained many recipes for delicate
sandwiches, including violet sandwiches composed of candied violets and
sweet butter spread on ladyfingers then garnished with fresh violets (132),
whipped-cream sandwiches made of whipped cream "spread quite thick
upon lady-fingers or sponge drops" (133), and cheese-and-Bar-le-Duc currant sandwiches, containing currants in syrup and cream cheese on wheat
bread (132).

Recipes for tea sandwiches filled cookbooks and women's magazine articles because a hostess preparing tea could use the dainty tidbits to demonstrate her artistic talent and her wealth. Due to their infinite variety, these
small sandwiches could easily be manipulated to suit the hostess's artistic
sensibility. Like the rest of the tea party, they also suggested the "proper"

femininity of the hostess and the lady friends who would presumably nibble such dainty foods.

"Gay, Sparkling, Quivery, Luscious-Looking": Jell-O and Ornamental Cooking

With their elegant and elaborate recipes, tea parties served as an ideal example of Veblen's theory of conspicuous consumption, being a display of wealth by the upper or middle classes. In addition, the fanciful items that filled tea-time menus in the popular media suggested that "proper" women should devote an inordinate amount of time to preparing such feasts. But what does Jell-O have in common with such fussy, frilly tea-time foods? After all, in the early twentieth century, as well as today, Jell-O was inexpensive (ten cents a package), a dessert that could be afforded by almost anyone. Jell-O appeared to be the quintessential dessert for the masses, not the elites.

Jell-O in some ways represented the democratization of the daintiness fad. Although delicate, Jell-O could be bought by most Americans without putting too much of a squeeze on their pocketbooks. Any woman could serve her friends or family a glimmering, shimmering Jell-O tower. The gelatin dessert represented a break from the nineteenth century, when molded desserts and their fanciful designs suggested a family's high economic status, as food historian Susan Williams notes in *Savory Suppers and Fashionable Feasts: Dining in Victorian America* (1985): "Foods that required a great deal of time and labor to create or elaborate utensils to produce and serve carried with them the prestige of elevated purchasing power. Fancy molded desserts, for example, commonly expressed status, wealth, and, at times, manual dexterity and industriousness" (122). What a change Jell-O represented! No longer did a molded dessert or salad require skill or a large outlay of money; now any woman could be proud of her molded Jell-O salad or dessert.

Even though it was not as expensive or elaborate as many of the foods that cooking literature suggested as appropriate for tea parties, however, Jell-O operated in similar ways, no matter how much it democratized the dessert- and salad-making process. Considered a feminine food, Jell-O helped to identify women as essentially different from men, who were depicted by the media as disliking frou-frou foods. Although Jell-O sped up many meal plans, women still had to spend a great deal of time in the kitchen, composing ever more elaborate Jell-O recipes; as is often the case with ornamental and decorative cooking, Jell-O cooking affirmed that the woman's place was in the kitchen, "naturally" enjoying such cookery.

When Pearl B. Wait invented Jell-O in 1897, he could not have foreseen the fantastic recipes that future generations of cooks would create. Jell-O, after all, was a simple, inexpensive gelatin dessert, homely and old-fashioned. When he sold his business for $450 to Orator Woodward, Wait did not know that his invention was going to become an "essential ingredient in our national festive life, both public and private. Jell-O dishes, from a simple sheet of lime Jell-O with bananas to towering, layered, whipped-creamed creations, have signaled to countless Americans times of gathering or celebration—funerals, potlucks, family reunions, church suppers, baby and wedding showers, Christmas and Thanksgiving" (Newton, 251).[11] A massive advertising campaign brought Jell-O into the spotlight, bringing sales to almost one million dollars in 1904 (Wyman, 85). Food scholar Betty Wason describes the "spectacular advertising" that spread the Jell-O name in *Cooks, Gluttons, and Gourmets: A History of Cookery* (1962). She notes that Jell-O recipe booklets were printed in the millions, up to fifteen million in a single year (301). The delights of Jell-O were touted in advertisements that popped up everywhere, from advertising booklets to cookbooks. One 1931 Jell-O cookbook exclaimed: "Jell-O dishes have 'looks'—gay, sparkling, quivery, luscious-looking, they lend appetite appeal to a meal!" (*Greater Jello*, 3). A General Foods advertising brochure promoting Jell-O assured the housewife that the booklet contained "the liveliest, gayest, loveliest surprises that you ever saw. . . . The kind of dishes that make the family think, 'She's a wonder, a cook in a thousand!'" (*Thrifty Jell-O Recipes*, 3). Advertising and cooking literature reiterated the message in countless ways: Jell-O was not just an ingredient, but an addition that would revolutionize your cooking from the first course to the last. In the 1920s, Jell-O's six flavors (lemon, orange, strawberry, raspberry, cherry, and chocolate) appeared in recipes ranging from appetizers to desserts (*Through the Menu*, n. pag.).[12] Sylvia Lovegren estimates that by "the Jazz Age, almost one-third of the 'salad' recipes in the average cookbook were gelatin based. Filled with chopped, cubed, cooked, canned, and otherwise mutilated vegetables or fruit, or with cream cheese mashed or balled, congealed salads were the 'bee's knees,' in the slang of the period" (8). Jell-O was an ideal method for an aspiring hostess to create a dish that was dainty and delicate, but not overly expensive.

Roland Barthes's theories about ornamental cookery in *Mythologies* (1957) help to explain the popularity of dainty cooking with Jell-O in the early 1900s. He defines ornamental cookery as endeavoring "to glaze surfaces, to round them off, to bury the food under the even sediment of sauces, creams, icing and jellies" (78). Barthes describes this cooking as being "based on coatings and alibis" and forever "trying to extenuate and even to disguise the primary nature of foodstuffs, the brutality of meat or the abruptness of seafood" (78). A perfect example of ornamental cookery, Jell-O is always engaged in concealing foodstuffs. Foods are buried in the middle of a Jell-O dessert and look distorted through the translucent gelatin. In nontranslucent recipes, foods are hidden entirely or only partially revealed. But such dainty cooking is not only about moving food away from nature. It is also about constituting femininity as distinct from masculinity, since the "natural" preference for ornamental cooking is one way of identifying women as gendered beings.

Barthes describes ornamentation as "one of the major developments of genteel cookery" (78). "Ornamentation proceeds in two contradictory ways . . . : on the one hand, fleeing from nature thanks to a kind of frenzied baroque (sticking shrimps in a lemon, making a chicken look pink, serving grapefruit hot), and on the other, trying to reconstitute it through an incongruous artifice (. . . replacing the heads of crayfish around the sophisticated béchamel which hides their bodies)" (79). Jell-O is an ideal dainty substance with which to conceal the "brutality" of food and also lends itself easily to ornamentation. Ornamentation is a way to distinguish women's tastes as antithetical to men's. At the same time, ornamentation—whether represented by a 1930s molded Jell-O salad or by today's gingerbread house created by Martha Stewart—assures that women will remain for longer hours in their kitchens, bound by the rigorous demands of such decorative cooking.

Dainty ornamental cooking involved more than covering a Jell-O molded salad with a layer of mayonnaise and decorating it to look like a melon or dyeing marshmallows in festive colors before they decorated a Jell-O salad. The very names of the Jell-O recipes in the early 1900s frequently emphasized lightness, airiness, and delicacy.[13] For example, the pamphlet *Your*

Electric Refrigerator and Knox Sparkling Gelatin (1929), a collection of recipes geared especially to the electric refrigerator, contained recipes for ethereal delights such as aspic jelly (5), perfection salad (11), snow pudding (15), and angel parfait (23). Similarly, *The Greater Jell-O Recipe Book* (1931) contained numerous recipes that emphasized lightness and delicacy, including fig fluff, Jell-O raspberry foam, banana fluff, prune whip, and strawberry whip (34, 35). Lightness, airiness, and daintiness were all important in gelatin recipes. Such delicate, lighter-than-air names suggested all the qualities that were supposed to be associated with women; thus, by consuming such recipes, women associated themselves with the very characteristics that were supposed to identify femininity and womanliness. Whether consuming tea party foods or Jell-O salads and desserts, a woman not only nourished herself; she constituted herself as feminine.

Jell-O names also suggested the exotic and fantastic. *Jell-O and the Kewpies* (1915) included a recipe for tropical dessert, which contained lemon Jell-O, figs, dates, and bananas (5), as well as cream fig pudding (12), banana layer Jell-O (18), and paradise pudding, with almonds, marshmallows, maraschino cherries, and macaroons folded into raspberry or lemon Jell-O combined with whipped cream (18). Another pamphlet from the 1920s contained recipes for Jell-O desserts with names like magic ice, raspberry delight, and paradise charlotte (*Through the Menu*, n. pag.). A recipe booklet from the 1930s, *Gayer Mealtimes with the New Jell-O*, contained recipes for springtime delight (6), raspberry twinkle (7), sea dream salad (18), and even prune perfection (7).[14] The exotic names of Jell-O recipes made ornamental cooking appear exciting. A woman creating sea dream salad or tropical dessert presumably would voyage far from her mundane kitchen experiences, at least in her imagination. These names showed a woman that even such a humdrum affair as making the family's dessert for dinner could be transformed into an adventure with Jell-O.

Dainty ornamental cooking with Jell-O also lured women into assuming that a "natural" part of being a woman was desiring to create decorative masterpieces in the kitchen, despite the arduousness of endeavors. Cooking literature and advertisements assured millions of women that Jell-O was more than merely an ingredient; it was a substance that magically helped women to transform themselves into more artistic cooks.[15] For decades, advertising has promoted Jell-O as providing endless creative opportunities for bored women cooks. Presumably, they could enjoy some of the same creativity in their kitchens that their husbands enjoyed in their offices. At its simplest, dainty cooking with Jell-O could be quick and easy. For instance, an advertising pamphlet suggested that women should cut Jell-O into festive shapes for holidays, including turkeys for Thanksgiving, pumpkins for Halloween, and shamrocks for St. Patrick's Day (*Through the Menu*, n. pag.). The sky was the limit for fanciful cooking with Jell-O. Cookbooks and women's magazines sometimes seemed to assume that *anything* would be more aesthetically pleasing in an elegant casing of Jell-O.

Women's magazines and other food literature commonly depicted salads and desserts as two of the best ways to show off a woman's dainty cooking skills with Jell-O. One advertisement for Jell-O discussed how it could give "a touch of magic to . . . salads. . . . Crisp slices of cucumber imprisoned in a shimmering crystal! Vivid shreds of pimento—toothsome bits of onion—fruits—meat or fish 'left-overs'—all these are glorified in taste and appearance by the magic of Jell-O!" (Jell-O, 150). Jell-O's advertising promoted the notion that even the humble leftover could be an opportunity for a woman to expand her artistic abilities. Salads were a good way to get rid of the scraps of food that lurked in the nether regions of the refrigerator: "Jell-O salads are a perfect boon! Thousands of women who used to think of 'leftovers' as a problem now welcome them as an opportunity" (*Through the Menu*, n. pag.). The cagey woman, this booklet suggested, could transform the most unappealing leftovers into delicacies such as salad supreme or golden glow salad. Why stop with leftovers? Cooking literature encouraged women to explore new and exotic combinations for their Jell-O salads. For example, *The Greater Jell-O Recipe Book* contained a recipe for salad novelty, which required two bottles of Coca-Cola and a package of lemon Jell-O (26); Coca-Cola dessert called for two bottles of Coca-Cola, one package of raspberry Jell-O, nutmeats, and dates (28). Jell-O salads offered women countless opportunities for experimentation, for creating wonders out of anything available in the kitchen.

Jell-O could also be used in an infinite variety of ways in desserts. *Gayer Mealtimes with the New Jell-O* observed: "When your family cut their spoons into a tender, shimmering Jell-O mold, and greet its miracle of flavor with enthusiastic praise . . . then you realize what deliciousness the New Jell-O has brought to your table! And your imagination starts working, devising different tempting desserts, salads, relishes, or entrées to take advantage of this luscious fruit flavor, to serve it in attractive new ways" (n. pag.). Almost any sweet ingredients could be mixed into Jell-O. One recipe pamphlet proclaimed:

> Plain Jell-O is a perfectly delicious dessert—a clear, sparkling, lusciously fruit-flavored dessert. But it can be varied in dozens of ways, as shown by the recipes in this book. Fresh or canned fruits, nuts, dates, figs, raisins, whipped cream, marshmallows, macaroons—these are some of the dainties that clever women have learned to combine with Jell-O to make desserts that are temptingly novel. (*Through the Menu*, n. pag.)

Marshmallows were a particularly common and dainty adornment for Jell-O desserts. This is perhaps no surprise due to the popularity of marshmallows in the early 1900s.[16] "They popped up in salads, in desserts—and in cakes as well. . . . They appeared frequently in frostings, especially ones topped with coconut, to make an ethereal, delicious confection, sweet enough and dainty enough for any feminine gathering" (Lovegren, 24–25). Another way to make a plain dessert fancier was to conceal ingredients in the Jell-O. For example, a recipe named peach surprise called for hiding a peach half filled with nuts in the middle of a peach Jell-O mold (*Jell-O and the Kewpies*, 8). *The Greater Jell-O Recipe Book* contained a recipe for Jell-O petits fours decorated with frosting made with Jell-O: "Blithely gay and delicately beautiful are cake cubes or tiny cakes dipped in a rainbow of pastel Jell-O frosting. Dainty petits fours with the inimitable French touch, but made in your own kitchen!" (43). Jell-O salads and desserts were a way for a woman to demonstrate her talent at dainty cookery. Elaborate and fanciful desserts were complicated culinary displays of a woman's adherence to daintiness—a Jell-O dessert represented everything that the woman herself was supposed to be, dainty, elegant, and decorative.

Of Cucumber Sandwiches . . .

I remember my mother teaching me how to make cucumber sandwiches as a very young child. We purchased a loaf of firm fine-textured white bread, usually Pepperidge Farm brand. When we arrived home, we trimmed off the bread's crust. We lightly spread each square of bread with softened butter. Then we topped the buttered bread with a thin, translucent slice or two of cucumber from which we had pared the skin. (Thinly cut radish or watercress could be used in place of the cucumber.) We completed the sandwich with another slice of buttered bread and cut the whole sandwich into—not the prosaic rectangles of my daily lunches—but what I thought were far more elegant triangles. In my adult life, I have never once actually made cucumber sandwiches, yet the recipe lingers in my mind, ready to be pulled out at a moment's notice if I ever give an afternoon tea party—for I still recognize, without even pausing to reflect, that such dainty sandwiches are better suited to the appetites of women, not men.

My youthful lesson on preparing cucumber sandwiches demonstrates that the issues brought up in this chapter did not vanish in the first few decades of the twentieth century. Even today, making and consuming delicate ornamental fare is one way that women are constituted as gendered subjects. My experience making cucumber sandwiches—a lesson, I'm sure, that I share with many women—is one example of how my girlhood cooking lessons also taught me how to be feminine and how to be a woman. Cooking lessons were also gender lessons.

A more contemporary lesson about dainty cooking can be found by perusing a Martha Stewart magazine or cookbook. In one of her books she suggests the following menu for a tea party:

> *Pear and stilton tartlets*
> *Orange madeleines*
> *Apple rosemary tea bread*
> *Molasses ginger scones*
> *Currant scones*
> *Poppy-seed cake*
> *Crumpets*
> *Neapolitan Sandwiches*
> (*Holidays*, 49)

Stewart's menu for a Pink Peony Dinner Party includes such delicate delights as endive and roasted beet salad with rice wine vinaigrette, lemon granita, iced lemon mousse tart, and lemon meringue tart in a macadamia nut crust (*Martha Stewart's Menus*, 25). What are her elaborate and complex menus and recipes but dainty cooking in a trendy and updated form? Although

Stewart proclaims that her recipes are simple enough for anyone to make, they are often so complex and expensive that it is doubtful that anyone but upper- or middle-class women with the luxury of leisure time could prepare them. In Stewart's recipes and menu suggestions, dainty cooking thrives today.

Chapter 4

Waffle Irons and Banana Mashers

Selling Mrs. Consumer on Electric Kitchen Gadgets

"Cookery by electricity is swathed in mystery and surrounded by . . . many phobias," wrote Ethel R. Peyser in a 1924 *House and Garden* article ("Some Aspects of Electric Cookery," 82). She stated the concerns of many. In the early years of the century, numerous women (and men) felt anxious about the unknown powers of electricity, which seemed almost magical. Some feared that electricity, if used in domestic homes, could actually harm the health of the inhabitants. For many reasons, people were wary about wiring their homes and exposing their loved ones to such a mysterious threat.

During this period, other authors were writing with tremendous enthusiasm about electricity's wonders. Electricity, some assumed, was going to result in a new era of freedom for housewives since electric gadgets and appliances would reduce women's domestic workload. Amy Hewes, a professor at Mount Holyoke College in the 1930s, wrote in rapturous terms about the benefits of electricity: "Only Fairyland can vie with the bright prospects pictured by the heralds of the Age of Electricity. . . . Women are to be especially blessed, for household drudgery will be no more" (235). Despite the fears of some, many housewives were fascinated by the new technology that (according to the advertising propaganda) would set them free from the burden of housework or at least lighten that load considerably. In the early 1920s, when the Edison Electric Appliance Company sponsored a series of talks in Seattle, Tacoma, Spokane, and Portland about the pleasures of owning and using an electric range, over 10,000 women attended, showing the wide-spread interest among middle-class women in using electricity in their kitchens (Turnbull, 171). During the years between World War I and World War II, electric gadgets and appliances filled the middle-class kitchen. This was a huge change—a shift so major that its ramifications are still being felt today in the typical American kitchen, bursting with electric devices ranging from popcorn makers to hotdog steamers.

This chapter examines how the media promoted the spread of electricity in the kitchen (as well as electricity in the entire household) in the form of gadgets and appliances. Although a number of scholarly studies have focused on technology, women, and the kitchen, little scholarship exists specifically about women and electric kitchen appliances.[1] Christina Hardyment's *From Mangle to Microwave: The Mechanization of Household Work* (1988) provides a broad overview of technology in the home, but does not focus exclusively on how electric kitchen devices were made more palatable to a mass audience. It is particularly important to study such kitchen devices—no matter how frivolous a waffle iron or electric grill might seem—because all mechanical devices carry an ideological burden, as Ellen Lupton makes clear in *Mechanical Brides: Women and Machines from Home to Office* (1993). "Mechanical devices, from the washing machine to the typewriter, are designed to perform work; the work they do is cultural as well as utilitarian, helping to define the differences between women and men" (7). The most seemingly insignificant gadgets can imply a great deal about gender roles in our culture; for instance, an electric beater is associated with a woman and her kitchen, just as a power saw is associated with a man and his garage. The correlation between women and kitchen gadgets and appliances is one of the ways that cooking is maintained as primarily women's work.

In the early twentieth century, the media made mechanical kitchen devices appealing to women by making them seem stylish and fashionable. Women were seduced by the supposed glamor of kitchen work. As Lupton observes, "By glamorizing appliances as partners in achieving health and happiness, advertising and design have encouraged women to embrace housework as women's 'natural' calling" (15). Advertisements, cooking articles, and cookbooks made electric kitchen gadgets attractive to women in four ways. (1) Electric appliances were touted as being modern, something that up-to-date housewives would wish to own—appealing to their desire for social stature. (2) Electric cooking was made to appear fun and interesting, appealing to bored housewives. (3) Electric kitchen devices were promoted as graceful and elegant additions to the dining experience, appealing to the women's desire for status. (4) Cooking with electric gadgets was supposed to offer women greater freedom and more time to pursue hobbies and other interests, appealing to the housewives' desire for more personal time, without sacrificing their roles as homemakers and cooks. This chapter focuses on how the media depicted electric technology as so appealing to the middle-class housewife that any woman would wish to be responsible for the kitchen tasks, as long as she had the help of her "electric servants."

"A Push-Button Maid": Electricity and the "Servant Problem"

Before examining the popularity of electrical kitchen gadgets between World War I and World War II, we need to understand some of the social problems that encouraged the spread of electricity in the domestic sphere, including what was referred to as "the servant problem."[2] Throughout the nineteenth century, servants were commonplace in upper- and middle-class homes. In a larger household, ten or twenty servants ran the home. In a smaller house, one to three servants would suffice. It was relatively easy for the middle-class woman in the 1800s to hire servants, for numerous reasons. Millions of immigrants had flocked to the United States. These new Americans found that domestic service was one of the few jobs open to them, especially if they were women. Even for native-born American women, domestic service was one of few employment opportunities available and represented the largest job category for women throughout the 1800s. Hence employers could find many workers who sought jobs in private homes.

The taken-for-granted presence of servants in many middle-class homes changed dramatically at the turn of the century; in the early decades of the twentieth century, it became increasingly difficult for families to hire such workers. Domestic service carried a stigma, and a growing number of young women decided not to enter domestic employment in favor of jobs in factories and shops. Gone were the days when domestic service was the sole job possibility for women in many cities and towns. World War I also provided an impetus for working women to go from private households to wartime factories. After this experience, many of them never went back to domestic labor. Due to these factors and others, people willing to work as servants became ever scarcer. No matter how much middle-class women lamented about the servant problem, they could do little to alter the fact that the ranks of potential workers were dwindling. Middle-class women were forced to change the way they perceived household work. Formerly considered a labor-intensive activity, which involved domestic servants performing myriad household tasks with the lady of the home supervising, housework was now seen as a much lighter activity, which could be performed with ease by the lady of the house and the help of what one writer referred to as "a push-button maid" (Dunbar, 10).

With the increasing shortage of servants in households, advertisers promoting electric kitchen gadgets (and other household electrical devices) had a tailor-made opportunity to encourage their purchase in homes both modest and grand.[3] Electric "servants" became the fashion, as women's magazines and cookbooks touted kitchen devices as superior to human servants.[4] In an article in *Sunset* magazine in 1923, one writer proclaimed: "Electricity is the first assistant to the housewife at the present time. Almost unconsciously she has seized this aid when good personal service failed her and she now finds herself freer than ever before, for convenience is always on the wire, day or night, year in and year out, by the simple turning of the switch" ("Convenience," 84).[5] The author of "Push-Button Mary" (1923) in *Country Gentleman*, made grander claims for the new servant:

> There is a new hired girl on the farms. She is wageless and strikeless. She is swift and neat and silent. She never tires at the washtub. She irons without keeping the house like an oven. . . . When she bakes, no one has to carry wood for her. After the family is seated at the table she supplies them with fresh, fragrant coffee, golden-brown waffles or toast, piping hot. . . . Farm women don't need Martha now. They have a Mary who is not cumbered with much serving. . . . Mary is electricity. (Dunbar, 10)

For these writers and many others, the new electrical maids promised to revolutionize housework. No longer would women be dependent on a servant's moods. Now they employed a new servant who was always eager to work.

The popular media promoted electrical gadgets and appliances of all kinds as being less cantankerous than servants, depicted by the media as lazy, foolish, and inefficient. *Edison Monthly* observed: "Every woman who has electricity in her home can have at least seven servants, seven days a week, never tired and never grumbling" ("Electrical Servants," 11). In an era when many maids, well aware that they could find positions elsewhere if their employers grew too exacting, demanded better working conditions, electrical gadgets appeared easier for a woman to handle than disgruntled servants.[6]

By pointing out the time and effort women would save because they would not be responsible for managing the idiosyncrasies of a household of servants, the media encouraged them to believe that electric appliances would make their domestic workload much lighter. Of course, no woman expected all of her kitchen work to vanish as if by magic, but many were lured by the promise in women's magazines, newspapers, advertisements, and cookbooks that electrical cooking devices would make kitchen chores easier and less time-consuming.[7]

The Dawn of the Electrical Age

The servant problem was not the only cause for the spread of electrical kitchen equipment in the early twentieth century. This technological change would not have occurred without the invention that made such devices possible. In 1889, Nikola Tesla developed a small electric motor that could power small household appliances. People in the 1890s displayed a keen interest in electricity and its potential to change the running of the entire household. Electricity seemed modern—all the glamor and promise of a new century rested in it—and people came by the thousands to visit the Model Electric Kitchen with an electric kettle, range, and broiler at the 1893 Chicago's World Fair. Despite the appeal of electricity, it remained out of the price range of most middle- and lower-class families. As late as 1916, a writer for *Countryside Magazine* lamented the high cost: "Astonishing as has been the development of electricity throughout the past decade, we have, as yet, hardly sounded its possibilities as a kitchen servitor. Its manifold advantages are admitted and admired everywhere, but the price is still so high that the housewife whose budget is modest cannot often permit herself the pleasure of experimenting with them all" ("Pantry," 150). Electricity was expensive, as were the kitchen gadgets that it powered. One 1927 advertisement listed the cost of a Hotpoint electric percolator as $12.50 (Hotpoint Appliances, 191). An advertisement from 1931 listed the cost of a Wafflemaster as $14.50, while a two-slice Toastmaster was $17.50 (Toastmaster, 227). In 1928, over 80 percent of American families earned less than $2,000 a year, so purchasing a toaster could easily cost half a week's wages, a prohibitive sum for many (Wandersee, 21). High costs helped to explain why only 4.54 million out of the total 27 million homes owned electric toasters in 1928 (Wandersee, 17). Many middle- and lower-class families could not afford the high-priced electric kitchen gadgets or had to budget carefully.

Although electricity and electrical gadgets were costly, their prices did fall enough during the interwar years to make many middle- and even lower-class families consider wiring their households (Cowan, 93). The number of wired houses and homes with electrical kitchen appliances rose rapidly: "while only 8 percent of the nation's residences were wired for electricity in 1907, this percentage had doubled by 1912 and doubled again (to 34.7 percent) by 1920. At first, houses were wired just for lights, but by 1920 there were also a significant number of electric appliances on the market" (Cowan, 93). By 1928, approximately 17.6 million homes were wired for electric current (Wandersee, 17). By 1941, 80 percent of households had electricity (Cowan, 94). Looking at these figures, we can only agree with Morris Llewellyn Cooke's words in the foreword to Electricity in the Home (1927): "It does not require much imagination to realize that we are on the threshold of an electrical age" (quoted in Beard, Electricity, 9). America was on the verge of a new era.

Electricity would soon become a necessity taken for granted rather than something rare and expensive, affordable only for the elite. One place where this new era was most visible was in the kitchens of millions of American homes. Electric devices both big and small proved popular in the kitchen for many reasons. Kitchen tasks could be performed more easily with the aid of electricity, and electric gadgets could display a family's modernity and class status, especially since the kitchen was the most used room in the house.

Two of the first major kitchen appliances that gained in popularity were the electric range and the refrigerator. In her 1921 article "The Facts about

Electric Ranges," Ethel R. Peyser considered electric ranges so popular that she wrote about "the vogue of the electric stove" (54). Ranges, however, were still expensive, making them slow to spread in the 1920s and 1930s. More popular than the range was the refrigerator, which, like the electric range, represented a major purchase for most American families. "Making an intelligent choice of an electric refrigerator is no trifling matter these days," cautioned one writer in 1934. "For most families an electric refrigerator represents a sizable investment" (Adams, "The Best Electric Refrigerator," 533). To sell such expensive appliances, refrigerator manufacturers had to convince potential buyers that their money would be well spent; a "massive selling campaign for refrigerators [began] in the early twenties; the industry's advertising expenditures, about $45,000 in 1923, grew twenty-fold in the next five years, peaking at around $20 million in 1931" (Strasser, 265). The advertisers and manufacturers sold Mrs. Consumer on the refrigerator's merits, promoting the idea that every woman needed one in order to cook the best meals. An article from the 1940s discussed the delights of preparing meals ahead of time with the aid of a refrigerator: "Meat and vegetables, fresh and safe for several days, waffle batter made Saturday night for Sunday-morning breakfast, ice cream ready and waiting in the freezing compartment, eliminating that hurried trip to the corner before Sunday dinner— these are some of the surprises of today's food storage" (Kendall, 147).[8] Alice Bradley also described the delights of owning a refrigerator in *Electric Refrigerator Menus and Recipes: Prepared Especially for General Electric Refrigerator* (1929):

> To many people electric refrigeration is still such a novelty that they scarcely realize the range of its possibilities. It is almost like having an Aladdin's lamp and not knowing the right way to rub it. With a General Electric Refrigerator, simple recipes, easily prepared, produce delightful results. . . . The owning of such a refrigerator is a form of health and happiness insurance which every homemaker in America should have the privilege of enjoying. (8)

Countless advertisements, cookbooks, and cooking articles touted the electric refrigerator as priceless to any homemaker, and millions of women listened to this message, flocking to stores to purchase the exciting new appliance.[9] The number sold went from 20,000 in 1923 to 850,000 in 1933. By 1936, 2 million had been sold. By 1941, that figure was 3.5 million (Celehar,

10). By 1941, 52 percent of families owned electric refrigerators (Cowan, 94). Although the electric refrigerator was not as ubiquitous as it would become in post–World War II America, it was still a common item displayed prominently and proudly in millions of households—a dramatic change from the mere twenty thousand of these appliances in 1923 homes.

For Americans who could not afford to purchase an electric range or refrigerator, there were many smaller and less costly electric gadgets that shared their larger cousins' pleasing aura of modernity. Small electric appliances were not the first new gadgets to invade the home and kitchen. In *Savory Suppers and Fashionable Feasts*, historian Susan Williams describes some of the many inventions that women adopted in the second half of the nineteenth century, including vacuum cleaners, carpet sweepers, meat grinders, and cast-iron ranges (95). Upper- and middle-class kitchens had been well stocked with gadgets in the 1800s; what was new in the early 1900s was the vast variety of electrical devices and the multitude of tasks that could be simplified by such devices—or at least the manufacturers and advertisers of electrical appliances hoped that women would believe this. Although people in the early decades of the twentieth century had not "progressed" to the level of sophistication of modern Americans, they still had a wide range of electrical devices, "attractive, ingenious and of fascinating complexity," from which to pick when they visited the appliance store (Hardyment, 157). Popular small electrical devices included waffle irons, percolators, table stoves, electric mixers, and electric grills. Members of the Cleveland Electrical League mentioned a number of electric devices in their book *Electrical Homemaking with 101 Recipes* (1928)—"tea samovar, toaster, grill, waffle-iron, kettle, chafing dish, table-stove and egg boiler"—that were de rigueur for the well-set breakfast table (38). (Many households kept numerous electric devices on the table, where they could best advertise a family's class status and ability to afford such devices.) The authors of *Household Equipment* (1934), an informative book on modern domestic equipment, listed a number of small electrical devices for the kitchen, including "electric cookers and grills of several varieties, percolators, toasters, waffle irons, egg cookers, and a dozen or more different mixers" (Peet and Sater, 120). It was increasingly difficult to avoid noticing kitchen gadgets in the interwar years, as they moved from luxurious extras to must-have necessities. Even during the Depression, they continued to sell, as Sylvia Lovegren points out: "Electric gadgets were the darlings of the Thirties, evidence of the Modern Age even in the midst of the Depression. Waffle irons, chafing dishes, . . . electric snack servers, and hot plates, all were guaranteed to 'serve you with efficiency.' The lucky lady who had an electric mixer could even order her own banana masher attachment from one major manufacturer" (47). Although electrical devices were expensive to purchase and operate, they proved irresistible to many women, even during a period of great economic hardship.

In popular cooking literature, housewives were encouraged to buy not simply an electric refrigerator or other device but a whole new way of life associated with modernity, glamor, and high status. Electricity in the kitchen, the media promised, would transform the kitchen. Millions of women were encouraged to believe that their satisfaction should stem from the sparkling, brand-new electric devices that they could buy, which would make cooking into a glamorous task, rather than merely unappreciated drudgery.

Modernity and Electrical Cooking

The media sold electric kitchen appliances to women (and men) by stressing the modernity of electricity, suggesting that any woman who wished to be considered up-to-date had to own the right electric kitchen equipment. A magazine article from 1921 emphasized that every housewife should modernize her old-fashioned kitchen appliances: "There is not one woman in a hundred who would not like to have an electric range. There is not one housewife in a thousand who has not thought about it and wondered how long it would be before she, too, could stop using the old-fashioned stove and cook electrically" (Whitehorne, 128). Estate Electric Ranges were sold in *Good Housekeeping* by linking them with modernity and progress: "In thousands of communities progressive women have proved the practical advantages of electric cookery" (Estate Electric Ranges, 246). Everywhere they looked, women and men were bombarded with advertising messages that any household that wished to be considered modern needed to be equipped with electricity and be filled with electric gadgets: vacuum cleaners, fans, electric percolators, toasters, sewing machines, irons, and dozens of other items.

Advertisers claimed that electricity was not only a necessity but also a right for the modern American housewife. A prefabricated speech appeared in a 1921 edition of *Electrical Merchandising*, a magazine tailored to the electrical industry. The writer claimed that "electricity in the home . . . is within the easy reach of every man and woman. And the 'service,' comfort and convenience that it offers is the *right* of every modern woman who is faced with the problem of saving and carrying on a home" ("Electricity," 68–69). If having an electric home was a "right," it became the responsibility of every husband to make sure he provided his wife and children with a house wired for electricity and the appliances to use in such a home.

Popular media also promoted electric kitchen equipment as reducing a woman's workload. One article from *Illustrated World* observed: "The modern housewife always is on the lookout for new electric appliances that will save her work or inconvenience" (Grinde, 65). Another article focused on the time saved, as "the intelligent home-maker of today adopts distinctly modern ways of performing routine work by pressing an electric button or turning a switch. A household routine performed electrically requires no concentrated attention or effort and eliminates monotony" (Hausman, 340).[10] And advertisements were filled with claims about the speed and simplicity of electric cooking. One advertisement for a Hotpoint range showed an attractive young woman showing off her new appliance, with the caption: "Why I cook electrically—Electric cookery *is* Modern." The advertisement continued: "Like all modern women, I want as much time free from household cares as possible, but I don't want it without well-prepared meals" (Hotpoint Servants, 142). Another advertisement for a Hotpoint range announced: "Wives, Mothers! Learn about this MODERN way to cook. . . . Electrical cookery is MODERN. It is cooler, cleaner, more convenient, saves time" (Hotpoint Electric Range, 154).

Modern kitchen appliances, however, accomplished more than merely speeding up the cooking process. Women were also assured that their shiny new appliances would be the envy of everyone. In the 1920s, the Cleveland Electrical League marketed electric kitchen appliances to women by claiming: "There's something wrong with your kitchen . . . unless it is envied by your friends" (quoted in Redmann, 39). One advertisement for the Hughes Electric Range proclaimed: "It's so modern! Your kitchen will be your pride, the envy of every housewife who sees it, when you install the Hughes Electric Ranges [*sic*]" (Hughes Electric Range, 117). An advertisement in *Electri-*

cal Merchandising in 1935 featured a gleaming, shiny white refrigerator, surrounded by a group of smiling faces, with the caption: "All eyes are on this new refrigerator for the Streamline Age" (Westinghouse Streamline Refrigerators, 41). In these advertisements, it was clear that kitchen appliances did more than perform their assigned tasks with speed and ease: they served as the latest status symbol, representing modernity and everything that was up-to-date.

Electric Appliances: Making Food into Fun

In the early 1900s, electric kitchen devices had to do more than just make the neighbors envious in order to spread to millions of American households. Manufacturers and advertisers needed to convince women that electric appliances would make cooking pleasurable, changing the image of cookery as drudgery into cookery as play. Suggesting that electric gadgets would improve women's work experience in the kitchen was one strategy that sellers and advertisers used to sell electricity. As Philip Bereano, Christine Bose, and Erik Arnold point out in their essay "Kitchen Technology and the Liberation of Women from Housework" (1985), "Appliances are bought because people believe they save time and because they have symbolic value: if a woman believes that the latest equipment increases the quality of her housework and home life she has a powerful incentive to want a well-equipped home" (176–77). Convincing women that a kitchen gadget—whether a toaster or a Cuisinart—improved their life and made cooking more enjoyable helped kitchenware companies assure themselves of a market.

The media promised women that electric cooking devices would "lighten labor and make cooking a game instead of a tiresome task" ("Cooking at the Table," 70). Cooking literature and advertisements were filled with promises of the enjoyment that housewives would discover in cooking if they used electric kitchen appliances. One *Good Housekeeping* advertisement promoted a table stove with the promise: "Housework becomes a real joy when the young bride can get meals right at the table the modern way" (Armstrong Table Stove, 131).[11] An article in *Pictorial Review* proclaimed that large electric appliances could make even clean-up enjoyable, promising the housewife that the "work of preparing, serving, and cleaning up after any meal would be a joyous part of your job as a home maker" (Swann, 30).[12] In an *American Cookery* article, "Electric Equipment in the Home" (1932), A. F. A. Hausman made a larger claim for the pleasures of owning electric equipment: "Home-making is the greatest of all professions. . . . Just how much modern electric equipment has done to restore genuine pride and interest in home-making cannot be estimated accurately, but home-making is on a firm and inspirational basis and there is less monotony and drudgery in the average home than has existed since the World War" (340). For Hausman and others, electric kitchen equipment held the promise that it would keep women in the household or lure them back, because such devices made cooking and other domestic tasks much more pleasurable than they had been in earlier decades.

Owning electric kitchen appliances was supposed to be more than merely enjoyable—it was expected to be fun, as many advertisements mentioned. One in *Good Housekeeping* in 1931 depicted a former domestic science instructor discussing why she bought an electric refrigerator, which she considered a "wise investment." She observed: "I like the 'feeling' of owning an Electric Refrigerator. It's fun to own one" (Electric Refrigeration Bureau, 187). A young woman in a 1941 Frigidaire refrigerator advertisement gushed: "I fell in love with Frigidaire! It's beautiful, INSIDE AND OUT." Buying a refrigerator was not only about keeping food cold; the female consumer also showed that she appreciated the pleasure of having a "fun looking" refrigerator (Frigidaire, 62). (You feel that this woman's husband probably came a distant second to her love for her fun Frigidaire.)

Grace and Elegance: Electric Appliances

Electric refrigerators and other appliances did more than show the fun-loving side of a woman and demonstrate her modernity. They also revealed a family's social standing and showed the father's ability to afford such goods. In her article "My Adventures With Electricity" (1922), Nell B. Nichols put social advancement first as a reason why women should own electric kitchen appliances. "I have five reasons for believing in electrical cooking devices: they better women socially, add charm to dining, make meal preparation easier, simplify the service, and lessen the number of dishes to be washed afterward," she observed (50). For Nichols and other women, electric appliances served as an ideal way for a hostess to show her breeding and wealth. She did not have to say anything—her expensive, elegant appliances would do all the talking.

Men also could display their business acumen by demonstrating that they could afford to fill their houses with electric gadgets. Men and women did not have identical reasons for purchasing appliances before World War II, as historian Mark H. Rose observes in *Cities of Light and Heat: Domesticating Gas and Electricity in Urban America* (1995): "Men played different roles [than women] in the diffusion of household appliances. Consequently, those appliances held different meanings for them. Men perceived appliances as another arena in which they had to provide for women and children" (142). Purchasing electric appliances demonstrated men's power, prestige, and wealth. Electric appliances were a highly visible display of the husband's ability to be a successful breadwinner.

Like tea parties, for many families electric kitchen appliances served as a symbol of conspicuous consumption. In *The Theory of the Leisure Class*, Veblen wrote:

> Goods are produced and consumed as a means to the fuller unfolding of human life; and their utility consists, in the first instance, in their efficiency as means to this end. . . . But the human proclivity to emulation has seized upon the consumption of goods as a means to an invidious comparison, and has thereby invested consumable goods with a secondary utility as evidence of relative ability to pay. This indirect or secondary use of consumable goods lends an honorific character to consumption and presently also to the goods which best serve the emulative end of consumption. (111)

Veblen also noted: "The more reputable, 'presentable' portion of middle-class household paraphernalia are, on the one hand, items of conspicuous consumption, and on the other hand, apparatus for putting in evidence the vicarious leisure rendered by the housewife" (69). Due to their steep prices, electric kitchen appliances served as a sign of a family's ability to afford such goods. The fancier and more expensive the electric items, the better they displayed a family's wealth, particularly because they were used in some of the most visible domestic rooms (the kitchen, the dining room).

Since electrical appliances served as a sign of a family's upper-class status between the world wars, it comes as little surprise that the popular media emphasized the glamor of the devices themselves and the people who used them.[13] An advertisement in *Good Housekeeping* depicted an electric perco-lator with the accompanying copy: "The real fortunate bride has a Manning-Bowman electric percolator urn set among her gifts. . . . It makes perfect coffee, of course. But its fitting place among the 'loveliest gifts' is held by reason of its beauty—its harmonious design and superb finish" (Manning-Bowman Quality Ware, 245). An advertisement in *Good Housekeeping* for an electric toaster declared that the machine was an ideal present for the aspir-ing hostess: "Enhancing the faultless charm that characterizes the Breakfast service of the exquisite hostess. . . . The STAR-Rite Reversible Electric Toaster combines beauty with utility, and is a graceful complement to the perfectly appointed Breakfast service" (STAR-Rite, 301). One writer empha-sized the beauty of electric gadgets: "Bright electrical cooking appliances, polished and well kept, . . . are not merely useful but beautiful as well" (Nichols, "My Adventures," 50).

The elegance of the people using these appliances was also stressed. The cover of the trade magazine *Electrical Merchandising*, for instance, showed a graceful woman lighting the candles in a candelabrum. On the table were electrical gadgets such as a toaster and a waffle maker. The caption read: "Table appliances are not all drug store specials. People are paying good prices for this merchandise and finding a new way to smarter living" (n. pag.). An advertisement for Frigidaire Electric Refrigeration depicted an elegantly attired couple taking something out of a refrigerator, with the caption: "Whether you entertain simply or elaborately you will find Frigidaire a de-lightful aid to hospitality. Every dish served in your home will have a new richness of flavor . . . " (Frigidaire Electric Refrigeration, 127). The implica-tion was clear: to be considered as elegant as this couple, a housewife needed to purchase a Frigidaire.

Electric devices were also advertised as a necessity for the hostess wishing to prepare a fabulous meal for guests. If a woman used electric appliances, the media assured her that her cooking would delight the most discriminat-ing connoisseurs. The pamphlet *Electric Cooking at Its Best: Instructions and Recipes for Electromaster Ranges* (1939) declared: "In your new electric range you have the facilities for the finest cooking you have ever experienced— literally 'the finest cooking that money can buy!'" (2).[14] Electric cooking was guaranteed to improve even a simple food like toast: an article in *Electrical*

Merchandising (1923) asserted that "electric toast is the best breakfast food" ("A Toast to the Toaster," n. pag.).

All foods could be made more glamorous, the media promised, with the aid of electricity. An automatic refrigerator was particularly useful for a hostess trying to make her cooking more elegant. The delights of an automatic refrigerator were explained in the article "You and Your Automatic Refrigerator" (1929) in the magazine *Delineator*: "Delineator Home Institute feels that automatic refrigeration has almost inexhaustible possibilities. . . . [It] makes possible smart and attractive refreshments for the hostess" (36). Alice Bradley's *Electric Refrigerator Menus and Recipes* (1929) elaborated on how the refrigerator could help out a hostess preparing an after-theater lunch: "Place beverages to chill and put a delicious mousse or parfait in the chilling unit of the General Electric Refrigerator immediately after dinner and it should be ready to serve upon your return from the theater" (27). The cookbook also offered refrigerator-aided luncheon menus: toasted lobster sandwiches, coffee float, and frosted cookies or creamed sardines and eggs, tiny baking powder biscuits, and loganberry mousse (28). Electric appliances were supposed to help middle-class women aspire to an upper-class way of life by making it easier for them to prepare and serve elegant, stylish recipes. The media promoted electrical appliances as a simple strategy to appear high-class.

Kitchen Appliances and the Lure of Personal Freedom

Dozens of books, articles, and advertisements promoted the idea that electricity would speed up cooking, leaving harried housewives more time to enjoy their families and pursue their favorite hobbies. One advertisement for a Servel refrigerator declared: "SERVEL electric Refrigeration frees women for their families!" (Servel Electric Refrigeration, 102). But perhaps more appealing was the advertisers' promise that electric cooking would allow women more time for pleasurable pursuits. One advertisement for a Frigidaire depicted two attractive women with golf clubs, closing the Frigidaire before taking off for a day on the golf course, with the caption: "Frigidaire gives carefree refrigeration—*more time to play*" (Frigidaire Corporation, 161). Similarly, the cookbook *Meals Go Modern Electrically* (1937) proclaimed the wonders of the electric oven:

> Time out of the kitchen at the time you want it most—that's your reward when you plan whole meals for your electric oven to cook. Time to linger longer at your favorite shop . . . time to relax and primp in cool comfort before a company meal . . . time to appear as a gracious hostess to afternoon bridge guests, while a hearty dinner for the family is unobtrusively cooking in the oven. Time after time, this before-dinner freedom can save the day for better things. Once you discover the utter luxury of walking out on your dinner, and coming back hours later to a cool kitchen where that dinner is waiting—hot, appetizing, ready to serve—well, the chances are that you'll let your electric oven do the work of meal-getting several times every week.[15] (5)

Electric cooking promised not only to improve a woman's cooking but also to improve her social, emotional, and family life—no wonder millions of women purchased refrigerators and ranges. They were buying more than a mere appliance—they were purchasing a dream.

Electric appliances, however, did not always offer women the personal freedom that the advertisements promised. The availability of appliances made it possible for many cooking articles and cookbooks to emphasize that women should strive to reach loftier culinary heights. One *Sunset* article, "Your Obedient Servant" (1926), proclaimed: "Think of the good things you do not make, either because they take too much effort—like beating popovers, or beaten biscuit—or because you are not sure of a good result in the case of a cake filling or delicate dessert" (76). Although electric gadgets could help women achieve cooking triumphs, the message was clear that they had to aspire to ever grander ones.

Kitchen Appliances: Gendered Messages

During this period, electric kitchen appliances served as more than just devices to simplify a cooking task—they were a sign of the cook's modernity. Cooking literature made electric kitchen equipment appear so glamorous that any woman would salivate to own such technology. In addition, manufacturers and advertisers of electric kitchen devices suggested to women that they should want to stay in the kitchen, since it was equipped with all the newest gadgets and appliances.

What did not change was that the media depicted mom, not dad, as the person in charge of operating such equipment. The kitchen was transformed by the addition of everything from electric toasters to refrigerators, but this did not alter traditional gender relations to cooking. Mom might have had the help of a table stove and a waffle maker, but she remained the one responsible for the majority of cooking-related tasks. Professor Amy Hewes was mistaken when she said that the Age of Electricity would make household drudgery vanish for women. Even with electricity in the majority of American homes, the drudgery remained, and it was still, for the most part, women's responsibility. Electricity sped up many kitchen tasks, but it did not cause them to vanish.

It is important to study not just cooking, but the equipment that makes it possible. When women buy kitchen equipment, they are also buying a vision of their relationship to cooking and their correct gender roles. Today manufacturers of electric cooking equipment still usually target an audience of women, implying that women should be the ones who wield such devices and that their place is in the kitchen.

Chapter 5

"Fearsome Dishes"

International Cooking and Orientalism between the Wars

We do not often think of the years between World War I and World War II as a period when foreign foods were widely consumed; after all, this was a time when America stood for apple pie, not sushi. If Americans ate foreign foods during this era, we assume, it was usually in ethnic enclaves— safe niches where Italians could relish lasagna or Mexicans could consume tamales without the disparaging comments of other Americans who viewed such foods as scarcely edible. Foreign foods, however, were not as ghettoized at this time as we might first assume. People living in urban areas could pick from many different ethnic restaurants, and any large city had specialty grocery stores where adventuresome cooks could pick up the ingredients to make a meal that reflected one of a host of different cultures, from Spain to Hungary to Japan.

During this period, it was not uncommon for mainstream cooking literature to include a number of food-related articles and recipes from different nationalities.[1] A 1930 *Woman's Home Companion* article contained recipes for *empanadas de hornos* (Chilean meat pies), *pastel de puerco* (Mexican pork pastries), and *salad de pepino* (a cucumber salad from Portugal) (Salvail, 117). Writing for the magazine *American Home*, Merle Lamborn described the delight of an Indian meal for Americans: "You may not be able to take the next boat for India, but you can do something pretty fancy in the way of an Oriental dinner. Why not try a curried dish, complete with all the fixings, for your next Sunday night supper party?" (49). Ethnic foods were common enough between the wars that even the American classic Irma S. Rombauer's *The Joy of Cooking* (1936) included a number of foreign recipes: spaghetti (topped with a can of tomato soup mixed with butter, onion, green pepper, and milk [51]), Italian macaroni (pasta topped with grated cheese and melted butter; a clove of garlic was rubbed in the bowl and discarded [52–53]), Italian meatballs (90), chili con carne (a can of tomato soup added to beef, kidney beans, onion, and chili powder [91]), chow mein with fried noodles (96), chicken chop suey (96–97), and Mexican avocado salad (279). Of course, the foreign recipes that appeared in *The Joy of Cooking* and other cookbooks were Anglicized and were vastly outnumbered by recipes with an Anglo-American or northern European background. But how are we to understand the inclusion of *any* foreign recipes during a time of great xenophobia in America? And what do they imply about the way American women between World War I and II were expected to perceive foreigners and foreign influences? Does a recipe for chop suey or spaghetti suggest anything about women's roles in this era?

Exploring the depiction of foreign foods in the popular media during this period helps to explain how such cooking literature played a role in constituting American women.[2] The previous chapters have focused predominantly on Anglo-American women, since they were the ones who filled mainstream cooking literature; other ethnicities and races sometimes seemed invisible. This chapter seeks to locate those "missing" women by analyzing the messages about ethnicity and race that popular cooking literature conveyed. The depiction of foreign food, particularly Italian, Chinese, and Mexican food, provided the media with a way to indoctrinate women readers with the belief that the ideal American woman was white and middle class. As we shall discover, popular cooking literature did not exclude foreign foods entirely, but they were often included with the clear understanding, whether implicit or explicit, that they were inferior to American foods with a northern European background. Cooking literature popularized eating foreign foods as an experience in what cultural theorist Edward W. Said's calls "Orientalism"; foreign food could be consumed by middle-class Anglo-American women, but only as an experience of the exotic, the foreign, and the strange.

It is important to study ethnic cooking literature because we need to recognize that cookbooks (and other cooking literature) not only form bonds among people; they also exclude people, as food historian Jefferey M. Pilcher observes in *Que Vivan los Tamales! Food and the Making of Mexican Identity* (1998): "Cookbook authors help unify a country by encouraging the interchange of foods between different regions, classes, and ethnic groups, and thereby building a sense of community within the kitchen. But these same works also have the power to exclude ethnic minorities or the lower classes by designating their foods as unfit for civilized tables" (2). We recognize the important role that cookbooks play in building a regional or national cuisine; while some foods are accepted into the national or regional cuisine, however, others are rejected as undesirable. This power of exclusion was a significant force in mainstream American cooking literature in the early twentieth century. Repeatedly, such literature focused on the upper- or middle-class white woman; this emphasis through the decades asserted that the "right" American woman was white and middle class. In addition, the "right" American food was what middle-class white Americans consumed. Readers learned what foods were considered acceptable (not too exotic or unusual) and what foods were excluded. Simultaneously, American women were taught what ethnic groups were more or less acceptable (for instance, Italians were judged more acceptable than Mexicans or Chinese).

"Mysterious and Repulsive": Attitudes about Ethnic Foods

Since the United States has always been a land of immigrants, it has always possessed a cuisine based on foods from a wide variety of cultural backgrounds, as Donna R. Gabaccia points out in *We Are What We Eat: Ethnic Food and the Making of Americans* (1998). A number of ethnic groups (including, among others, the Spanish, Native Americans, and blacks) have significantly influenced the foodstuffs associated with America. Like Gabaccia, food historian Richard J. Hooker notes the long history of foreign foods in the United States: Eliza Leslie's *New Cookery Book* (1857) contained recipes for an Indian pickle, country captain, curry powder, Italian pork, and a number of curried dishes. These foods, however, were consumed by only a few brave souls; as Hooker observes, the United States was still a land of beef and potatoes rather than more exotic dishes (108). Historian Susan

Williams also writes about America as a land influenced by many different cultures and their foods, particularly in the latter part of the nineteenth century; she notes that one typical chef's guide from the turn of the century included information on Chinese, Jewish, Russian, Italian, and Turkish cuisines (114). This interest in foreign foods, however, has not necessarily been widespread, and mainstream white America has had (and continues to have) a cautious relationship with foods from outside its borders, particularly foods that were distant from Anglo cultural traditions. French and Italian foods might have been cautiously accepted in the nineteenth century—at least as a special restaurant meal—but Chinese and Japanese foods had less success.

To understand the role of foreign foods in early-twentieth-century America, we need to recognize these two strands of thought from the past. There have always been people who welcomed foreign tastes and flavors; there have also been those who viewed new tastes and flavors with dismay. These two opposing cultural attitudes played important roles in the popular media in the early twentieth century.

In this period, some writers argued that foreign foods should be welcomed to America since they offered opportunities for learning about different cultures and broadening food tastes.[3] In the 1930s, one cookbook writer observed: "Since variety has long been reputed to be the best spice of life, the American housewife may find that the pleasures of living, and more particularly of the table, would be increased by taking a peep into the households of other lands" (Stewart, *One Hundred Favorite Foreign Recipes*, xv).[4] A 1940 cookbook stressed the importance of learning about foreign cuisines and the cultures that produced them: "no matter what the ethnic differences are or the boundaries of one country or another, in this troubled world, among the cooks at least, there is a 'League of Nations.' Real hospitality and good cooking can be found in every country on earth and from each we can learn something to enrich our American table" (Metzelthin, xiii). For these writers and others, foreign foods offered an easy way to bridge cultural differences. Without going abroad, Americans could experience at least a little of the world's cultures, even if that meant only eating an enchilada dinner.

Other writers perceived a different reason for adding foreign foods to the American table: they were inexpensive and nutritious. One cookbook from 1917 observed: "With the present discussion regarding the necessity for saving time on the home cookery processes, it may be that Americans may learn much from the study of the foreign 'one dish meals'" (Van Arsdale, 4). The author of another cookbook wrote in its preface: "I hope my book will dispel this bugbear about 'foreign cookery' and prove that it is often plainer and simpler, less 'rich' in many cases, and far more economical than some American cooking" (Morphy, 9). For many food writers, foreign foods were alluring because they promised to feed millions of families for very little money. The foods might have tasted a bit peculiar, redolent of garlic and other unusual odors, but food economists considered that a small price to pay in order to feed the hungry masses in America's burgeoning cities and towns.

Given this interest in foreign cuisines, it comes as little surprise that a number of cookbooks were published between the wars that included a wide range of ethnic menus and recipes.⁵ International cookbooks had existed before World War I, but their contents varied tremendously and tended to be less foreign than the title conveyed. Alexander Filippini's *The International Cook Book* (1906), for instance, contained foreign-influenced recipes such as chicken sauté Mexicaine (804), Madras chicken curry (838), Sumatra lamb curry (848), and chicken Udaipur (902), but also included a number of American recipes: fried ham and eggs (793); Virginia stuffed okras (808); Baltimore oysters (816); American tomatoes (871); and Atlantic City halibut (980). American, English, and northern European dishes greatly outweighed the recipes from China, Japan, Mexico, Italy, and other countries. Many of Filippini's recipes, such as Atlantic City halibut, contained little or no foreign influence. Although his book was identified as "international," it did not take too many risks with exotic foreign foods that Americans might have viewed with dismay.

After World War I, foreign cookbooks grew increasingly adventuresome, perhaps due to the increased international influences brought back by doughboys returning from the war. During this period, international cookbooks seemed to include every nationality under the sun. L. L. McLaren's *Pan-Pacific Cook Book: Savory Bits from the World's Fare* (1915) contained recipes for sauces such as chile colorado (42), curry sauce (43), Dutch sauce (126), and wow wow sauce (an Old English recipe that included vinegar, butter, mustard, parsley, port wine, and pickled cucumbers [46]) as well as recipes for Chilean corn pudding (79), Mexican enchiladas (81), Peruvian chicken picante (101), Hindustan chicken curry (101), Spanish pancakes (123), and

Italian polenta (129). *Food at the Fair* (1939), a cookbook from the New York World's Fair of 1939, featured foods from around the world, including Albanian, Brazilian, Cuban, Finnish, Italian, Norwegian, Swiss, and Venezuelan dishes, among others (Gaige, 9). The cookbook encouraged people to try the new dishes that they would find at the fair: "Diners at the Italian Line Restaurant will want to try the *agnolutti* of Piedmont, savory sachets of *pasta* filled with minced meat and vegetables . . . and the famous *fonduta*" (39). If Italian foods were too tame for hungry customers, they could have ventured elsewhere, consuming Turkish pilau at the Turkish Restaurant (59), arroz con pollo at the Cuban Village (20–21), feijoada at the Brazilian Restaurant (16), Albanian shashlik at the Albanian Pavilion (12), or Norwegian prune pudding at Norway's Pavilion (43). Yet another interwar cookbook, Pearl V. Metzelthin's *World Wide Cook Book: Menus and Recipes of Seventy-five Nations* (1940), included recipes from a host of countries, including Albania, Arabia, Argentina, Australia, Bulgaria, Egypt, Estonia, Haiti, Hungary, Japan, Korea, Lithuania, New Zealand, Nicaragua, Romania, and Syria. The message of these two cookbooks and others was clear: the world was a vast and exciting place filled with different cultures and foods; the cook should welcome such culinary adventures, rather than shun them.

The vast majority of Americans, however, remained dubious about such adventures when it came to their stomachs. While some people embraced foreign foods, many members of mainstream American society were cautious about these mysterious foods associated with strange peoples and stranger cuisines. Even authors who wrote positively about some foreign foods remained suspicious of others that seemed too exotic and unusual. In *Dainty Dishes from Foreign Lands* (1911), Louise Rice wrote, "I have . . . gradually incorporated into my daily life, the habits of eating of French, Germans, Italians, Swiss, and even Chinese. . . . I have found my health and that of my family improve under this management; while the simple fact of eating the dishes of The World has seemed to bring us into closer sympathy with mankind, even in its most foreign guise" (8–9). Still, she cautioned: "I have omitted many distinctive dishes because they are seldom liked by Americans" (9). Rice was not the only writer who found some foreign flavors too unusual to enjoy. Other authors found the strong flavors and odors of some foreign foods to be distinctly unpalatable. One article in *American Cookery* in 1929 praised foreign travel as especially delightful because it gave travelers an opportunity to sample foods from different lands. The same article, however, warned against the excesses of Italian cookery: "The malodorous garlic taints practically everything served, from the salad up, and down. The Italian diet likewise includes a bewildering variety of cheeses and sausages, many of which smell even worse than they look, which is saying a great deal. Not a few are so mysterious and repulsive in appearance that it requires considerable bravery to dare an attack" (Stemple, 279). Cultural uneasiness with foreign foods stretched across the United States; many people felt uncomfortable with these new foreign foods, which seemed too closely linked to the immigrants who brought them, who, like the foods themselves, had yet to be assimilated into American culture. These new immigrants and their strange foods, some assumed, endangered American values and traditions, including traditional foods. In 1939, one Federal Writers' Project author lamented that traditional foods had been forced out by immigrants' foodstuffs. At the grocery store, for instance, "cans of Boston baked beans and codfish cakes" stood right next to "cans of spaghetti and chop suey" (quoted in Gabaccia, 122). This author expressed uneasiness not only with unusual foreign foods, but also with the people who brought those foods to American shores.

Between World War I and World War II, widespread uneasiness existed in America about the "new" immigrants from China, Japan, Italy, Mexico, and other nations, who were often perceived by Americans who had lived in the United States for a longer period as threatening to change the country. These new immigrants gathered together in groups in many of America's cities and appeared more difficult to assimilate than earlier immigrants (Matthews, 163). Millions of Americans believed that this flood of foreigners threatened to swamp America and its traditions, so laws were passed to try to stem the flow of immigrants. As early as 1882, the Chinese Exclusion Act had already greatly reduced Chinese immigration to the United States; it would not be repealed until 1946. In 1921, a system of quotas seriously limited immigration from many nations. In 1924, the Johnson-Reed Act lowered the number of immigrants even further. Asians and southern and eastern Europeans suffered the most from such restrictions, since these were the immigrants who were perceived as posing the greatest danger to American values.

Such exclusion acts kept millions of foreigners off America's shores, but what about the millions of immigrants who already lived in America? How could these new Americans be assimilated? For many social workers and other concerned people, the answer seemed to be "Americanization"—a catch-all word that referred to teaching immigrants American values and mores as quickly as possible so that they would blend into the cultural melting pot. To many of the teachers, social workers, and home economists charged with transforming the new immigrants into Americans, food seemed to be the best place to begin. In *Revolution at the Table* Harvey A. Levenstein notes:

> Many of these "Americanizers" were convinced that the immigrants could never be weaned from their old-country attitudes toward work, society, and politics until they abandoned their old-country ways of living and eating. The acrid smells of garlic and onions wafting through the immigrant quarters seemed to provide unpleasant evidence that their inhabitants found American ways unappealing; that they continued to find foreign (and dangerous) ideas as palatable as their foreign food. (104)

Numerous people involved in Americanization viewed foreign foods as un-American. Changing such food preferences, the reformers thought, was the best method to help immigrants assimilate into mainstream American culture.[6] These reformers gave little or no thought to the notion that other cultures' foods might have been superior to traditional Anglo foods; the reformers believed that foreigners possessed a few useful food ideas, but, overall, American foods were better. One international cookbook author in 1917 observed: "Helping the foreigner . . . means understanding his point of view and then educating him according to American standards" (Van Arsdale, 4). In 1923, after studying the eating habits and nutritional deficiencies of Italian immigrants in different cities, Gertrude Gates Mudge wrote in the *Journal of Home Economics*: "In view of dietary conditions found in this survey, it is evident that the Italian kitchen is a fertile field for education in the proper selection of foods. The Italian diet has features which may well be incorporated into our experience and in return the nutrition specialist will do real 'Americanization' work when she aids the Italian women in the adjustment of old dietary customs to the new environment" (185). Both of these writers and others clearly expressed the idea that American ways and American foods were superior to anything that immigrants brought from their native lands. Although not all food reformers felt this way, the belief was widespread that America's blander, more neutral foods were healthier than the spicier and more robust flavors of Italy, Mexico, and other nations.

The social workers engaged in Americanization were often ignorant or scornful of the foodstuffs and cooking habits brought from other countries and quick to suggest changes to make the diets of immigrants more economical and more American. Such changes frequently entailed casting out traditional foodstuffs without understanding their cultural significance. For instance, Lucy H. Gillett wrote about the dietary habits of the Italians she studied in New York City in the article "Factors Influencing Nutrition Work among Italians" (1922): "Cheese is used freely but during the last few years, when Italian cheese was $1.50 a pound, they preferred to use less rather than to substitute American cheese at 50 cents. They could not see that $1.50 spent for American cheese would buy three times as much nourishment" (17). In a similar study by home economists Velma Phillips and Laura Howell, the authors lamented that even the poorest Italian families bought one or two ounces of Italian cheese and small amounts of virgin olive oil (397). These home economists did not pause to reflect on the possibility that many Italians might have received more than mere nourishment from the familiar cheese of their homeland.

Popular media images of foreign foods, particularly those from Italy, China, and Mexico, reflected the ambivalent social reactions to foreign food and foreigners. The broader societal attitudes about foreigners played themselves out in popular cooking literature, which instructed women that ethnic food might be an exotic surprise for a Sunday night party, but it was no match for mainstream Anglo cooking. Cooking literature played a role in constructing different images of foreign foods: while Italian food was broadly acceptable to Anglo-Americans, Chinese and Mexican foods were less widely accepted.

Urbane and Sophisticated—Italian Food

Italian food was the first ethnic cuisine to gain broad acceptance in the United States (Levenstein, *Revolution*, 146). Between World War I and World War II, it went from being something of an oddity to becoming a broadly accepted part of American food culture. A person searching for an Italian meal would find numerous restaurant choices in big cities like Boston, Chicago, New York, and San Francisco; by the 1930s, New York City alone offered the hungry diner a choice of over 1,000 Italian eateries (Gabaccia, 81). The authors of the Federal Writers' Project book *The Italians of New York* (1938) praised the contribution of these restaurants: "There is no disagreement about the contribution made by the Italian restaurants to the gaiety and physical well-being of New Yorkers. For gastronomic color, invention and subtlety, Italian dishes and wines compare favorably with any other variety" (204). Preparing an Italian meal at home was also relatively easy, since macaroni, spaghetti, and other dried pastas, as well as other Italian ingredients, were becoming common items in many grocery stores. Italian food gained broad cultural acceptance in America much earlier than other foreign foods, in part because of its depiction in the popular press. Cooking literature presented Italian food as glamorous and cosmopolitan, deserving a place on every American dinner table; while some other foreign foods were too exotic, Italian food should be perceived as a beneficial addition to American cuisine.

Italian food was not new to the United States in the twentieth century. Italians, who played an important role in the restaurant business, were already dishing out Italian foods such as spaghetti in Gold Rush California (Williams, "Foodways," 1337). By the 1890s, a broad range of Italian foods, including pasta, pastries, and salads, were popular with a large audience of Americans from diverse cultural backgrounds (Hooker, 238–39). By the Progressive Era, as Gabaccia notes in *We Are What We Eat*, Italian food was popular at restaurants, and it grew more popular in the early decades of the twentieth century.[7] Since people associated Italian food with rebellion and bohemianism, it was an ideal dining experience for those seeking culinary adventure (Gabaccia, 99–100).

Before World War I, Italian food was still not widespread in non-Italian American homes. It continued to be viewed as exotic, a bit too peculiar for the mainstream dinner table at home. After the war generated favorable feelings toward Italy, American attitudes toward Italian food changed; by 1920, "a revisionist tide was in full flow. Now social workers, reformers, and food writers portrayed Italian immigrants as people who abandoned the sunny abundance of a varied and heathful diet for the meager fare of the tenements of America" (Levenstein, "The American Response," 14). Since Italy had been an ally in World War I, it was perceived as only fitting that Americans now accepted the Italian foods that many soldiers savored while in Europe. In "Peppers and Garlic" (1918) in *Good Housekeeping*, Elsinore R. Crowell observed: "Ravioli, favorite dish of our Italian ally, should be served on every American table" (63). Ravioli was not the only Italian dish accepted by urban Americans. In the 1920s, at least in America's cities, many people would have been familiar with a range of dishes, including minestrone, cannelloni, antipasto, and lasagna; by the 1930s, pizza was beginning to spread in urban areas (Hooker, 292). Italian food went from marginal to mainstream.

Obviously, many reasons existed for this change, but one influence was popular cooking literature, which gave Italian food a desirable image as cosmopolitan and urbane.[8] The popular media presented both Italians and Italian food positively. Murray Manning noted in *American Home* that an Italian dinner was "different without being strange" (47). Similarly, in *House Beautiful* magazine in 1939 Mary Grosvenor Ellsworth wrote that "pasta is no insipid potato substitute. It is an important and delicious meal in itself" (32).[9] Many writers suggested that pasta and Italian food in general should make a frequent appearance on American dinner tables. They promised that Italian food would provide a pleasant change from meat and potatoes, even if many Americans had to adjust to the notion of pasta composing an entire dinner.

Cooking literature also promoted Italian food by depicting it as elegant and refined. In 1933, Mary Martensen wrote in the trade magazine *Macaroni Journal*: "Spaghetti—a continental favorite—is rapidly becoming equally popular in America." She referred to spaghetti as "the most cosmopolitan of dishes" (7).Presenting Italian food as especially for sophisticates was an effective way to sell macaroni products. For example, one article from *Woman's Home Companion* by Elisabeth G. Palmer in 1935 featured an elegantly clad man and woman preparing an Italian picnic to be served to guests along with a game of *le boccie*: antipasto, green noodles con burro, veal scaloppini, cheese, and coffee (60). In the accompanying photographs, the dinner guests were all nicely dressed and upper middle class; an Italian dinner was depicted as a gala affair. By presenting Italian food as a glamorous treat, cooking literature played a role in making Italian food (and Italians) more accepted in the United States.

It was not always an easy task, however, to persuade Anglo-Americans to sample Italian foods. Many still viewed all foreign foods as suspect; as Levenstein observes, most Anglo-Saxons were particularly suspicious of garlic ("The American Response," 6). No doubt numerous Americans would have agreed with Francis E. Clark's assessment of Italian food in *Our Italian Fellow Citizens: In Their Old Homes and Their New* (1919): "Nothing is too coarse or repulsive for the Italian peasant to eat, if it is not absolutely poison" (174). The many Americans who viewed garlic with abhorrence, like Clark, did not want to be served authentic Italian recipes such as those found in Maria Gentile's *The Italian Cook Book* (1919): polenta pie (31), corn meal with sausages (30), curled omelet (47), and pigeon surprise (98). They wanted dishes adapted to Anglo-American tastes, with the foreignness watered down considerably; cooking literature took an active role in achieving this diluted Italian cuisine (Lovegren, 40). American cooks were reassured that any Italian foods that were too strong, too pungent, too peculiar could be replaced or removed entirely. Garlic too odorous? Skip it. Olive oil too pungent? Replace it with corn oil. An article in *Woman's Home Companion* with a recipe for an Italian antipasto including anchovies, sweet peppers, olives, salami, and tomatoes is one of the more striking examples of the lengths to which this replacement practice went. If these ingredients were not readily available, the American cook was encouraged to substitute Spanish onion for the pepper, salmon for the anchovies, and bologna for the salami (Fenderson, 42). The lesson in this article was clear; American women needed to recognize that they could tame the undesirable aspects of Italian food (or other foreign foods). Food scholar Lucy M. Long refers to this process as "recipe adaptation," which often happens to foreign foods that might be unusual in appearance and taste. According to Long, the process involves "the manipulation of the ingredients and preparation methods of particular dishes in order to adapt to the foodways system of the anticipated consumers. Potentially offensive ingredients may be omitted or replaced with more familiar ones" (194). With recipe adaptation, a foreign recipe, no matter how peculiar it might first seem, can become a familiar addition to America's food culture. By suggesting that foreign recipes should be adapted in this way, cooking literature assured readers that Anglo-American tastes were superior and that foreign foods should be adjusted to Anglo-American standards.

The popular media assured American women that Italian food was acceptable because it was urbane and glamorous. It was also reassuring to recognize that Italian food was similar in many ways to Anglo-American food; if any flavors were too robust, too foreign, they could easily be changed by the imaginative cook armed with a package of bologna or a can of salmon. It was acceptable to experiment with Italian food, as long as women remembered that such foreign food in no way replaced traditional American foods.

Since Italian food was not too unlike Anglo-American food, it is understandable that it became an accepted part of America's food culture between World War I and II (even if in often altered and adapted forms). But what about Chinese and Mexican foods, which were less familiar to Anglo-Americans than Italian food? How were these spicy and unfamiliar cuisines presented in the media? Popular cooking literature conveyed different lessons about Mexican and Chinese food than about Italian food; Mexican and Chinese foods were portrayed as too foreign, too unusual, not something that American women should necessarily welcome into their kitchens. In a similar fashion, readers received the implied lesson that Mexican and Chinese people were inferior to Italians.

Requiring "a Cast-Iron Throat and Stomach"—
Chinese and Mexican Food

Countless Americans went out for dinner at Mexican and Chinese restaurants or prepared Mexican or Chinese meals at home, but the majority of Anglo-Americans still viewed these foods with suspicion. Chinese and Mexican foods appeared in the popular press less frequently than Italian foods such as spaghetti or ravioli and were not accepted as readily as a part of the American cuisine. Even if they accepted Italian food, many Anglo-Americans perceived Chinese and Mexican food as too exotic for the dinner table.

We can better understand the Anglo-American population's apprehension about Mexican and Chinese food in terms of Edward W. Said's theory in his famous book *Orientalism* (1978). Although Said is particularly interested in charting the growth of Orientalism in the nineteenth century as a support for Western imperialism and its development as an academic area of study, his theory is also germane when considering the role of foreign foods in the United States. Said writes: "The Orient was almost a European invention, and had been since antiquity a place of romance, exotic beings, haunting memories and landscapes, remarkable experiences" (1). He notes that, "as much as the West itself, the Orient is an idea that has a history and a tradition of thought, imagery, and vocabulary that have given it reality and presence in and for the West" (5). Thus, foreign foods in the United States are a way for Anglo-Americans to experience the foreign, the unfamiliar. Anglo-Americans were taught by popular cooking literature between the wars that they could experience the exoticism of places like Mexico or China by consuming Americanized versions of these foods. At the same time, however, Orientalism also suggests that the Orient is the opposite of the Occident and that the two will always be separate. In a similar fashion, early-twentieth-century cooking literature established foreign foods from Mexico and China as antithetical to Western tastes. Cooking literature taught women readers about the expected norm (Anglo-American tastes) and what was outside the norm (other ethnicities and their food preferences).

Perhaps because Mexico was America's neighbor and Mexican foods had long been part of southwestern U.S. culture, Mexican foods were not portrayed by the media as negatively as Chinese foods were. Still, Mexican food was depicted as less desirable than Italian food, and cooking literature taught women readers that Mexican foods, as well as Mexicans themselves, were "naturally" of a lower caliber than Anglo-Americans. Mexican food appeared fairly commonly in popular cooking literature during this period, although it was not as common as northern European or Italian recipes. Popular women's magazines contained numerous recipes for Mexican dishes. In "Mexican Cookery" (1920) in *Ladies' Home Journal*, Caroline Cook Coffin discussed the correct way to make tamales, enchiladas, stuffed chiles, and chile con carne.[10] Other authors seemed less knowledgeable about how to identify Mexican foods; Pauline Wiley-Kleemann's *Ramona's Spanish-Mexican Cookery: The First Complete and Authentic Spanish-Mexican Cook Book in English* (1929), for instance, contained authentic Mexican dishes such as albondigas, atole, turkey mole, and tamales. But it also included recipes such as beefsteak a la tartar a la mexicana, boiled dinner a la mexicana, hamburger a la mexicana, and chicken-spaghetti a la mexicana as well as "authentic" Spanish-Mexican dishes such as German sour roast, chicken giblet German style, Syrian chicken, English chicken croquettes, German donuts, and chop suey (!).[11] Since many authors felt unsure about exactly what Mexican food was, they felt free to change menus to suit North American tastes. One article in *Good Housekeeping* entitled "Mexican Dishes for American Meals" (1939) suggested making cornmeal pancakes if tortillas were not available; the only thing Mexican about the Mexican rice described in the article was the clove of garlic and the onion added to the concoction—the condensed tomato soup detracted from the recipe's dubious claim to authenticity (Barber, 177). "Seasonable and Tested Recipes" in *American Cookery* called for cornmeal muffins to replace the more traditional corn husks (Hill and Chambers, 612). Like Italian food, Mexican food was portrayed as needing to be adapted to Anglo-American preferences.

Many Americans, however, remained less comfortable with the tastes of Mexican food than with those of Italian food. Mexico seemed more foreign than Italy, and this feeling was apparent in cookbooks and magazine articles, which approached Mexican food with trepidation. Repeatedly, readers were warned that Mexican dishes were too strong and too hot for American tastes. In *Dainty Dishes from Foreign Lands*, Louise Rice commented: "Spanish and Mexican cooking is so 'hot' that only a cast-iron throat and stomach can endure it" (51). Similarly, one author writing for *Ladies' Home Journal* in 1920 observed: "While there is much in Mexican cookery to be recommended as an addition to our own by way of variety, there is much to be said against it as a regular diet. The use of so much chile cannot but help having a detrimental effect on the organs of digestion, and through them on the general system" (Coffin, 112). These authors expressed a commonly held belief of the period: Mexican foods were too hot and strong-flavored for people in the United States to stomach. Implicit in this belief was the idea that Mexicans as a people were too exotic, too foreign. By portraying Mexican foods as unpalatable, cooking literature also suggested that the Mexican people might also be too different for Anglo-American tastes.

Sometimes cooking literature went even further in portraying Mexicans in a negative light, frequently mentioning that Mexicans were a crude and unrefined people with "primitive" tastes. For example, in the article "A Mexican Kitchen" (1923), Kate Peel Anderson discussed a Mexican home with "a tiled floor kept only reasonably clean with the rather inadequate looking bunches of twigs tied nonchalantly together which pass for a broom" (628). The disparaging note was obvious, and she was not alone in belittling Mexicans. The assumption was prevalent in the popular media that Mexicans and southern Europeans were among the worst of the immigrants to America. In a 1924 issue of *Sunset* magazine, for instance, Maybel Sherman commented positively about many immigrant groups, but she wrote negatively about Mexicans, stating that it was "almost impossible to keep them in school beyond the fourth or fifth grade" (39). Mexicans were also patronized as innocent children: one writer dedicated her 1935 cookbook to "Maria Luisa the gay little maid who brightens my Mexican Kitchen" (Scott, n. pag.). These racial slurs show how cooking literature often instructed readers to treat other ethnic groups in a patronizing or belittling fashion. Cookbooks indoctrinated women about the desirability of cooking and staying in the kitchen; they simultaneously taught them that Anglo-American mores and foods were superior to all others.

Middle-class Anglo-American women also received a lesson about race and ethnicity when they read about Chinese food in cookbooks and magazine articles. They were taught that Chinese food and the Chinese people should be perceived as even more exotic and mysterious than their Mexican counterparts. This racist lesson was particularly interesting because Chinese food was not new to the United States in this period. Chinese restaurants were among the oldest ethnic restaurants in the United States, getting their start during the California Gold Rush, when miners proved eager to try modified Chinese meals such as chow mein and chop suey (Pillsbury, 161). The Chinese restaurant grew to become a part of most American urban areas. Chinese restaurants were especially popular in the early decades of the twentieth century; Gabaccia notes: "No enclave businessmen enjoyed greater success attracting culinary tourists in search of inexpensive exoticism than Chinese restaurateurs in the Chinatowns of New York and San Francisco" (103). Even in the 1890s, however, Chinese food was still perceived by many Anglo-Americans as a somewhat risky dining experience, as historian Richard J. Hooker observes:

> For a few New Yorkers it was an adventure to go to a Chinese restaurant. It was said in the mid-1890s that sometimes two or three men might go into such a restaurant out of curiosity, but they seldom remained for long. The best method, one man wrote, was to make up a party, order dinner before hand, and have a private room. Sometimes, he added, women were taken along to enjoy the novelty. (259) [12]

Eating out at a Chinese restaurant was still perceived as a colorful, but potentially dangerous, experience by most Anglo-Americans.

By the twentieth century, many Chinese restaurants were successful in altering their dishes enough to appeal to Anglo-American tastes; thus, they transformed their restaurants into must-visit places for the adventuresome tourist:

> By the 1920s Chinese restaurants dotted the American landscape, and one was as likely to find a "chop suey parlor" in Kansas City as in New York or San Francisco, even though the typical menu in such places bore small resemblance to the food the Chinese themselves ate. Many dishes were cloyingly sweetened with caramel and sugar, inundated with pineapple chunks and maraschino cherries, and fried in thick batters. (Mariani, *America*, 79)

Despite the popularity of Chinese restaurants (albeit ones serving foods that many Chinese might not have recognized or wished to acknowledge), Chinese foods remained an exotic treat in Anglo households in this era, and women did not always know how to react to them.

Some popular cooking literature praised Chinese food, offering it as a dinner surprise for jaded palates. Dozens of articles mentioned that women should try preparing a Chinese dinner for family or guests.[13] As Alice Moore observed in 1923, "No one need be afraid of Chinese cooking. It is perfectly balanced and very wholesome and, we think, delicious" (x). Hosting a Chinese luncheon was portrayed as exotic in an article from *Harper's Bazaar* entitled "Giving a Chinese Luncheon Party" (1913) written by Sara Bossé. She raved about the merits of such a party: "Served in the real Chinese fashion, with Oriental embellishments and decorations that seem a part of the very food itself, one's guests become imbued with that quaint far-away feeling, as if you had transported them into a new and charming land" (135). In another article written the same year, Bossé discussed the benefits of giving a Chinese dinner: "A Chinese dinner, properly served, proves a delightful and novel form of entertainment. It should be served, of course, in the purely Chinese fashion, which lends an added charm and mystery to the dishes themselves" ("Cooking and Serving," 27). Cooking articles such as these perpetuated an image of the Chinese as mysterious Others. By discussing Chinese food as "far away," Bossé emphasized the gap between her presumably Anglo readers and the Chinese (and other Asians). Like Bossé, Helen Powell Schauffler promoted the idea that Chinese food was perfect for an unusual treat. In her article "Oriental Cookery Makes for Economy" (1928), she urged readers to forget the idea that foreign foods were difficult and expensive to prepare and asked them to "fling convention and prejudice aside some evening" so that they could treat their family to a "genuine Oriental dinner" (72). For Schauffler and others, Chinese food might be an exotic dinner surprise, but that did not mean it should become a standard addition to weekly American dining.

Popular cooking literature sometimes gave Chinese food a more sinister image. This vision of Chinese food was common during a period of deep hostility toward Asian immigrants in the United States, when Chinese immigration to the United States was sharply curtailed.[14] As so often happens, society's view of a people's food habits coincided with the vision of the people themselves. Anglo-Americans had a deeply inculcated fear that Chinese food was unpalatable, barely edible—they feared what they thought was hidden under the concealing Chinese sauces. In 1876, for instance B. E. Lloyd's guide to San Francisco "scarcely mentioned Chinese food as a viable option for visitors. It noted that the Chinese . . . staged great banquets where exotic and rare, but sometimes also disgusting, foods were consumed" (Gabaccia, 103). This belief that Chinese food, unlike Italian food, was unpalatable and even disgusting to Western tastes thrived in the media during the years between World War I and World War II. One article in *Catholic World* in 1927 proclaimed:

China being a country of topsy-turvydom, it is not surprising that the Chinese menu contains many fearsome dishes which would turn the stomach of the average foreigner. And, in addition to serving up meat which the white man would not give to his dog, or to his cat, nearly everything is cooked in oil or fat, while an enormous quantity of garlic is added. (Cecil, 176)

The author of an article entitled "Try This on Your Chopsticks" (1937) wrote that women should only try Chinese cookery when they felt "reckless and nobody that matter[ed was] coming to dinner" (Marshall, 38). The idea was clear that Chinese food was just too unusual to serve as more than a risky surprise for one night's dinner; on other evenings, the cook should stick to more acceptable cuisines. For most Westerners, Chinese food was too different and strange to be appealing, as Countess Marcelle Morphy described in her international cookbook *Recipes of All Nations* (1935):

> Racial and climatic factors are responsible for the wide divergencies in national cookery and food, and the study of comparative cookery shows the unbridgeable gulf which exists between peoples. North, South, East, West—learn what they eat, and you will realize why they have always clashed. In Europe itself, the abyss between the palates of one nation and another explains the enmity and hostility which exist between human beings whose conception of feeding is completely antithetic [sic]. As to the food and cookery of the older Eastern civilizations—India, China, and Japan—they are too remote to be fully understandable. (7)

Morphy was not alone in thinking that Eastern foods were too exotic for Western preferences; many Americans thought exactly the same. In this fashion, they helped to support the notion of an intrinsic difference between East and West, which made it impossible for the two ever to understand each other. This was a lesson that much cooking literature supported and passed on to women readers. Thus, this literature played a small role in perpetuating the beliefs that Said identifies as Orientalism.

Cookbooks also expressed the fear that Chinese food was apt to be dirty and unsanitary. Writing for *American Cookery*, Addie Farrar addressed this issue by assuring her readers that Lo, the Chinese chef about whom she was writing, was "proud of the fact that he is so Americanized" (518). She went on to mention that his kitchen was "spotless," and the cooks he employed were "as clean as a person can possibly be" (518). The belief that Chinese were not clean was repeated frequently in cooking articles and cookbooks that featured Chinese food. For instance, M. Sing Au's cookbook *The Chinese Cook Book: Covering the Entire Field of Chinese Cookery in the Chinese*

Order of Serving, from Nuts to Soup (1936) contained an advertisement for La Choy's Chinese foods proclaiming that all its foods were "packed on automatic equipment in the United States by American men and women in a spotlessly clean plant under supervision of municipal, state and federal inspectors" (n. pag.).[15] Another advertisement for La Choy meals mentioned that La Choy Vegetable Chop Suey was prepared under "strict sanitary conditions in America" (La Choy Chow Mein). La Choy had to combat the stereotypical view of Chinese food as dirty, contaminated.

Chop suey and chow mein, especially the canned variety produced by La Choy, perhaps represented the epiphany of sanitizing Chinese food. Although chop suey was a staple at nineteenth-century chop suey restaurants, it reached its height of American popularity in the amorphous concoction that La Choy canned and identified as Chinese food (Williams, "Foodways," 1341). Although many Chinese would have claimed that La Choy's products bore little or no resemblance to real Chinese food, such pseudo-Chinese food proved popular with many Americans. La Choy dinners promised safe exoticism and meals that were—at least according to La Choy's advertising—identical to those available at the fanciest Chinese restaurant; one La Choy advertising brochure from 1937 proclaimed: "Ravenous or jaded appetites alike are tempted by the alluring goodness of genuine Chop Suey and Chow Mein, and it is possible for you to prepare authentic Chinese dishes in ten minutes that will rival the magic creations of those practiced in the art of the Chinese cuisine" (*The Art*, 1). La Choy's products could easily be purchased at any local grocery store. By the 1930s, La Choy's chop suey and chow mein were sufficiently omnipresent that one writer for *American Cookery* could write: "Oriental food is no longer uncommon on American tables, for its unusual combinations and tastiness make it appealing to nearly every one. Chop suey and chow mein have reached the tin-can stage of popularity" (Leung, "A Chinese Luncheon," 154). But this food had little in common with "real" Chinese food; it was so homogeneous, so altered from any authentic Chinese recipes, that chop suey and chow mein were often difficult to tell apart (Lovegren, 93). With chop suey and chow mein, American women could provide exotic meals for their families without going too far away from home. They were also taught to assume that most Chinese foods were apt to be unappealing, however; cooking literature sent messages that were easily applied not just to Chinese food but to Chinese people: Chinese were still too unusual, too different, to think of them as "regular" Americans. The divide between East and West loomed wide.

Cooking, Race, and Ethnicity

Cookbooks (and cooking literature in general) play a role in constructing the desired racial and ethnic identity of the United States by suggesting how American women should react to different cultures and their foods. Whether promoting the general acceptance of Italian foods between the wars or the American cultural ambivalence toward Chinese foods, cookbooks teach lessons about what constitutes the "proper" American woman and what her race and ethnic identification should be. Even cookbooks that focus entirely on northern European foods teach a lesson about race by excluding foods from around the globe. As Pilcher noted, cookbooks are not only about inclusion, but also about exclusion, keeping people regarded as undesirable out of a community or nation.

In this examination of how early-twentieth-century cooking literature encouraged women to stay in the kitchen, we need to remember how many women were left out of the picture. The focus of mainstream cooking literature was almost exclusively on middle-class white women; this excluded millions of American women who were not considered to be "ideal" representations of American women because of their class, ethnicity, or race. As we read about women and cooking, we need to remember these silenced women.

Chapter 6

"It's Fun Being Thrifty!"

Gendered Cooking Lessons during the Depression

What do lima beans au gourmet, grilled macaroni, lima beans supreme, and baked bean croquettes have in common? They were all Depression-era recipes suggested as possible replacements for the expensive main meat course that many families could not afford ("Why Not," 43).[1] These inexpensive meatless main dishes were one small sign of an economy that was no longer roaring. Countless women who never had to economize in the kitchen were forced to think about strategies to stretch their household budgets, whether by serving lima beans supreme or by other means. During a time of widespread social upheaval, the housewife serving good food in an economical fashion did more than make her nickels and dimes go further. More importantly, at least according to the popular media, she also preserved the American family by keeping its members together around the hearth with her home cooking.

Popular cooking literature taught women that they played an important part in the difficult task of keeping the American family together during the bleak years of the Depression. First, the media taught them that their roles as cooks and nurturers to the whole family were vital. Despite hard times, women had to ensure that their families were fed healthy, nutritious foods. Since they were frequently the ones in charge of the family budget, women also had to make sure these meals were economical; the media presented thriftiness as essential for a woman trying to feed her family. Second, although preparing these nutritious and thrifty meals could be particularly arduous during the Depression, the American housewife had to be creative with her cooking. After all, in those dark years it was especially important that her home-cooked meals be creative, interesting, and savory, even though the ingredients were simple and inexpensive. The media's message to American housewives was clear: by serving economical, nutritious meals that were simultaneously creative and tasty they played a part in ensuring that the American family stayed together during a period of tremendous economic and social stress. With such an important role to play for both family and nation, women were encouraged to continue to perform their domestic tasks and to remain responsible for the majority of work in the kitchen. It was here, the popular message went, that they could do their best work to fight the Depression's woes.

Women and Work in the Depression

We must remember that the reality of women's lives during the Depression was seldom accurately reflected in cookbooks and cooking articles.[2] Such literature transformed America's economic plight into something that could be solved simply through some good old-fashioned thrift in the household. Cooking literature did not explicitly address the changes occurring in both men and women's societal roles. The Depression was a time when both men and women questioned traditional gender roles, which no longer seemed to work in many households where men's positions as the providers were weakened significantly by the tough economic times. The Depression "created a tension between traditional domestic roles and challenges to those roles. The prevailing familial ideology was gravely threatened during the thirties, when women and men adapted to hard times by shifting their household responsibilities" (May, *Homeward Bound*, 51). During the Depression, a conflict arose between the demand for the woman to work outside the household in order to bring in money and for her to remain in the domestic realm. Historian Winifred D. Wandersee describes this tension in *Women's Work and Family Values, 1920–1940* (1981):

> As the household economy lost its productive role and increased its consumption of purchased goods, additional income beyond that of the principal wage-earner became more important rather than less. There was a basic dilemma in this need for additional wage-earners at a time when the role of women and children in the home was glorified, and when women's domestic role, with respect both to housekeeping and to child care, was greatly intensified. (55)

We need to remember this social tension about traditional domestic responsibilities as we explore Depression cooking literature. Even though this literature did not address the tension openly, it lurked beneath the surface. As Depression-era cookbooks and cooking articles discussed the importance of the woman being a thrifty housewife, they were also entering into the public discourse about what roles women (and men) should have in the home and outside it.

One of the places where the tension about women's roles was most visible was in the debate about women working outside the household. During the 1930s, the weak economy made it a necessity for many women to seek a paycheck (Scharf, 139). A relatively large number of women (25 percent) worked during the Depression, with the numbers being much higher for unmarried than for married women (Nash, 76). The number of working women was also higher among some ethnic and racial groups. For instance, twice as many black women as white women worked outside the home (Nash, 76). Despite the numerous women in the workforce, a vitriolic debate emerged about whether or not women should be allowed to work when millions of men did not hold jobs. The issue at stake was not only who would bring home the paycheck, but also what were acceptable roles for men and women.

The public debate about working women grew particularly heated when it focused on married women who held paying jobs outside the home. In *The Paradox of Change: American Women in the Twentieth Century* (1991), William H. Chafe writes about the antagonism directed at these women: "The Depression had fostered a wave of reaction against any change in woman's traditional role. Legislatures enacted laws restricting the employment of married women; labor, government, and the mass media joined in a campaign urging women to refrain from taking jobs" (121). Although some Americans accepted that unmarried women might need to work outside the home because no one else could support them, married women were a different case entirely. After all, they had husbands who could bring in paychecks. Was it fair that these women also worked, bringing in money that, many feared, would be spent on frivolities, not necessities? Even though many of these wives worked to make ends meet for their families, strong social antagonism was directed at them. Many Americans assumed that these married women did not need the money they were earning and should exit from the paid workforce, leaving the jobs for the millions of unemployed men who desperately needed such positions in order to support themselves and their families.[3] During a time of massive unemployment, many Americans assumed that married women should "sacrifice personal ambitions and accept a life of economic inactivity" (Chafe, 115). This belief was widespread and received broad support from both individuals and institutions, including schools, banks, and government offices. In almost every place of employment, a strong antipathy existed toward hiring married women. "The Gallup poll found, in 1936, that 82 per cent of the people were opposed to married women's working. In 1939 Gallup found that 78 per cent were opposed" (Shallcross, 5). This antagonism was particularly powerful in teaching and government work. The government put into law Section 213 of the Economy Act of 1932, which stated that only one person in a couple could be employed by the federal government. This usually resulted in the woman losing her position if both she and her husband were employed by the government. In teaching, too, many married women lost their positions, and numerous states had clauses in teaching contracts stating that marriage was cause for dismissal (Scharf, 76). In 1940, only 13 percent of cities and towns hired married women as teachers (Scharf, 79). Married teachers "were accused of inefficiency, irresponsibility and failure to keep abreast of new developments because their dual responsibilities at home and at work were so time consuming" (Scharf, 79). Many reasons existed to justify why a married woman could not be a schoolteacher, government worker, or business employee.

One reason for the antipathy toward the married woman working outside the household was the fear about who would take care of her domestic tasks. She would abandon these domestic responsibilities, many Americans assumed, and a whole generation of young people would grow up poorly nurtured and poorly fed. The belief was widespread that women with paying jobs outside the home could not contribute sufficiently to their husbands and children to help the American family thrive.

Some people defended the married woman who worked outside the home. For example, Edith V. Cook wrote in a National League of Women Voters pamphlet in defense of married women workers. If they were not allowed to work, Cook warned, the United States faced a "serious crisis in the position of married women—and therefore of all women—which threatens the social and economic position of women" (22). In *Should Married Women Work?* (1940), Ruth Shallcross wrote positively about married women who worked outside the home: "Working women also make a contribution to their homes and children by having interests in the outside world" (22).[4] For Cook, Shallcross, and a minority of other commentators, the married woman benefited her family by holding an outside job. But Shallcross was aware of the negative image of the working mother and had to counter the popular myth that this woman slighted her domestic responsibilities. "Contrary to the usual impression, working women usually eat freshly cooked food when at home rather than food out of cans," Shallcross noted (14). The belief was widespread that mom's good cooking would diminish or vanish entirely if she held a job outside the home and that the entire family (and America) would suffer because of her lapse.

With the Depression-era hostility toward married women working outside the home and the belief that such women could spell the downfall of the American family, a glorified image of motherhood and domestic life arose in the media. Everything about a mother's responsibilities was adulated. This idealized vision of the household and the housewife had little to do with reality for millions of American women: "The Great Depression left its mark upon American women in a variety of ways. It propelled more women into the workforce. . . . But although working women managed to take a small step forward during the Depression, they were also faced with what had become a highly romanticized concept of home and family" (Felder, 145). The home and family had always been romanticized in American history, but this was especially true during the Depression (and other periods of economic or social turmoil, such as World War I and World War II). The media were filled with pictures of rosy-cheeked mothers feeding and taking care of healthy and happy children and husbands. They also featured glowing accounts of the merits of domesticity, including mom's home cooking. America looked back to a romanticized vision of home and hearth—everything Americans believed in and worked for. Perhaps the media depicted home and family in such glowing terms in an attempt to reassure Americans that, despite difficult times, the family, with mother keeping everyone together with her old-fashioned cooking, would survive any hardship.

In this romanticized image of home and family, the role of housewife was depicted as the "natural" and "best" career for a woman.[5] It is hardly surprising that such messages cropped up frequently since during this period there were not enough jobs for men, let alone women. If housekeeping could be made to appear appealing, such media images would at least encourage women to continue acting as housewives and cooks.

In particular, the media celebrated the role of the housewife as a cook and encouraged women to view their cooking talents as essential to keeping their families well fed and content. Even when she was a new bride, a woman had to worry about whether or not her cooking skills were good enough to keep her man happy. One author writing for *Delineator* magazine in 1932 noted: "The first meals in the new home are vastly important" (Batchelder, "Those Important First Meals," 26). Another article entitled "Advice to Brides . . . by Experts" (1933) in *Better Homes and Gardens* warned the new bride that "her happiness depends upon her dedication to the cause of good food right in the very beginning. So we have drafted six experts to give her certain very high standards for biscuits, for cake and pie, for coffee and tea, and for steak—those foods by which every woman's success as a cook is measured, whether or not she is conscious of it herself" (24). These articles spelled out the general belief of many Americans that a marriage depended on a woman's cooking talent. Even during the difficult years of the Depression, a woman had to be a good cook, the myth went, or else she risked her family's health and well-being. The popular media encouraged women to be good cooks during the Depression, but also to be thrifty ones. The media message was clear: only women were equipped to be the cooks during a time of great economic hardship. Thus, women had to stay in the kitchen performing their domestic chores (including cooking) because this work contributed to the stability of America's family in a period of tremendous social stress.

"Every Penny Counts": The Thrifty Housewife

During the Depression, the popular press idolized the thrifty housewife who stayed within her budget.[6] She was presented as someone who could keep a family financially solvent in the most difficult times. Otherwise, the media warned, she could cause a family's fiscal ruin. Everywhere readers looked in Depression-era cooking literature, they were likely to encounter this thrifty housewife doing her home canning, growing her own vegetables, saving heels of bread to turn into breadcrumbs, serving inexpensive meatless meals, and using leftovers rather than discarding them—anything to stretch money a little further. This Depression paragon was doing her part to keep the American family together, the media informed women readers. How could they do anything less?

The reasons for the emergence of this idealized thrifty woman are many. She gave millions of women hope that they could play a small part in ending the Depression if they were just economical enough. This image also humanized the face of the Depression, suggesting that the stagnant economy would not be cured by New Deals and other nationwide economic plans; it would be ended by women who saved a few dollars by doing their own home canning instead of buying canned goods at the stores and by similar thrifty acts. Countless women were provided with a role model that they could emulate.

This figure also served other purposes. She was a domesticated image of womanhood. The thrifty housewife seemingly spent all her time running her household and taking care of her family. She served as a reminder to women that they should be in charge of the kitchen because only they could operate it in the most economical fashion. She also suggested that women belonged in the kitchen because it was there (at least according to the media's logic) that the Depression finally could be vanquished if housewives managed to economize sufficiently. Ultimately, the thrifty housekeeper affirmed for women that their "correct" and "best" place was the home and kitchen. This ideology was difficult for millions of women to combat. It proved remarkably durable even when many other social and gender roles were being questioned, changed, or undermined. Mom's place was still in the kitchen, preparing her family inexpensive, but savory, meals.

Lessons about being a thrifty cook and housekeeper appeared frequently in Depression-era cookbooks and cooking articles.[7] Everywhere, it seemed, women were discussing how to economize in the kitchen, as historian Jeane Westin observes: "During the Great Depression decade, interest in recipe collecting and cooking reached the boiling point. The desire of the American homemaker to give her family high nutrition at a low cost helped her create ingenious new recipes which were often passed from one woman to another" (2). Even the radio jumped on the bandwagon of popular interest in inexpensive and nutritious cooking. Radio food programs that emphasized economical meal plans were popular during the Depression, including Betty Crocker representing General Mills, Aunt Sammy distributing government recipes, Ed and Polly East hosting "Kitchen Quiz," and Eleanor Howe sharing kitchen tips in "Homemaker's Exchange" (Westin, 3).

Perhaps the most visible sign of the nationwide interest in thrifty cooking was Eleanor Roosevelt's book *It's Up to the Women* (1933), which argued that women had to play an essential role in helping the United States out of its doldrums: "We are going through a great crisis in this country and . . . women have a big part to play if we are coming through it successfully" (vii). She emphasized the important role of the mother as a food preparer, commenting: "At the present time there is so much less money to be spent on food in most families, it is fairly important that the mother study all the latest suggestions in the way of inexpensive and yet nourishing meals" (64). Eleanor Roosevelt expressed the thoughts of many other women in the Depression. Thrifty cooking and housekeeping were essential to keeping the American home going. No wonder millions of women stayed in charge of the majority of tasks in their households during the Depression and did not seek outside employment; society's message was that every household needed a woman who was willing to devote all her energies to economizing.

The thrifty housewife knew that, at all costs, she had to avoid becoming the dilettante housewife, as described by Hazel Young in *Better Meals for Less Money* (1940):

> It's the little woman down your street—and ours—who doesn't let her housekeeping or her husband's small salary bother her too much. . . . She never takes the time to get a good old-fashioned dinner with a meat pie or a beef loaf or a thrifty stew. She runs to the delicatessen at the last minute for some chops, and

potato salad, and cream puffs for dessert. It's strange, but she is always behind on her housekeeping allowance. (60)

This specter of the dilettante always appears when an American housewife does not perform her own cooking but, instead, relies on convenience foods to feed her husband and other family members. There was a cultural antagonism toward such pre-made foods, and the belief was strong that mom's cooking was always best. If a woman during the Depression wanted to be considered a "good" mother and wife, the message was clear: she had to serve her family members economical home-cooked meals.

Thrifty cooking could include a wide variety of recipes that relied on inexpensive and nutritious ingredients. Depression-era cookbooks suggested hundreds of such economical recipes. Like *The Joy of Cooking* (1931), many Depression cookbooks were tailored to "meet the needs of the average household, to make palatable dishes with simple means and to lift everyday cooking out of the commonplace" (Rombauer, n. pag.). Irma S. Rombauer's famous book contained numerous simple and inexpensive recipes that even those forced to economize could afford: baked bean soup (26), oxtail soup (27), meatless vegetable soup (29), leftover vegetable soup with croutons and cheese (29), hamburger steak (209), liver stew (227), "very economical" plain cookies (425), economy spice cake (387), and crumb muffins, made with a cup of dry bread crumbs (307). The book included a recipe for lobster canapés, with expensive lobster meat and rich cream sauce, but Rombauer assured readers that tuna fish could be an easy and economical substitute for the lobster (9). Other Depression-era cookbooks also emphasized inexpensive recipes. *Grandma's Cook Book: Designed to Meet Present Day Conditions* (1932) provided families on tight budgets with basic recipes: vegetable soup, Irish stew, fish chowder, fried pork chops, fried salt pork, stewed parsnips, broiled pigs' feet, and fried liver and bacon. Budget recipes from Ida Cogswell Bailey Allen's *The Budget Cook Book* (1935) included fried bread (29), browned cereal slices (46), rice fritters (47), shredded codfish balls (70), and Mexican fish loaf (70). Ruth Berolzheimer's *How to Feed a Family of Five on $15 a Week Cook Book* (1942) contained recipes for hearty, practical, inexpensive dishes such as chili con carne, macaroni and cheese, meat pie, peanut roast, shepherd's pie, Brunswick stew, stuffed prune salad, which could "double for a dessert too" (33), jellied cabbage salad, corn chowder, cream of tomato soup, navy bean soup, gingerbread, chocolate pudding, and baked apples.[8] All of these cookbooks were filled with simple yet nutritious recipes that the thrifty cook was supposed to make for her family.

By preparing such recipes, the housewife was not only reducing her weekly grocery bill, she was helping to end the Depression—a task more important than any other. This was such a crucial responsibility that the media encouraged women to stay at home and not work outside the domestic sphere because they could be more valuable to their families (and America) if they concentrated their efforts on thrifty living. Winifred D. Wandersee writes: "The emphasis upon household thrift and its beneficial effects on the standard of living was so strong that some observers felt that married women workers would be better off financially if they left their outside jobs to those who really needed them and expended all their energies on thriftiness within the home" (53). The household was transformed into a battleground where the war against the Depression would be won or lost. With their domestic responsibilities raised to such an important level, it is no wonder that millions of women did not hold paying jobs outside their homes during this time.

Thriftiness became a demanding full-time job. One cookbook author observed that "many of us have to count our pennies and to stretch our dollars till they creak" (Young, v). Helen K. Bates wrote in an article in *Good Housekeeping*: "Planning three meals a day, seven days a week, is job enough by itself, goodness knows. It becomes a truly Herculean task when your budget allows a rather limited amount for food and every penny counts" (109). The lesson in this article was that women had to devote the majority of their time to work in the kitchen and the rest of the household, making their budgets go further. It is interesting to note that men were seldom mentioned in such articles; the emphasis was always on women needing to be the economical ones, at least when it came to domestic concerns. Men, presumably, would not be able to do the important work of running a thrifty household; thus, women had to be responsible for kitchen (and general household) thrift.

Thriftiness was a demanding task that required more than just staying within a budget. The housewife had to make sure that every scrap of food counted, as Allen warned in *The Budget Cook Book*: "If care is taken to buy seasonable fruits and vegetables and to prepare them by the recipes given in this book; and if every scrap of food is utilized, every Food Budgeteer will soon find herself in that enviable position—in control of the food budget, with interesting meals and an enthusiastic, satisfied, robust family to her credit" (113). Allen was not alone in emphasizing that a cook needed to learn how to use parts of food that she might have discarded in earlier years. "A 'good cook' is not one who can take the choicest and most expensive of ingredients and from them concoct a delectable dish, but rather one who can combine the cheaper products and make a dish that is 'fit to set before a king,' savory and delicious," observed one article in *Good Housekeeping*, which described a variety of ways to prepare cheaper cuts of meat (Taylor, "Why Not Buy," 90).[9] Women were urged to change any habits that resulted in wasted food. "Much so-called 'waste' finding its way to the garbage can could have been used to produce appetizing and nutritious dishes," another Depression-era article in a women's magazine observed. "The green stems surrounding the head of cauliflower, so often discarded, make a delicious vegetable, and so do beet greens. Trimmings from chops prepared by the butcher make delicious stews. How many order these sent home?" (Fisher and Taylor, 81). The cook had to be careful to use every food item in the most economical fashion possible and had to be aware of innovative ways to stretch food even further. The media's message was that the thrifty cook's job was never done; she always could improve the way her home and kitchen were run.

Such emphasis on thrift often ended up in increasing the hours real women spent on their domestic responsibilities. Historian Gerald D. Nash observes that such tasks grew during the Depression for many women:

> In many instances, the tribulations of the Depression tightened the bonds of family. The majority of women centered their lives on their homes and families and devoted more than sixty hours to them. When money was scarce, women often increased giving of their own time and labor. So instead of purchasing canned fruits and vegetables, an increasing number of homemakers reverted to canning. (75)

Deborah G. Felder also cites the many new kitchen-related responsibilities that filled women's lives: "Wives . . . practiced such economies as buying day-old bread, warming several dishes in the oven at the same time to save gas, buying cheaper cuts of meat, and substituting cheap ingredients for some recipes" (143). If housekeeping before the Depression demanded many hours from the average housewife, it grew to be an even more laborious task during the Depression. Despite the longer hours for many women, most members of American society did not question that the wife should be in charge of such work. Her role was to be the one responsible for the majority of kitchen-related tasks, no matter how many hours they might have required. The thrifty housewife had a job that was impossible to complete because it could always be done a bit more carefully. Her standards could never be as high as those promoted by the popular media, which showed an economical housewife cooking cheaper cuts of meat, making her own canned vegetables, using beet greens, buying day-old bread, and doing a hundred other chores. Any woman reading about the thrifty housewife's exploits was left feeling that she was not accomplishing as much as she should be.

"Don't Let Yourself Slump": Creative Cooking in the Depression

The media also taught Depression-era women that they needed to present food in a creative and original fashion. This was especially important during the Depression, cooking magazines and cookbooks informed their readers, because mom's creative cooking kept the family together during difficult times. A creative dinner showed everyone in the family that, despite the economic and social hardships, mom could be counted on to produce a creative and tasty home-cooked meal, despite her reliance on budget ingredients. Mom had to keep up her enthusiasm and interest in cooking; her attitude presumably would influence everyone in the home. She also had to serve her meals with grace and elegance, with decorations, nice china and silverware, and candles—anything to make a dinner appeal to her family members and guests. Such messages about the importance of decorative cooking are never as simple as they might first appear. They assure that women will spend even more time in the kitchen, striving to produce ever more creative meals.

The Depression-era media suggested that women had to view their kitchen responsibilities as a creative challenge. If they did not approach cooking in this fashion, their families would suffer. Young wrote in *Better Meals for Less Money*: "Good foods need not be expensive foods. Ingenuity and really liking one's job can work wonders" (44). This message was repeated frequently in the popular media. But liking her job was not enough for the thrifty house-wife; she also had to think of it as an exciting challenge. One Depression-era article urged readers to "bring enthusiasm and a fresh interest to your meal planning each week. Don't let yourself slump and get into ruts. Hunt through your recipe files for old favorites, and be on the lookout for new ones. Meal planning can really be great fun!" (Bates, 124). Advertisements also proclaimed that cooking could be enjoyable for a woman, even when serving something as prosaic as the common lima bean. The caption for one 1931 advertisement read: "It's fun being thrifty when I can serve dishes like these!" (California Limas, 212). The advertisement contained recipes for lima puree, limas Louisiana, flavory lima loaf, and limas and lamb stew, all guaranteed to help the woman give her family "a real treat in wholesome goodness and flavor" (212). The media stressed the importance of finding pleasure in cooking throughout the twentieth century (and earlier), suggest-ing that any woman who does *not* find enjoyment in such culinary activities is somehow less a woman, less a mother. This message has long been used to ensure that women remain the primary cooks in American kitchens.

Women were encouraged to add a special touch to make even a simple meal more appealing. Blanche Seder wrote in a *Better Homes and Gardens* ar-ticle in 1933: "A few . . . tricks in preparing and serving everyday foods will enable the homemaker to stay within her food budget, yet serve meals which are more intriguing" (14). One article asserted that familiar foods required just "a dash of bright magic from the imagination of clever women. And lo! what was yesterday's monotony becomes tomorrow's surprise" (Hussong, 357). The same article suggested that "lowly garden vegetables [could be] transformed into such alluring shapes as flowers and balls and cubes," and "ring moulds and fish moulds and shell moulds [could] make the familiar meat dish a decorative triumph" (357). Potatoes could be formed into "little white marbles" with the help of a melon scoop (358). Beets could be cut with a grater into "perfect cubes" (378). Ice box-puddings could be made more interesting by forming them in molds "shaped like turkeys or mounds of cherries" (378). Even the lowly onion could be raised to new heights as Andrea Channing noted in "Stretch the Budget by Using Onions" (1936) in *American Home* magazine. She encouraged homemakers to try adding on-ions to their budget menus. "The inexpensive, healthful onion is always on the market and lends itself nicely to variety in preparation. Try introducing this 'friend of the budget' to your family" (55). She provided budget-pleasing and creative recipes for scalloped onions and corn, baked onions with rice and nuts, and sour onion and tomato salad (56). Particularly creative was her recipe for onion mix-up, using cooked rice, four onions, almonds, chopped hard-boiled egg, toasted coconut, butter, olive oil, and two sweet pickles. The cook mounded the rice on plates and then cooked the other ingredients, except for the egg and pickles, until the onion was golden brown. The cooked onion mixture was heaped on the rice and then garnished with the hard-boiled egg and chopped sweet pickle. Onion mix-up was exactly what the Depression-era cook was supposed to prepare, a dish that was creative and appealing to her family members but used inexpensive ingredients. Such meals showed that a housewife believed in economy, but had not forgotten that it was her responsibility to provide food that her family found palatable and interesting. She had to remember that her home-cooked meals provided more than nutrition during the dark Depression years; they also kept her family members together.

The cook's responsibility did not end with turning beets into perfect cubes and being able to cook one hundred different recipes with onions. Women also had to make sure that their meals were presented in a festive fashion, whether they were serving family members or entertaining guests. One Depression article gave the following rule to budget-minded housewives: "Serve every meal nicely, no matter how simple. A bouquet on the table, the silver shining and set in orderly fashion, and a smiling mother make every meal an important occasion" (Smith, "We Help You," 16). Entertaining, of course, called for special efforts from the thrifty cook, as Allen noted in *The Budget Cook Book*: "Today simplicity has become the height of elegance, so any Food Budgeteer may entertain without worry over cost and without overwork. The simplest foods, well cooked and seasoned and hospitably served, are the vogue. Table decorations are simple—a few flowers arranged in Japanese style or even a basket of perfect vegetables is the mode" (117). The ideal housewife during the Depression was supposed to turn her meal into an experience in which everything from the beets to the silverware was arranged in an artistic fashion. This emphasis on creativity suggested that women who scorned these activities were less womanly than those who thrived on them.

Such artistic cooking was increasingly difficult to achieve for many real women in the Depression—and completely unobtainable for millions of poverty-stricken women who could not aspire to such middle-class goals as they set out a meal of cornbread and salt pork or plain porridge. What the media suggested was a middle- and upper-class ideal of dining, which did not have a basis in reality for many women. This ideal was set forth in popular cooking literature as "normal" for the American family. Women were encouraged to devote their energies to achieving it, which was an effective way to prevent them from agitating about other social problems.

The Thrifty Housewife

During a time of economic and social chaos, the thrifty housewife in the media assured millions of Americans that the family had not been destroyed by the Depression. She was a reassuring reminder that mom's place was still in the kitchen and that she would perform her cooking tasks no matter what changes occurred. Even though many women, due to ethnicity or class, might have been unable to achieve what the thrifty housewife did, she acted as a symbolic norm, showing women what was expected of them. She suggested that their place was in the home and the kitchen. This conservative ideology assured that millions of women stayed in the home. How could women change their domestic duties when they were taught that economical cooking was a key ingredient in ending the Depression?

Now it is time to turn to another period of great turmoil for the United States: World War II. During the war, cooking literature again created images of women's thrifty cooking as a heroic duty during a time of hardship, essential to the country's survival. But the message changed. Before the war, the stay-at-home mother was praised; during the war, she had to perform all the cooking (and other domestic chores) and at the same time act as Rosie the Riveter, doing her part in the war efforts.

Chapter 7

"Wear This Uniform Proudly, Mrs. America!"

Rosie the Riveter in the Kitchen

"Wear this uniform proudly, Mrs. America!" declared a World War II advertisement for Stokely's tomatoes. "It's just a kitchen apron. Not a bit dramatic. Yet you who wear it perform a service without which this war cannot be won. . . . Planning good meals with rationed foods. Keeping everyone on the job. Holding home together, no matter what" (Stokely's Finest Foods, 126). In a similar vein, a 1943 advertisement for Chef Boy-ar-dee spaghetti dinner observed: "Not just in overalls or a uniform—but even more in an apron—the American woman is serving her country today as never before. . . . If you are one of the millions who share this essential job, you are serving where *you* are needed most" (Chef Boy-ar-dee, 174). These are two examples of the flood of advertisements, cookbooks, and magazine articles published during the war that emphasized the importance of the American woman in the kitchen. According to the media, she played a vital role by feeding the millions of men, women, and children caught up in the war effort; without her labor in the kitchen, the war could not be won. At a time when millions of women were working outside the private home, frequently in nontraditional jobs making steel, airplanes, and bombs, how were these Rosie the Riveters simultaneously persuaded by the media to keep up their kitchen tasks as well as their other domestic responsibilities? Cooking literature instructed women that kitchen work and other domestic tasks came before labor outside the home, but it also promoted the idea that during the war women should be *both* housewives and workers in war-related industries across the United States. Finally, cooking literature suggested that women should continue to be responsible for cooking and other traditionally feminine domestic tasks after the war ended. To lure Rosie the Riveter back to the kitchen, the postwar kitchen was depicted as a pleasure palace to which any woman would yearn to return.

Of course, wartime media images of women did not necessarily reflect the lives of real women during the war, as historian D'Ann Campbell notes in *Women at War with America: Private Lives in a Patriotic Era* (1984):

> Doubtless the image of Woman that was presented to the public bore some relation to the experience of American women, whether as distorted reflection or prescription or ideal, and few people were unaware of those images. Yet studying the image of the American Woman, whether that projected by the movies, soap operas, novels, billboards, women's magazines, daily press, or government propaganda, only offers a very indirect access to American women's actual experiences. (10)

Although the American woman as depicted in popular cooking literature was not necessarily a realistic representation of millions of women's lives and experiences of the war, it is important that we recognize the tremendous influence of such media-created visions of womanhood in swaying public opinion. Even if many women might not have followed these dictates, it is difficult to question the influence that such ideals have on any society in any historical epoch.

Women as War Workers

Before turning to popular cooking literature, we must first understand the wartime conditions that made it necessary for such literature to address woman's place both in the home and in the workplace. World War II caused an upheaval of social and gender roles greater than any seen before in American history. The shifting of roles and responsibilities was profound, affecting every class, racial, and ethnic group of women who were called to perform wartime responsibilities, from folding bandages for GIs to wielding rivet guns at the local shipyard.[1] Chester W. Gregory notes that war gave "American women new training programs, new jobs, new experiences, new responsibilities, and practically a new way of life" (xxi). Historian Karen Anderson concurs with Gregory, writing that "no war in American history has had as profound an effect on American society and American women" (4). World War II dramatically altered the lifestyles of millions of women, but this change did not come without profound cultural anxiety about women's shifting roles. Many Americans worried that it might be difficult to send women back to their quiet homes and domestic responsibilities after the excitement (and paychecks) of working in wartime factories. Yet, it was felt that they needed to return to the home front, thus making jobs available for the millions of soldiers coming back from the war.

At the beginning of the war, however, little public rhetoric existed that supported women staying at home, unless they had very small children. As wartime production began to gear up in the United States, it was evident that America faced a serious shortage of wartime workers unless women joined the workforce in unprecedented numbers. The media message was widespread that women should work outside their homes for the good of the nation. In the informational booklet *Women in War Production* (1942), author Thelma McKelvey wrote that "women are an immediate reserve of potential producers which will and must be used as our armed forces are increased and our working forces consequently depleted. In a war period it is imperative that there should be wise use of women" (3). In the pamphlet *Is There Enough Manpower?* (1942), Harold W. Metz proclaimed: "The greatest reservoir of additional manpower is the 29.8 million women who are . . . homemakers" (6). Millions of these homemakers heard the call to find jobs producing war materials and left their homes to work long hours in factories, shipyards, and other industries that provided the enormous volume of supplies needed by a war fought on two fronts. Other women took up jobs that were not specifically war-related but vital to the American economy, jobs left vacant by the departing soldiers. By 1944, one out of three war workers was a woman (Gregory, xvi). In 1944, nineteen million women worked outside their homes, 47 percent more than the year before (Anderson, *Wartime*, 4). Millions of women's lives were turned topsy-turvy by the war efforts. Many worked the midnight shifts at local factories, returning to care for their children during the day. Some women moved to other states to take up new jobs in cities with booming wartime economies like San Diego and Baltimore. Other women trained for new wartime jobs, ferrying airplanes or making ammunition, jobs they would never have considered performing before the war broke out.[2] Women workers were everywhere, doing jobs that needed to be accomplished despite the severe shortage of men.

The tremendous need for women as wartime workers called forth a deluge of official and unofficial propaganda touting the importance of women venturing outside their homes.[3] The message was clear: women had to work if they wished to be considered loyal Americans. One writer noted in 1942: "The loyalty and patriotism of the women of America are unquestioned. When they are needed, they will do their share in turning out the essentials of war" (McKelvey, 32).[4] The message was omnipresent that women workers were vital to the war effort and would serve as an important line of defense against the enemy. The chairman of the U.S. War Manpower Commission, Paul V. McNutt, suggested that housewives "constitute our principal last-ditch battle line in industry today. They hold the balance of power. They must win the victory, those of them who are strong enough to do the work" (25). He urged women to find jobs: "If you are an employable miss or housewife in an area where war workers or essential civilian workers are needed, get a job. Regardless of the sacrifice, it cannot be a greater one than dying on a battlefield" (101). In *What Women Can Do to Win the War* (1942), Albert Parry described America's women as the nation's secret weapon: "The Axis forces often boast of a 'secret weapon.' America's secret weapon is its millions of trained, wide-awake women, who stand ready to take their places, shoulder to shoulder, with the men of America until the world is again made free for all men and all women—and all children—everywhere" (4). Many voices reiterated the idea that women should work in wartime jobs or face being responsible for losing the war. Such wartime rhetoric sent millions of women into jobs outside their homes.

World War II altered women's work lives dramatically, a shift that changed the fabric of American society. Many Americans worried that this change would be permanent. After women left the workforce, some people feared, they would not easily return to their peacetime occupations. D'Ann Campbell writes: "Successful achievement in jobs that had traditionally been closed to women made for dramatic publicity photographs and fostered an image of 'wonder woman' in khaki, but it raised doubts on the home front about the wisdom of having the nation's future mothers and homemakers in service" (31).[5] What woman would wish to go from riveting airplanes to preparing dinner for her family? There was a very real social fear that women's participation in the wartime workforce would remove them forever from their domestic abode, the American home.

The media needed to confront this fear because, after all, the GIs were fighting for the American home and the American housewife. The soldier wanted to come back to a home where his wife cooked the dinners and cared for the children—a place he could gratefully return to after a hard day of work, a safe haven from the world's ills. The illusion had to be perpetuated that this life still existed and would continue to exist after the war. Thus, the media were careful to temper the image of Rosie the Riveter that they presented. She worked a wartime job, but she still managed to keep her feminine side; she was depicted as eager to return to her domestic role after the "abnormal" years of the war concluded. The media assured readers that women's roles had not changed drastically, even though women might be picking up rivet guns in airplane factories or using welding torches at shipbuilding facilities: "Although women were exhorted to take war jobs as a patriotic necessity, they were also warned that men do not want to marry career women and that competence in 'woman's realm,' the home, was a woman's greatest asset" (Anderson, *Wartime*, 60). Historian Leila Rupp notes:

> The War Manpower Commission and the Office of War Information forged ahead with their policy of selling the war to women, and in the process the image of American women underwent major transformations. Yet these changes were in a larger sense superficial, because they were meant by the government, and understood by the public, to be temporary. It was a tremendous change for Rosie the Riveter, who was always a housewife in the public image, to leave behind her peaceful home existence and take up riveting, but everyone understood that it was only for the duration. (138)

As Rupp observes, the belief was widespread that women's roles would return to "normal" after the exigencies of wartime life ended; still, there were those who feared the opposite.[6] The media played a major role in assuring Americans that women would return to the delights of their homes and kitchens after the war was over.

Cooking literature assured a nervous public that the American woman would not abandon her cooking duties and similar domestic responsibilities during or after the war. It emphasized that a woman's domestic responsibilities always came before any other duties she had outside the home. Additionally, cookbooks, cooking articles, and advertisements portrayed cooking as essential to the war effort; thus, women would "naturally" wish to keep up their kitchen tasks because they were cooking not only for their families but also for the nation. Finally, this literature created an alluring picture of the kitchen after the war that would persuade the most reluctant Rosie the Riveter to put down her rivet gun.

"Forward to Victory!": Wartime Cooking Literature

"We are the Pinch-Penny Privates of Uncle Sam's Army. We housewives of the nation have adopted as our slogan: Waste not, and win the war!" wrote Tekla Barclay for *American Home* magazine in 1943 (68). She exhorted housewives to make use even of foods that would have formerly been considered scraps. Potato peelings could be baked and served as a vegetable. Leftover vegetables could be turned into savory patties with the addition of an egg or two and spices. The article concluded by urging readers to "train with the kitchen as our barracks, the stove as our anti-axis gun, and food as our ammunition. Forward to victory!" (68). Writing for *Good Housekeeping* in 1943, Katharine Fisher reminded women to remember the importance of their food-related domestic tasks: "Food fights for freedom! That's not just a slogan. . . . You and your kitchen have a big job to do. And a proud one, too" ("It's Harder," 92). In *Thrifty Cooking for Wartime* (1942), Alice B. Winn-Smith proclaimed that the role "played by American housewives in their own kitchens is no less important than that of the worker in the munitions plant or the soldier advancing with the tanks" (vii).[7] "American housewives of today are united in one great army, for one noble purpose—VICTORY. Just as necessary as shouldering a rifle, is the shouldering of our responsibilities in the home," Winn-Smith asserted (ix).[8] Many other writers of cooking literature also emphasized the importance of taking charge of the home front.[9] Housewives performed an essential job in the war effort, equally important as the task performed by their husbands, brothers, and sons in the trenches. This message, of course, also served the dual purpose of keeping women in the kitchen. Cooking literature was not the sole source that influenced women to stay in the kitchen; it played a significant role, however, in depicting cultural norms about how society expected women to behave.

The kitchen was transformed into a battleground, in which American women served as the frontline troops. In *Eating for Victory: Food Rationing and the Politics of Domesticity* (1998), Amy Bentley writes that "messages specifically regarding food were clear and uniform: women's real and most important battlefield was the kitchen. There women could—and should—fight the war and prove their patriotism by cooking and serving the right kinds of foods in the right kinds of ways" (31). The task of buying, preparing, and serving food during wartime was prodigious, however. Women had to confront many difficulties that did not exist prior to the war. Even before shopping, a woman had to discover if she had enough ration points to buy goods ranging from coffee to sugar to meat.[10] Meals had to change when meat or sugar ran short; rare items had to be hunted down at different shops—the cooking task had never been easy, but wartime conditions made it much more complex (Anderson, *Wartime*, 86).[11]

In a wartime article, Esther Heineman wrote: "To do her share in the war effort, the American home-maker must be adaptable, adjusting herself easily to new deficiencies in the food supply" (284). This is exactly what home-makers were forced to do: change recipes and meal plans to fit the available ingredients. Sugar was particularly scarce; with America's sweet tooth, that demanded special creativity from women.[12] One wartime cookbook suggested a number of ways to cut out rationed white sugar from meals: "Lemon drops in hot or iced tea; cinnamon drops or balls for coffee and for sweetening cooked apples whether baked, coddled or made into sauce; peppermint candies for pears, ice cream or sherbets; cream patties, when you can get them, for frostings. The imaginative budgeteer will find endless uses for these and protect her sugar ration at every point" (Berolzheimer, *250 Ways to Save Sugar*, 4). Prudence Penny's *Coupon Cookery* (1943) contained numerous recipes that used sweeteners other than white sugar, including honey chocolate cake (87), carrot-honey cookies (88), steamed ginger fig pudding sweetened with molasses (91), honey frosting (94), and never-fail frosting sweetened with corn syrup (94).

Meat was another scarce commodity, forcing women to resort to all kinds of tactics to put a main course on the dinner table. One strategy was to serve meatless meals, but they did not always meet favor with an American population used to meat and potatoes. In *Cooking on a Ration: Food Is Still Fun* (1943), Marjorie Mills made it clear that the housewife had to become a master deceiver to convince her reluctant family to eat the changed fare of wartime: "Now it takes cleverness to make the family taste and say rapturously, 'What did you do to THIS?'" (57).[13] It must have been difficult to elicit such a rapturous response, because meatless meals were often far different from more familiar meals based on a main course of meat. Meatless meals proposed for wartime dinners sound like menu items at contemporary health food restaurants. Mills's *Cooking on a Ration* included recipes for peanut butter loaf, cottage cheese loaf, and nut vegetable loaf.

Demetria Taylor's *Ration Cook Book* (1943) included recipes for meatless main dishes such as curried eggs (42), baked soya beans (43), baked bean loaf (43), and walnut sausage (43).[14] The need to prepare such meatless dishes no doubt made wartime cooking a greater travail, especially when the cook not only had to prepare the dish but also had to ensure that her family members ate it. Clearly, these dishes would be a hard sell, as Florence La-Ganke Harris declared in *Victory Vitamin Cook Book for Wartime Meals* (1943): "It is quite possible (although not probable) that your family will grow so fond of the meatless dishes you concoct during this meat shortage that they won't want to go back to meat abundance—but we're still betting on the popularity of steaks, chops, and roasts after our boys are back home, after the starving nations have been fed, and after peace is once more back upon this troubled world" (104). It was a difficult task for mother to turn the thoughts of meat-loving Americans from steak and potatoes to walnut sausage and soybeans.

Given the tremendous difficulties confronting any woman during the war who cooked for a family and grappled with everything from ration points to soybeans, wartime cooking was a vexing responsibility. Yet millions of women performed their domestic duties, and millions of women worked double duty, cooking for a family and also maintaining wartime jobs outside the home. The reasons for this devotion were many, but women stayed the primary cooks in the family during a time of tremendous upheaval in part because of the popular media, which assured women that their domestic duties should be performed with zeal, despite all hardships. The media conveyed five major messages about how the American woman should think about the wartime responsibilities of feeding her family: (1) she had to recognize that her good cooking would hold the family together; (2) she needed to feed her family nutritious meals; (3) she had to use food in a scientific, rational fashion; (4) she should be proud because she was following in her foremothers' footsteps; and (5) after the war, she would be rewarded for her hard labor with a dream kitchen equipped with all the latest appliances and gadgets. These five messages constituted a wartime cooking ideology that suggested women's place was in the kitchen both during and after the war.

Historian Mark H. Leff discusses the ethos of sacrifice that pervaded wartime culture. Sacrifice on the home front did not always involve tremendous hardship: "During World War II, Americans gloried in the feelings that they were participating in a noble and successful case by making 'sacrifices.' In common parlance sacrifice did not require the suffering of terrible loss. It instead comprehended a range of activities—running the gamut from donating waste paper to donating lives" (1296). He continues: "In the home front war, the politics of sacrifice prevailed" (1318). Cooking literature fit into this larger discourse about the virtue of sacrifice. Women spent long hours on their cooking responsibilities during the war—far more effort and time had to be expended than during peacetime—but these efforts and sacrifices were acceptable because they were part of the larger ethos of sacrifice that pervaded society.

According to this ethos, a woman never could shirk her food responsibilities; she had to embrace them with energy and spirit. This was particularly important since many men were giving their lives to protect the homes in which women worked and lived. One cookbook author wrote: "We owe it to our families to keep the home fire burning as comfortably as possible, while they are so willingly doing everything to protect it" (Winn-Smith, xvi). The message was loud and clear: when women prepared good food for their families, they helped keep that fire burning. Cookbooks and cooking articles affirmed that the family should come first, even if that meant having no wartime job outside the home. One cookbook writer warned: "Family deterioration is too dangerous a price to pay for holding down two jobs" (Allen, Double-Quick Cooking, 21). In an article in American Home in 1943, Jessie Hooper wrote:

Since two members of my family work in a defense factory, I decided that keeping them well fed and happy is my patriotic contribution to the war effort. The
hours I had been devoting to volunteer services would have to be curtailed
because my two defense workers and family now come first in my duties. I still
find time to do some volunteer work and the hours devoted to it give me a peace
of mind because I know that my first job of making a home for my family is
being efficiently done. (74)

In another article from the same magazine, Lilliace M. Mitchell warned her
readers: "Work on the homefront, by caring for her children, is one of the
most patriotic duties mothers can perform if juvenile court records are any
criterion. . . . The mother who rushes in ten minutes before dinner time
to . . . open three or four cans of rationed vegetables and fruit for a pick-up
meal is not coming in on the beam" (66). The message in Hooper's and
Mitchell's articles was that without good meals served by moms to American
families, chaos would ensue.

Mom's home-cooked meals also served another purpose; ideologically,
they reinforced traditional gender values. During the war, the media were
important conveyers of messages about acceptable gender roles. Amy Bentley notes: "During the war, media depictions of bountiful meals with women
as servers and cooks connoted stability to many Americans, in large part
because the images reinforced the status quo of traditional gender roles" ("Islands," 132). Bentley discusses the symbolic importance of what she calls the
ordered meal, the traditional American meal of meat, potatoes, and vegetable: "The image of the ordered meal unquestioningly promoted the long-
held assumption that women, as wives, mothers, and domestics, would serve
nutritious and abundant meals for their families, despite the fact that more
and more women were involved in work outside their homes as 'Rosie the
Riveters' or in other, more traditionally feminine kinds of work, both voluntary and paid" ("Islands," 132). To extrapolate from Bentley's argument, it
was not only the ordered meal that affirmed a woman's place in the kitchen;
any home-cooked meals that mom served her family reaffirmed that she was
not abandoning her domestic duties, despite the war's upheaval. Food and
meals played an important role in perpetuating the ideology of the united
American family. Women and their home cooking were "symbolic of the
home-centered life style soldiers were fighting to protect," notes one historian (Honey, 136). Thus, the wartime media worked to strengthen and sup-

port the belief in women's "natural" connection to home cooking and the kitchen since it was such a powerful ideological core of American life.

These messages about the supreme importance of mom's home cooking to keep the American family and home together did not mean, however, that mom would be given assistance with her food-related responsibilities either by family members or by the government. Cooking literature suggested that mom alone would be the hero, balancing a job outside the home with her cooking tasks. One magazine warned, "Join up . . . but don't let your family down" (Marsh, "Don't," 108). According to wartime propaganda, mother was supposed to keep up her responsibilities both inside and outside the private home. In a 1943 *Good Housekeeping* article, Dorothy Marsh wrote: "Clerk in a store, deliver milk, groom a locomotive, drive a bus—any job that will help keep the home front functioning. Many women find that, with planning . . . , they can fill a full- or part-time job and still have time for housekeeping and the meals" ("Tips," 85). Cooking literature suggested a difficult ideal; to be real wartime heroes, women had to juggle cooking duties and wartime job responsibilities without letting anything fall crashing to the floor.[15]

During the war, however, it was not enough to feed families home-cooked meals; the cook also had to ensure that the foods she served contained the correct nutrients and vitamins to keep her family healthy. The *Better Homes and Gardens Cook Book* (1943) informed homemakers: "We have a real war job keeping our families healthy and happy" (1). No longer could mom prepare whatever was inexpensive and convenient for dinner. Now she had to consider the nutritional needs of everyone from the future fighting man to the factory laborer to the teenage Red Cross volunteer. The woman cook was compared in the media to a general: she had to make careful decisions to make sure that her troops were in fighting trim for whatever their wartime duties required and had to make use of the supplies she had available. An article in *Good Housekeeping* observed: "A family fit and well fed forms the first line of defense in the grand strategy of the home front. You, as General, must plan your strategy with full knowledge of defense needs" (Fisher, "March Meals," 104).[16] This home-front general faced the tremendous task of feeding her family nutritious food, but this problem could be solved with intelligent planning. One cookbook stated: "American housewives have taken over the responsibility of feeding some thirty-five million families healthful and attractive meals with our share of the food supply. We are eager to win our part in the War, and by attacking our problems intelligently we will" (Voellmig, n. pag.). An advertisement with a similar theme read: "American housewives are responsible for keeping 18 times as many men properly fed on the Production Front as those who feed the men on the Fighting Front. . . . Vitamins, calories, balanced meals and ration cards may complicate the situation, but they do not daunt mothers and wives whose work is at home, but whose heart is 'at the front'" (Youngstown Kitchens, 50).[17]

Some cooking literature suggested feeding family members as though they were soldiers. Ruth Berolzheimer's *Military Meals at Home Cook Book* (1943) urged the reader: "Feed your family as well as Uncle Sam feeds his" (13); it included recipes for military specialties such as beef hash, creamed beef, spareribs, smothered ham, pork chops, and pork cutlets. "Military food provides vim, vigor and vitamins" (28) and "military recipes are designed to build men" (45), the book promised. Thus, women's cooking responsibilities were, at least rhetorically, raised to the level of military endeavors. How could any woman refuse such a patriotic responsibility?

The housewife also had to make sure that she used her foods in the most rational and scientific way possible at a time when food could mean victory or defeat in the war. One cookbook author declared that "the wise and patriotic woman will make of her marketing nothing less than an exact science. Neither the telephone nor a child will be a safe substitute for the trained judgment of the homemaker herself" (Berolzheimer, *Wartime*, n. pag.). The lowly domestic cook became a domestic scientist whose training was essential to win the war; such wartime propaganda suggested that women were the only individuals trained for food-related responsibilities; untrained shoppers and cooks could wreak havoc. One article from *Woman's Home Companion* entitled "No Time for Failures" (Kirk and Cahill, 1943) stressed: "This is no time for failures. We have to make the most of what we have. New recipes must be trustworthy. They must work one hundred per cent. Ingredients are precious. Time is precious. Strength is needed for so many things" (n. pag.). Such appeals suggested that the best-trained cooks were women.

One part of the crucial job of cooking during the war was to estimate with great care how much food was required. In *Cooking on a Ration*, Marjorie Mills proclaimed: "Use your wits and ingenuity and you'll be part of the great army of Kitchen Commandos who are doing an invaluable part to win the war" (166). Similarly, Katharine Fisher wrote for *Good Housekeeping*: "Keep variety in your meals, plan them carefully, don't cook more than you think will be eaten, and put your best food forward as a cook. Food saving has become one of the war's biggest musts. Use every ounce of food to best advantage" ("What You Should Know," 157). Mother played an important role as the kitchen commando in charge of doling out rationed commodities, making sure every ounce was used in the most appropriate fashion.[18] No wonder many millions of women stayed in the kitchen; they were taught that even ounces of food mattered and that women were the only ones capable of addressing the complexities of shopping and cooking. This belief that women are "naturally" superior at cooking-related tasks has long helped ensure that they are the primary food preparers in the United States. Even today, the belief is strong that women, not men, are the "natural" cooks; it is not uncommon to hear a man say that he lacks the training and knowledge to cook, which keeps him (and other men) out of the kitchen.

Another powerful way to persuade women that their duty lay in the kitchen was to inform them that they were following in their foremothers' footsteps. In *Coupon Cookery,* Prudence Penny observed: "Wars may come and wars may go, but real, red-blooded American Homemakers will put up a struggle to preserve that cherished custom of Good Eating!" (22). An advertisement from Youngstown Pressed Steel portrayed a housewife in her apron, with the caption: "The [women], in their kitchen aprons, are keeping step with all the other women in uniform who are serving the Nation at war. Ever since the Pilgrim Mothers landed at Plymouth Rock, this simple, unsung uniform has been the symbol of one of women's vital services to the Nation—feeding the family" (15). The language in cooking literature painted a vivid picture of World War II homemakers following the precedent set by their grandmothers and mothers. Serving a family meal became the quintessential icon of being a woman and a mother. A woman's responsibilities of feeding and caring for her family were more important than her other tasks. Cooking was a patriotic responsibility as old as the United States; this was not a task that most women would wish to delegate to others.

To follow in their foremothers' footsteps, women also had to keep up the feminine and social graces that should go with mealtime, as Mills commented in *Cooking on a Ration*: "In this troubled universe it's more than ever important to make mealtime loom up as a little island of serenity and contentment" (41). Mealtime was also a chance for a woman to show her feminine talents as a hostess. A cookbook observed: "Our meals can still be symphonies while our courage and our smiles maintain the relaxation and refreshment that mealtime should bring to all" (Winn-Smith, x). Despite wartime jobs riveting airplanes, building bombs, testing gas masks, and doing other masculine tasks, a woman had to adhere to feminine values and graces. After all, her husband was not fighting for a Rosie the Riveter in grease-stained overalls; he was fighting for an elegant, graceful wife to preside over his dinner table.

The housewife also had to make sure that she satisfied her man's food cravings. Catering to men's food requests and preferences was essential during the war. One article from *American Home* urged readers to give soldiers on leave the foods they longed for: "Note to all mothers, wives, and sweethearts: when your man comes home on leave, don't let him down on his expectations. Plan every meal around his best-liked dishes, even if this entails combinations that horrify you" ("On Leave!" 82). A sacrificing woman had to remember that her food desires were subordinate to a man's. She also had to recognize that her cooking was central to making her husband proud of her talents. "Do yourself proud in the lunch box you pack. Don't make the man ashamed when he opens his box in front of other workers," warned one cookbook writer (Harris, *Victory*, 33). If a woman wished to follow in her foremothers' footsteps, she needed to make sure to please her man.

All the sacrifices that a woman made during the war so that her family could be well fed, however, would pay off after the war when she would be repaid for her efforts with a shiny kitchen bursting with the newest and most exciting appliances and gadgets available. Scores of wartime advertisements described the postwar bliss of the woman with a new kitchen and shiny, gleaming appliances. An advertisement for Universal Appliances pictured a dreamy-eyed housewife thinking about the return of her husband-to-be: "When a certain gunner in Uncle Sam's Navy comes home to marry me—and stay—I'm going to need the very best appliances and housewares! Things will have to be right for that man. Home spic-and-span as a cruiser's deck, food cooked to beat the fleet" (Universal Appliances, 141). The advertisement included a long list of appliances and gadgets that the woman was supposed to purchase, including electric ranges, toasters, percolators, mixers, waffle irons, sandwich grills, ovens, kitchen cutlery, carving sets, table knives and forks, food and meat choppers, pressure cookers, and fruit juicers (Universal Appliances, 141). An advertisement for Magic Chef stove addressed the housewife: "When the right time comes, you'll want a cozy home, with an up-to-date kitchen—and that's going to mean, among the first things of all, a brand new postwar model Magic Chef gas range! That new Magic Chef will be a never-ending joy. It will be so modern—so good looking—so easy to use—so fast and sure and economical" (Magic Chef, 234). An advertisement for Kelvinator appliances pictured a young soldier and his wife or wife-to-be, who is lost in a daydream about their future:

> If I just close my eyes . . . The wonderful smell of coffee will wake me up . . . And all of a sudden I'll find myself in a magic place . . . A kitchen of white and gleaming tile. And the first thing I'll see will be a gleaming refrigerator with shining glass shelves and magic compartments to keep *all* the good things we'll order to eat . . . and there by the door will be something shining white—our new home freezer—a treasure chest of steak and chops, pheasant and trout, and all the green things our garden will grow. And over there a brand new electric range . . . a wondrous thing! We'll just flick a switch and go for the day, and when we come home . . . dinner will be ready and waiting! Or we'll go to bed and the aroma of breakfast coffee will tell us it's time to wake up. (Kelvinator, 111)[19]

The message in these advertisements and many others was clear: after the woman had fulfilled her wartime responsibilities and managed to keep her family healthy and well fed, it would be time for her to receive her reward: the dream kitchen that she had imagined during the frugal wartime years. This strategy was supposed to persuade women to return to their kitchen responsibilities. The modern kitchen was transformed into a place of magic, where the housewife effortlessly flicked a switch and dinner was ready with no effort. (This, of course, was not the reality of cooking dinner in even the most up-to-date kitchen in the 1940s or 1950s or today, but it was an alluring fantasy that no doubt lured millions of women back to the kitchen and its attendant tasks.)

Postwar Life and the American Dream

"American women are willing to scrub, work in defense plants, drive ambulances, and do hundreds of other things for . . . victory. But with it all, not one of us will neglect the home, to preserve which all this fighting is done," wrote Alice B. Winn-Smith in *Thrifty Cooking for Wartime* (x). Her words provide an accurate summary of the way wartime cooking literature operated. It conveyed the message that women should work outside the home; such responsibilities, however, should not interfere with their domestic duties, especially cooking. Cooking literature reinforced the lesson that, despite world turmoil, a woman's place remained in the kitchen. If women did not keep up the home in general (including its heart, the kitchen) during the war, the whole American way of life would be jeopardized.

Wartime cooking literature provided a map for women's behavior. Since it was one of the forms of literature most commonly read by women, it was an ideal venue to convey messages about society's expectations. Thus, cooking literature taught women lessons not only about how to cook but also about how to act as gendered individuals at a time of social stress. It conveyed the message that women's wartime tasks were important, but that women must still maintain their womanliness and femininity. Cookbooks made it clear that the family and domesticity should come before working at the local armament factory.

Women had to keep cooking and working in domestic homes because they were helping to shape the American dream that American soldiers sought to protect. "They show that they think life is worth living, worth fighting for. These modern American women believe in the American Way. They set themselves behind the fighting man who is at war for the preservation of the American Dream," wrote Gulielma Fell Alsop and Mary F. McBride in *Arms and the Girl: A Guide to Personal Adjustment in War Work and War Marriage* (1943) (259). It was this mythology that cooking literature sought to perpetuate by encouraging women to stay in the private home, despite the changes that had swept over U.S. society.

Wartime cooking literature was only a single node in a much larger cultural discourse during the war that emphasized the importance of domestic values and the American home, for which GIs were fighting. When they came home from the war, the propaganda went, soldiers deserved to find that dream still intact. No wonder millions of women left their wartime jobs and became full-time homemakers; they were inculcated with the belief that they played a crucial role as symbols of the American dream.

Chapter 8

Of Casseroles and Canned Foods

Building the Happy Housewife in the Fifties

In 1954, Richard Armour published a poem in *Better Homes and Gardens*:

Portrait of a Happy Housewife
She has a brand-new recipe,
A range that she can fricassee
  Or bake or broil or fry it on,
Ingredients, both fresh and canned,
Knives, spoons, and cups on every hand,
A dish on which to serve it, and
  A husband she can try it on.[1]

A few years earlier, *Betty Crocker's Picture Cook Book* (1950) appeared. Women lined up for hours to purchase a copy, and General Mills received scores of letters from women who were desperate for the company to produce more copies of the popular work (Marling, 203–4). By 1951, a million copies were already in print (Marling, 203). Armour's poem and *Betty Crocker's Picture Cook Book* serve as appropriate starting points for a chapter that focuses on popular 1950s cooking literature and the lessons this literature conveyed to women.[2] The poem and the cookbook both reveal the decade's emphasis on the central place of the kitchen and societal adulation of the housewife. This was a period when being a housewife was held up to countless middle-class women as the ideal, one that many accepted (at least on the surface), leaving wartime jobs in droves to pursue careers as stay-at-home mothers and wives. Why did millions of Rosie the Riveters become Armour's Happy Housewives within the span of a few short years? What role did the media play in this process?

Fifties cookbooks and cooking articles went beyond merely instructing a woman about how to cook a chiffon cake that would not fall flat or how to carve a radish into a rose. They also conveyed ideological messages about how she was expected to lead her life. *Betty Crocker's Picture Cook Book*, for instance, conveyed a variety of lessons about how women should behave in a list of shortcuts for the tired housewife:

> Harbor pleasant thoughts while working. It will make every task lighter and pleasanter. (431)
> Notice humorous and interesting incidents to relate at dinner-time, etc. (431)
> Every morning before breakfast, comb hair, apply make-up, a dash of cologne, and perhaps some simple earrings. Does wonders for your morale. (431)

Betty Crocker was passing on more than how to prepare a piecrust. She was teaching her readers how to act like "correctly" socialized women.

This chapter explores how cooking literature spread the ideal of the Happy Housewife and helped convince women to return to the kitchen.[3] Women who might have been repairing airplanes or building boats during the war were reassured by 1950s cooking literature that the home had challenges that were more rewarding emotionally (if not financially) than their jobs outside the home. This literature conveyed three important lessons. First, women should develop their creativity in the kitchen. This was easy to do by concocting a simple dish—the casserole—that allowed for tremendous variation. Second, women should recognize that the kitchen was no longer the stodgy, old-fashioned place it had been in their mothers' time but was instead up-to-date and technologically sophisticated. Third, women did not have to spend all day in the kitchen. Utilizing modern foodstuffs like freeze-dried mashed potatoes or frozen TV dinners, they could prepare meals and still have time for their own personal activities, such as shopping at the local department store or pursuing an afternoon golf game. Cultural critic Joshua Gitelson observes that, "cooking was a socially acceptable and potentially creative activity which could be performed at home without neglecting other responsibilities" (73). With such lessons about how alluring domestic cooking was, women flocked to the kitchens in droves.

This chapter focuses predominantly on white middle-class images of womanhood in magazines aimed at a white middle-class audience. Focusing solely on such a narrow group presents a problem, as historian Joanne Meyerowitz makes clear: "Especially in works on the 1950s, the sustained focus on a white middle-class domestic ideal and on suburban middle-class housewives sometimes renders other ideals and other women invisible" (4).⁴ While Meyerowitz's words are a reminder of the importance of considering how women from all classes, racial and ethnic groups, and backgrounds were living in this period, it is also essential to examine the stranglehold of the white middle-class domestic imperative, which appeared throughout mass culture. Cooking literature rarely questioned the preeminence of the white middle-class female, allowing her image to eclipse those of other women. Women from all classes and backgrounds were exposed to the idealized white and middle-class vision of femininity and domesticity that any "good" woman was expected to strive to achieve.

The Troubled Fifties

If any single experience can symbolize the importance of the 1950s American kitchen (and the American housewife), it is the famous "kitchen debate" that occurred at the 1959 American National Exhibition in Moscow between vice president Richard M. Nixon and Soviet premier Nikita Khrushchev. The two men toured a model of a modern American house. As they walked through the home's dream kitchen, Nixon praised its modern technology, but Khrushchev sneered: "Newly built Russian houses have all this equipment right now" (quoted in "Encounter," 16). The leaders also debated the merits of the modern washing machine. Nixon pointed one out, observing: "In America, these are designed to make things easier for our women." "A capitalist attitude," the premier retorted (quoted in "Encounter," 16). For

Nixon, the home—especially the kitchen bursting with new gadgets and sleek, streamlined appliances—represented a potent symbol of the superiority of American ways. After restricted domestic purchasing during the war years, the fifties was an era of abundance, when middle-class American women could glory in creating the dream kitchens that were impossible in the leaner decades of the Depression and World War II. The well-stocked kitchen became a signifier of the American dream.

Cooking literature tells only part of the story about life in the 1950s. It is easy to think of the fifties as an era that should not be taken too seriously. "Americans . . . think of it as a jokey, cartoonish decade, full of too-bright colors, goofy space-age designs, outlandish people and events, extreme ideas. We collect streamlined appliances, big-finned cars, poodle skirts and Hula Hoops as artifacts from an exotic and slightly ridiculous era" (Harvey, xi–xii). Despite its lingering *Leave it to Beaver* image, the fifties was a profoundly troubled era, a time of great social anxiety. The nuclear threat was omnipresent. Hiroshima and Nagasaki lurked in the shadows, and bomb shelters blossomed in backyards. The extremes of McCarthyism represented one reaction to communism. The Reds were hardly the only boogeymen lurking in the imaginations of white middle-class America. Racial unrest was increasingly common. In 1954, *Brown v. Board of Education of Topeka* outlawed separate but equal education for blacks, and the Montgomery bus boycott came on the scene in 1955. African Americans were not the only ones to voice their displeasure with the American dream. Jack Kerouac, Allen Ginsberg, and other Beat writers wrote about a dream that contained no room for them or other disenfranchised individuals. The disgruntled rumbles of rock 'n' roll roared onto the scene, and Elvis Presley's miraculous gyrating pelvis hinted that popular music would never be the same.

Women were not all happy and complacent homemakers. In 1953, the *Kinsey Report* suggested that Beaver's mom had more on her mind than providing a good home for her son. America heard the early stirrings of unrest by women, including Betty Friedan, that later would erupt into the women's movement of the 1960s. In *The Feminine Mystique* (1963), Friedan wrote about the fifties feminine ideal:

> The American housewife—freed by science and labor-saving appliances from the drudgery, the dangers of childbirth and the illnesses of her grandmother.

She was healthy, beautiful, educated, concerned only about her husband, her children, her home. She had found true feminine fulfillment. . . . She was free to choose automobiles, clothes, appliances, supermarkets; she had everything that women ever dreamed of. (18)

Friedan discussed how American advertisers and corporations created an image of the Happy Housewife to sell the endless supply of commodities that she would require to care for her family. This image was far removed from the bleak lives of the unfulfilled suburban housewives Friedan had interviewed for her book. She was one of many scholars and historians who emphasized the schizophrenic roles of women in the fifties. As Steven Mintz and Susan Kellogg point out in *Domestic Revolutions: A Social History of American Family Life* (1988):

A tension underlay women's needs for personal fulfillment and the sometimes conflicting demands of her family role. On the one hand, young women received the same education as men and were encouraged to develop their skills and intellectual abilities. On the other, women were pressured to maintain their "femininity" and to seek fulfillment as wives and homemakers, and they were cautioned against pursuing a career. The result was a deep sense of ambivalence and internal turmoil toward both homemaking and career. (195)

The fifties was a time of great ambivalence; women were caught between being the perfect wife, hostess, mother, and career woman—roles that seemed impossible to reconcile.

The threat of nuclear annihilation, the Red scare, hints of women's rebellion—all these social concerns and many others need to be kept in mind as we examine 1950s cooking literature, which seldom mentions any of these issues, despite their prevalence. We need to remember that cooking literature, even when it seems to be entirely isolated from social concerns, is never separated from the culture that produces it; a society's hopes, fears, and dreams are always evident, even through their omission.

We associate the fifties with food: Jell-O salads, Spam, elaborate casseroles, Cool-Whip, barbecues, meatloaf and potatoes.[5] Such foods might seem worlds removed from the larger societal conflicts playing themselves out, but this is far from the truth. Fifties food and cooking were sites to work through some of the conflicting gender ideals that were characteristic of the society in general. Cooking literature helped make the kitchen appealing for many women during a time of societal anxiety, when people feared that women would not return to their domestic responsibilities after holding wartime jobs outside the home.

Home and Hearth: Traditional Ideas about Cooking

In *It's Easy to Be a Good Cook* (1951), Jessie De Both glowingly described the delights of making a pie: "Truly a beautiful pie is a beacon to light a man's way homeward. It symbolizes so many things: the energy and effort of the woman he married; her wish to give him the utmost in eating enjoyment; her competence in fitting a pie into her never-ending day of homemaking" (111–12). De Both's words serve as a reminder that, troubled as the 1950s were, they were also a conservative time of looking back nostalgically at America's past and trying to keep traditional American values alive after the upheaval of World War II. As De Both points out, one way to keep traditional values alive was through cooking, emphasizing its age-old connection with mom and the American way.

Whether a woman baked a pie or braised a pot roast, she perpetuated traditional notions that the woman, not the man, was supposed to be the one working in the kitchen. After all, what woman would not want to be on familiar terms with the kitchen, since cooking literature suggested that cooking was the perfect way to attract a man. For example, *Ann Pillsbury's New Cook Book* (1954) included a recipe for a dessert called "Blueberry Boy-Bait" (Pillsbury Mills, 114). Fifties women were taught that males had to be considered at all times. De Both informed her readers: "I hope you will curl up with this book and find its rich sampling of delicious recipes not only readable, but realizable. When your husband begins to notice what he's eating, mark it well. When he undertakes to tell his friends how you prepare food (who in turn will spread your reputation), you've arrived" (8). De Both's words easily could have been taken from a cookbook of the 1920s or 1930s; the ideology still pervasive in the 1950s suggested that cooking was a serious matter for any girl or woman hoping to attract and keep a mate.

As in earlier decades, cooking was also a woman's crowning glory, as De Both described: "One of a woman's most beautiful moments . . . is the one which finds her arms floury, her face content and purposeful as she kneads yeast dough with strong fingers and graceful wrists. . . . And nothing in the kitchen ever smells so good or welcoming to homecoming men and hungry children [as home-baked bread]" (38). Cooking was the ideal way for a woman to express love for every member of her family. This notion was conveyed in the dedication in *Betty Crocker's Picture Cook Book*: "We dedicate it to homemakers everywhere—to all of you who like to minister to your dear ones by serving them good food. That's the age-old way to express love and concern for their welfare" (Crocker, n. pag.). Good cooking was also a way for a mother to encourage domestic happiness and ensure that the family stayed together. Food, according to Lily Wallace's *The American Family Cook Book* (1950), could "be used by every clever homemaker to influence persons and events which can enrich the happiness of a home and its members. Good meals, attractively served, go a long way toward keeping the family together. Those with a tendency to stray will spend more time in homes where every meal is an event to look forward to" (9). Like many other cookbook writers, Wallace was promoting the American family and traditional values. For her, a meal was the perfect time for a woman to exert her influence over her family. Following this logic, a woman had to cook or she would lose her most important pulpit for influencing her family and its members' values.

While cooking literature recalled traditional notions of a woman's "proper" relation to food and the family, there was also a keen sense in the 1950s that times were new, different, modern. The women who came back from building ships and airplanes in the war were not going to be satisfied with baking a pie or serving a good meal, no matter how adoring the audience might be. The modern woman of the fifties needed to be assured that her domestic workplace offered her as much room for creativity as her husband's downtown office did. She also needed to feel that cooking was as modern and up-to-date as her husband's shiny new auto.

Creativity in the Kitchen

One of the most important lessons that women learned from 1950s cooking literature was that cooking should be exciting and fun, a message that was stated repeatedly. The author of *Elsie's Cook Book* (1952) observed: "Most women, I think, really love to cook—to try new recipes on the family and friends" (Botsford, n. pag.). Another cookbook gushed that it was "dedicated to the aim of making your cooking a creative and rewarding pastime, rather than a necessary chore. It can be great fun, you know, and infinitely fascinating because there's no limit to what your imagination can do" (*Today's Woman Cook Book*, 3). The message was clear: women were fortunate to be responsible for such an exciting activity.

Cooking was also expected to be one of a woman's main creative outlets. Historian Benita Eisler describes the role of cooking in this period:

> [Women] who felt confined by the sandbox or routine secretarial jobs could express a stifled creativity in the kitchen. Motivational psychologists, led by Dr. Ernst Dichter, advised advertisers on how to exploit the discontents of the overeducated housewife. *Creative* and *professional* were the watchwords of campaigns to sell household products to women who were to be addressed as efficient managers and creative homemakers. The more demanding and time-consuming the chore, the more "satisfaction" was guaranteed. (192)

After all, if cooking was so creative, who would wish to leave the kitchen? Although millions of women in the 1950s might have enjoyed kitchen creativity, many other women no doubt felt trapped by this cultural imperative. Even today, many more women than men feel the need to display their creative talents in the kitchen. In most homes, it is still mom who is called upon to transform a chocolate birthday cake into a fairytale palace or make cupcakes into "ice cream cones" by cooking the batter in cones and then frosting the cakes.

Creativity in cooking represented a way for a woman in the 1950s to set herself apart from other women. Mildred O. Knopf's *The Perfect Hostess Cook Book* (1950) was advertised on its dust jacket as "the ideal cook book for every housewife who ever wanted to put that little-something-extra into a meal to endear herself to her guests forever" (n. pag.). This idea was conveyed by much 1950s cooking literature: a meal prepared with the right creativity could serve as a lasting sign of a woman's success as a hostess and cook.[6] Creative cooking was not only an act of enjoyment for the cook; it was also a highly competitive way to demonstrate her domestic talents.

Creativity did not necessarily mandate huge expenditures of time. The simplest meal could be made into a culinary triumph by the cook who challenged herself to try new techniques. *Betty Crocker's Picture Cook Book* urged women to try new sauces, illustrating the argument with a picture of a woman pouring a sauce over an entrée while her whole family looked on approvingly: "We know you will have fun serving [sauces] . . . and that your family will be very proud of your new skill" (Crocker, 353). A cook could liven up even the most plebeian food: liverwurst. One 1950s cookbook demonstrated that liverwurst could be far from dull as a party food:

> It can be a spread; a small broiled fritter, if dredged with flour; it can be a ball to garnish the salad bowl; it is an excellent ingredient for deviled eggs; you can make "dices" by dotting with mayonnaise and serving them on toothpicks at cocktail parties, or it can be a "rice," if pressed through the sieve, to be sprinkled on almost anything. . . . Try to think what other foods can contribute to your party—and parties will be fun. (Williams-Heller, 87)

(Liverwurst will never look the same to me again.) If dull liverwurst could jazz up a meal, even better was the marshmallow—an ingredient long used (and abused) by creative cooks. In "Take a Package of Marshmallows" (1956), June Towne urged readers to think about all the delicacies that could be created:

> You might go along with marshmallows in a salad. Even marshmallow center fill in acorn squash halves mightn't seem far-fetched. But who ever would dream that marshmallows would be so good cooked up in a peanut-butter sandwich? Then there's chicken—it blends well with marshmallows, and they're in this recipe and atop it. . . . And—most irresistible of all—make a delectable cake and decorate it with our marshmallow posies. (88)

The creative cook was supposed to think of all ingredients in the cupboard—no matter how ordinary or incompatible they might seem—as fodder for her imagination.

The 1950s ideal was for a woman to transform a humdrum meal into a memorable event, which sometimes demanded more than preparing liverwurst fritters or marshmallow posies. A meal had to become an aesthetic experience that encompassed shapes, textures, and garnishes. Food soared to new heights and "took on a shape of its own. Molds, rings, loafs and jelled salads did not just taste good; they were provocative visual events. Like the temples of the Acropolis, sculpted dishes commented emphatically upon their surroundings" (Gitelson, 75). Ornate recipes were a way to demonstrate a woman's aesthetic sensibility. The *Holiday Cook Book: Special Foods for All Special Occasions* (1959) from the people at *Better Homes and Gardens* included a recipe for cherry candle cake that called for one package of cherry angel-cake mix, a can of crushed pineapple, a package of lime gelatin, green food coloring, red food coloring, and a cup of green cherries. The cake was covered with pink frosting and had pineapple mixed with lime gelatin between its layers (82). A recipe for Jack Frost dessert in this book required three oranges, green grapes, a pear, bananas, pineapple tidbits, maraschino cherries, a cup and a half of tiny marshmallows, a tablespoon of brandy flavoring, a cup of crushed pineapple, a cup and a quarter of flaked coconut, and a cup of heavy cream (84). Even if recipes did not demand decorative ingredients like maraschino cherries and flaked coconut, a cook could always add garnishes of her own. As *Betty Crocker's Picture Cook Book* insisted, "It's the finish that counts" (Crocker, 37). The book admonished readers: "It may be only a ruffle of lettuce to set off a salad; a bunch of purple grapes for an accent note on a platter of roast chicken; a few tiny pimiento bells to add color to a bowl of oyster stew at Christmastime [*sic*]. . . . Take time to add that one little frill that can bring out color and appetite appeal of a special dish" (37). An article from *Better Homes and Gardens* offered the cook "special tricks" that would impress "family and friends" ("Smart Cook!" 100): a melon would be more interesting when cut to give each half a decorative edge, and "dainty toast cups" could be made in muffin tins and then filled with creamed chicken or tuna (100). Cooking literature taught readers that cooking was more than supplying a family with the correct nutrients. It was a complete aesthetic and creative experience that could be as challenging as sculpting or painting.

Casseroles

One place where women in the fifties could demonstrate their creative cooking skills was the wildly popular casserole. Dished out everywhere from PTA meetings to potluck suppers, the casserole was one of the dominant motifs of the decade's cooking.[7] Authors wrote dozens of articles and books that lauded the glorious dish and its creative possibilities.[8] It was an infinitely elastic recipe, yet could be prepared with the simplest of ingredients—potato chips, canned salmon or tuna, cream of mushroom soup, canned onions—items that any woman would have in her pantry. The flexibility of casseroles was a common theme. An article in *Sunset* magazine suggested that five basic meats or fishes (corned beef, pressed luncheon meat, boned chicken or turkey, salmon, or tuna) could be used interchangeably to produce new and intriguing versions of chili tamale casserole, crisp noodle casserole, curried rice casserole, noodle mushroom bake, olive-lima bean casserole, or scalloped potato bake ("The Flexible Casserole," 127). (It boggles the mind to think of corned beef or pressed luncheon meat being used in the chili tamale casserole.)

Although casseroles have existed throughout culinary history in the United States and in many other countries, they skyrocketed to prominence in the 1950s. For many reasons, including new varieties of glassware cooking dishes and the frequent appearance of casserole dishes in popular women's magazines, the casserole became the ultimate sign of the up-to-date wife and hostess (Mariani, *Dictionary*, 58). Due to the simplicity and speed of making casseroles, the cook could prepare one for family or guests and still have time to act as a charming hostess. An article in *House and Garden* proclaimed: "With several good recipes for casseroles under your thumb, you can escape from last-minute kitchen maneuvers and be free to enjoy your guests while the food stays hot and appetizing" (Brobeck, "Casseroles," 60). Cooks were warned: "Don't dismiss casseroles as simple cookery just because they are so easy to assemble. The right seasonings will turn a baked dish into an eating experience" ("Rich and Subtle Casseroles," 91). The casserole was the perfect all-around dish.

The casserole is particularly intriguing because it embodies two different aspects of 1950s ideology about women and cooking. On one hand, the casserole could be simple and straightforward, something to be whipped together in a matter of minutes. It symbolized how cooking in the 1950s had become streamlined and efficient: the modern housewife had nothing to fret about, because she could concoct a one-dish meal for her family in a jiffy. On the other hand, the casserole could be elaborate, a dish elegant enough to be served when a husband's boss came to dinner. The exotic casserole also provided the perfect opportunity for the cook to experiment, giving her a chance to use those creative talents that might be stifled in the domestic sphere.

The recipes collected in many casserole cookbooks demonstrated the dual impulse to present cooking both as simple and as challenging. John

Roberson and Marie Roberson's *The Casserole Cook Book* (1952), contained recipes for elegant specialties like oysters Rockefeller (153), lobster thermidor (150), squabs in casserole (145), and duckling with wine sauce (138), as well as simpler recipes for spring garden macaroni puff (202), noodles and frankfurters (203), onion pie (181), and curried cabbage (182). *Good Housekeeping's Casserole Cook Book* included a wide variety of both simple and complex recipes.[9] Many were for quick, easy foods: frankfurter supper quickie (7), ham-and-noodle casserole (24), zesty pork-chop bake (27), and crunch-puff pudding (30). There were also fancier recipes using expensive ingredients: oyster scallop (8), Swiss veal with limas (13), shrimp casserole Harpin (26), baked veal cutlets with mushroom sauce (31), and Jane's company lobster (12). Similarly, *Sunset* magazine's *Cooking with Casseroles* (1958) contained both fancy and plain recipes. The fancy recipes included wild rice casserole (57), curried veal (79), abalone and mushrooms (105), and crab artichoke casserole (111); the plain ones included ham and cheese loaf (67), "yummy balls" (i.e., meatballs) (63), and wiener mix-up (frankfurters, olives, corn, string beans, cheddar cheese, and two cups of catsup) (82). These varied recipes, from the simplest to the most complex, transformed the casserole into a wonder meal that could meet all the needs of the housewife foraging for a dinner idea. With the marvelous casserole on her side, the cook did not need to fret about the difficulty of her job.

Casseroles could be as basic as a few cans of soup, vegetables, and beans, dumped into a baking dish. The red-and-yellow casserole contained a can of kidney beans and a can of cream-style corn mixed with some onions and topped with American cheese and crushed corn flakes (Hagemeyer, 178). Simple recipes could be made even simpler with the addition of some of the many canned foods that crowded the grocery store shelves.[10] In particular, cooks and the media praised canned soups as the perfect casserole ingredient. "Casserole meals have long been favorites at our house but I really hit my stride the day I 'discovered' canned soup as a casserole ingredient," one cook announced (Whelan, 65). She described how a can of cream of celery soup in macaroni au gratin or a can of cream of tomato soup in chili con carne could make the most mundane of dishes special. If using canned soup was good, using all canned foods was better—it was popular to make casseroles that were entirely (or almost entirely) composed of canned foods. One recipe for surprise potato-tuna bake contained two cans of tuna, three cans of shoestring potatoes, a can of evaporated milk, a can of cream of mushroom soup, a can of mushroom pieces, and a can of pimientos (Stiers, 80). A recipe for California Burgundy supper called for a can of condensed tomato soup, a can of mushrooms, two cups of cream-style corn, two cups of grated American cheese, Burgundy wine, and spaghetti (Anders, 24). These simple, quick recipes promised the modern housewife of the 1950s that cooking was no longer the tedious, lengthy task that her mother or grandmother had confronted. Casserole cooking turned the daily drudgery of the evening family meal into a simple matter of opening a few cans.

Even better than the simplicity and speed of casserole recipes was the praise mom would receive from the family when she served one. Cooking literature reassured aspiring cooks that the family would rave about the meals that mom so rapidly concocted because all their food preferences could be satisfied. An article in *Good Housekeeping* entitled "Casserole Dishes Men Like" stressed that casserole recipes could be custom-tailored to ensure "downright good eating for the menfolks" (Callahan, 140). Another writer observed in *Better Homes and Gardens*: "Some casseroles are in the elegant gourmet class—white meat of chicken in mushroom sauce. Others are old-fashioned and homespun—baked beans rich with bacon. All are stick-to-the-ribs fare men approve" (Johnston, 72). Kids, too, the cookbooks promised, would love casseroles. One women's magazine described star casserole (macaroni and cheese with frankfurters) as a dinner that "will be voted tops by your small fry" (Johnston, 100). The simple casserole represented the promised food that would transform cooking into a game and would help mom earn the accolades from her family that, presumably, she had been lacking. Even if she prepared a recipe just a little differently—say, tossed in a handful of crushed potato chips or a cup of chopped black olives—her family would notice her innovation: "If you can take a familiar dish, add a little of this and that to change the flavor a bit, the family takes complimentary notice and your job as cook is infinitely more fun" (Shouer, "Casserole," 226). Casserole cooking became not a responsibility but "fun" for the housewife.

Casseroles served as an opportunity for the creative cook to experiment with the richest and most exotic ingredients, and fancy casserole dishes could be served to the most discriminating dinner guests. With the addition of high-priced seafood, a recipe like scalloped eggs and shrimp could be "just the thing for your next bridge-club luncheon" ("Casserole Combination," 299). Other casseroles were even more deluxe. Veal Divannini included cooked veal, asparagus pieces, fresh mushrooms, and a white sauce made with cream (Anders, 67). Champagne chicken casserole contained chicken breasts, champagne, and cream (Anders, 112). Lousene Rousseau Brunner's book *Casserole Magic* (1953) included recipes for delicacies such as baked lobster-stuffed eggs, coquilles Saint-Jacques, lobster au gratin, and baked veal with cream. But the recipe sure to send people's cholesterol levels soaring was one for oysters Claremont (supposed to serve six people) that called for half a cup of butter, three cups (!) of heavy cream, and two dozen fresh oysters (Brobeck, "Casseroles," 60). With the addition of a few oysters and a lot of cream, a casserole was transformed into a feast that signified good breeding, wealth, and abundance. Since many of these recipes, although full of expensive ingredients, were relatively easy to prepare, the gracious hostess could still have time to attend to her guests. Why would a wife complain when her husband brought eight unexpected business guests home to dinner?

Casseroles were also alluring because they frequently had a connection with faraway places.[11] Nedda C. Anders's *Casserole Specialties* (1955) contained recipes for eggs Bombay, Mexican flank steak casserole, Normandy casserole, Armenian hamburger casserole, tamale pie, Swedish veal and orange casserole, Danish pork chops and fruit, East Indian chicken curry, and turkey Monte Carlo. *The ABC of Casseroles* (1954) included recipes such as Austrian stuffed cabbage, Belgian meatballs with sour-cream gravy, Creole pork chops, eggs and scallops, oysters and macaroni, Kansas City franks, Mexican chili, Neapolitan lasagna, paprika oysters tetrazzini, shrimp curry, tamale pie, and veal chow mein. These recipes with roots in Mexico, Italy, Austria, or Kansas City helped consumers feel that they were daring as they sampled the wide range of recipes. Most of the casseroles, however, were not as adventuresome as their exotic names. For instance, the only seasonings that a recipe for veal chow mein called for were salt, celery salt, and Accent (*The ABC*, 59). A recipe for tamale pie was even tamer, requiring no spices at all, only cornmeal, water, ground beef, fat, tomato sauce, and cheese (*The ABC*, 53). A recipe for shrimp Creole was slightly bolder, requiring a "pinch of chili powder and a few grains of cayenne" for one and a half pounds of shrimp (*The ABC*, 51). *Arroz y queso mexicano* in one casserole cookbook contained over a cup of uncooked rice and two and a half cups of tomatoes but was seasoned with only pepper, salt, and half a teaspoon of chili powder. One and a half cups of American cheese topped this "Mexican rice and cheese meal [that] will do you proud as a company luncheon or supper" (Anders, 28). Casseroles could be made exotic by giving them foreign names and adding a half-teaspoon of chili powder. American families wanted to experiment, but they did not want to venture too far afield.

Each casserole ingredient provided an opportunity for artistic and creative exploration: "Every homemaker dreams—of creating memorable main dishes, even from leftovers; of cooking vegetables skillfully to produce subtly blended flavors; of serving distinctive desserts that take a minimum of time and effort. These dreams come true when she's cooking a casserole" (Culinary Arts Institute, 3). The casserole's decorations also offered room for experimentation. Even the lowly hotdog was not overlooked, since a wiener slice could be cut "on the bias [to] form [a] starry trim" (Johnston, 100). Casserole toppings offered an opportunity for a cook to personalize her recipes. "Do you always sprinkle crumbs over your casserole concoctions before you pop them into the oven? Why not try a topping that's a bit different, for a change? It's a simple way to add variety and a touch of glamour to everyday fare," observed an article in *American Home*. The author recommended a wide variety of toppings, including canned shoestring potatoes, chopped peanuts, torn chipped beef, parsley dumplings, toasted cheese, and "fancily cut luncheon meat"; the woman "in an artistic mood" could opt for piping a mashed potato border around her casserole creation (Boileau, 82). The creative cook could think of the casserole dish as her artistic palette; *Cooking with Casseroles* proclaimed: "All of the recipes [in this book] can be varied according to the whim of the cook. With a change in one or two ingredients or the addition of a few herbs or seasonings, the imaginative cook can make any casserole recipe her very own" (*Sunset Magazine*, n. pag.).

Whether frosting an elaborate cake or creating a new casserole, the cook was promised that her creative desires could be fulfilled in the kitchen. If the woman adopted the "correct" attitude toward her cooking tasks, they could be engaging rather than dull and repetitive. If her cooking lacked creativity, the fault lay with the woman not the cooking, according to the logic of popular cooking literature. She had failed to challenge herself sufficiently in the kitchen.

The Modern Kitchen: Technology and Convenience Foods

Cooking literature also endeavored to make domesticity appealing to women by representing the kitchen as an up-to-date room overflowing with innovative technology and new convenience foods. Cookbooks and women's magazines presented the modern kitchen as something very different from what earlier generations had been forced to endure. In the 1950s, at least according to popular cooking literature, kitchens had become streamlined places. No longer did a housewife appear frumpy and old-fashioned as she struggled with a coal-fired stove or old-fashioned icebox; her kitchen, equipped with the latest technological advances and convenience foods of all types, would dramatically reduce the time she spent cooking. This emphasis on the up-to-date kitchen encouraged countless Rosie the Riveters to go back to their households; they were promised that their new kitchens would be filled with the latest gadgets and appliances, guaranteed to make kitchen time into play time. One article in *Better Homes and Gardens* burst with enthusiasm about the joys of owning portable electric kitchen devices: "You can plug them into any outlet, cook where you'll feel the coolest and have the most fun" ("Take-It-Easy Meals," 72). Betty Furness also wrote about the joys of kitchen technology in the preface to her cookbook: "Until I began doing Westinghouse product demonstrations on television in May, 1949, I'd never realized what a delight and a marvel of convenience a really modern kitchen could be" (Furness and Kiene, n. pag.). For these middle-class women and others, the kitchen was transformed from a place of work to a place of relaxation and pleasure that could be as exciting and enriching as their husbands' workplaces.

Technology was feted everywhere in 1950s cookbooks. One typical example is John Roberson and Marie Roberson's *Complete Small Appliance Cookbook* (1953), which contained "more than 600 tested recipes for the popular new infra-red broilers, rotisseries, roaster ovens, casseroles, deep fat fryers, grills, mixers, blenders, and other portable electric cooking equipment" (n. pag.). The authors proclaimed: "This is the Golden Heyday of the Marvelous Mechanical Appliance. . . . So many and so helpful are these mechanical aids, and so varied their uses, that all but the most elementary hand labor may become obsolete in time" (xiv). Cooking was transformed from a lengthy, laborious task to something that could be done quickly and easily with the right small appliance; as the Robersons promised: "There's a small-but-gifted electric appliance today for almost every tedious 'hand' job" (263).

Cooking literature widely praised the blender, a device associated with modernity. *New Ways to Gracious Living: Waring Blendor* [sic] *Cook Book* (1957), made it clear that purchasing a blender would change a woman's life: "Your Blendor [sic] can add to party fun while it turns out exciting food" (101). "Your Blendor [sic] provides a dramatic new approach to baking" (48).[12] An article from *House and Garden* was more glowing about the machine's possibilities: "Now new techniques have been developed which actually enable you to prepare whole dishes, even meals, in a blender without recourse to range or refrigerator. The fine points: the blender speeds up and simplifies complicated cooking processes, cuts your cooking time to a jet-age schedule" ("Cooking with a Blender," 102). The blender was also a sign of the sophisticated cosmopolitan hostess who could whip up a variety of exotic delights. One article suggested making hollandaise sauce, vichyssoise, salmon mousse, cheesecake, and fresh butter with a blender ("Cooking with a Blender," 102). An article in *Sunset* magazine, "With a Little Blender Magic" (1959), suggested that a busy housewife might use her blender to make special dishes such as zabaglione, omelets, Mexican mole, curries, and guacamole (180).

This cultural interest in all that was new and modern extended beyond the kitchen devices that were supposed to fill a 1950s kitchen; food itself was expected to be equally modern. Gitelson writes that in this period "the suburban gastronomic world sprung from an obsession with Speed, Modernity, and Progress. Whereas today, we are told that we are what we eat, suburbanites ate what they were—or more precisely—what they wanted to be" (73). Convenience foods of all kinds, including the TV dinner, were an integral part of this image of modernity and progress. They came into their own in the 1950s, and the media celebrated them as a way to turn cooking into a quick and pleasant task. Cookbooks assured women that packaged convenience foods simplified cooking and left cooks more time for other tasks. Josephine McCarthy's cookbook *Josie McCarthy's Favorite TV Recipes* (1958) praised packaged foods: "The variety of convenience foods on the market today is a miracle of the era. They, with the modern kitchen appliances, have done away with the long hours of stirring, paring, and kneading and the big loads of dishes, pots, and pans. . . . Yes, the convenience foods with their built-in maid service are one of the bright spots on a modern woman's horizon" (3). For McCarthy and others, these foods promised to make kitchen work nearly effortless. Historian Laura Shapiro writes about the booming interest in convenience foods:

> During the years immediately following the Second World War, cooking—an activity long seen as so immutably female it was practically a secondary sex characteristic—became, for the first time, a choice. With the advent of packaged and semi-prepared foods, it became possible to put meals on the table while doing very little actual cooking. These new products were promoted on the premise that cooking was an odious chore, one that women couldn't wait to drop, and indeed many women greeted the arrival of gingerbread mix and dehydrated mashed potatoes with glad relief. ("Do Women Like to Cook?" 155)

Shapiro correctly notes the transformation that prepared foods wrought for housewives in the 1950s, but she makes it appear that they had a choice about cooking. Although they might have been armed with dozens of new convenience foods, women remained the ones responsible for purchasing those foods and preparing them. They were still the ones working in the kitchen; that arrangement had not been challenged. If anything, the convenience of modern foods made it more difficult for women to abandon their supposedly much "simpler" kitchen tasks, which were depicted in the media as much less onerous than those of a man.

In the 1950s, it was difficult for any woman to escape the message that convenience foods had dramatically changed cooking, making it a simple task of opening a few cans and defrosting a dish or two. Popular magazines were filled with articles that described convenience foods in glowing terms. Helen McCully wrote in an article "Short-Cut Foods Revolutionize American Cooking" (1955):

When the American housewife shops her super market, she has a choice of 4,693 short-cut foods—the most dazzling array of prepared, precooked and ready-to-eat foods the world has ever seen. . . . These amazing short-cut foods— in cans, glass and packages—have revolutionized cooking habits in every home in the United States. A boon to everyone, they're worth their weight in gold. (42)

A 1950s article from *Parents' Magazine* praised the pleasures of instant foods: "When minutes count at mealtime, it's a treat to turn to ready-to-heat-and-eat main dishes such as frozen TV dinners and canned meat pies. . . . And for real quick baked desserts there are both canned and frozen pies, which come ready to bake and serve. No small part of the treat is freedom from pots, pans and dishes" ("Treat Yourself," 62).[13] Even the lowly slice of American cheese was feted in the article "More Short Cuts to Dinner" (1954): "Of course you're using those fine packaged process-cheese slices that come all cut, ready to be separated and used in and on casserole dishes, hearty sandwiches, corned-beef hash, etc. They're so convenient!" (112). After reading all this praise of short-cut foods, any woman would think twice before complaining about her kitchen responsibilities. If she learned how to use the convenience foods that crowded grocery store shelves, the cook was promised a life of ease.

Although canned foods had existed for many decades, in this era they were omnipresent. More foods were packaged in cans; they cost increasingly less and were available for a wide audience; and they expressed the jet-age image that was so desirable to housewives of the period. Today it is easy to disparage this 1950s fetish for canned goods. Historian Glenna Matthews writes that "the nadir of American cookery came in the fifties. This was the heyday of prepared foods and the cream-of-mushroom-soup school of cuisine whereby the cook could pour a can of this product over anything that was not a dessert and create a culinary treat according to the standards of the day" (211). But it is important not to view food in the fifties with contemporary eyes. Actually, canned foods were generally seen as expanding a cook's repertoire, rather than narrowing it. One 1950s writer commented: "If she's gourmet minded [the home cook] can vary the menu every day of the year, choosing from among more than 500 different canned foods. . . . With such a wide variety available the year around there's no need for any child to grow up with a limited knowledge of food" (Stover, 51). Another writer observed: "Best of all—canned foods know no season: January, February, June and July—who ever stops to think nowadays whether anything is in season! They're available all year long and offer a wealth of variety and excellence that were never dreamed of by our grandmothers and that help make us the best-fed nation in the whole wide world" ("Canned Food," 115). For many women, canned foods offered possibilities to cook new and exciting menus without expending a great deal of time.

Canned foods were also exciting because they were associated with modernity and speed. One article from *Better Homes and Gardens* praised the benefits of canned foods: "Meals fast as space travel—that's the modern way. These minute-saving specials are from your canned-food shelf. Keep a supply for unexpected guests or jiffy family fare" (Heffington, 72). Even opening canned foods could be an up-to-date experience if a woman used a wall can opener. A whole article in *Good Housekeeping* discussed how to prepare canned vegetables; in "Susan Serves Canned Vegetables," Susan takes us through the process of cooking a can of peas, complete with a description of opening the can with a wall can opener: "Susan thinks it's slick, because it opens round, square, and oval cans" (128). Everything about canned foods was new and up-to-date. No wonder one magazine writer observed that "canned vegetables, soups and sauces make exciting side dishes" (Stover, 53).[14] Canned foods were the perfect symbol for the modern 1950s kitchen, and writers wrote scads of cookbooks and articles about their delights. In "Canned Food Picture Book" (1954) in *Woman's Home Companion*, Mrs. Harriet Heneveld of Syracuse, New York, shared with readers some of the reasons that she felt enthusiastic about canned foods:

> Glamorous Meals Come Easy with Help Like This
> Canned Foods Are so Thrifty and Easy to Shop for
> They Can Be Varied in so Many Interesting Ways
> They're so Packed with Year-round Goodness
> They're Always There When You Want Them
> My Idea Shelf Is Such a Help in Planning Meals. (105)

After reading this list, no 1950s housewife would feel that she could overlook canned foods. Having canned foods in the home was not just a shortcut, it was a sign of how streamlined and up-to-date cooking had become.

No longer did a woman have to struggle with difficult menus; she could just combine the right cans and prepare a gourmet meal in minutes. Countless cookbooks, articles, and advertisements promoted the idea of complete meals made from cans. One cookbook made a cheese sauce from a large can of Carnation evaporated milk, two cups of grated American cheese, and a dash of salt (Blake, *Fun*, 29). The same book suggested "making" soup by combining a can of instant soup, a can of Carnation evaporated milk, and half a cup of water (10). The American Can Company published an advertisement in *Good Housekeeping* in 1954 that raved about the delights of cooking when a busy housewife could "use today's fine canned food" (American Can Company, 46). The advertisement contained a recipe for chicken pie with biscuits that called for one can of chicken soup, two cans of boned chicken, one can of peas, one can of sliced mushrooms, and one container of refrigerator biscuits (47). In these recipes composed solely of canned foods and maybe a pinch of seasoning, the fifties cook was promised that she could perform her kitchen duties far more quickly than her mother did. Yet friends and family members would still rave about her recipes and the "creative" ways she utilized canned foods.

The creative housewife could also experiment with ethnic recipes prepared with canned foods. An article from *Parents' Magazine* listed countless ways for the industrious housewife to use "wonderful canned foods that make getting family meals real fun" ("Treat Yourself," 74). The article enthused: "Think of the treats you can make by using canned and frozen condensed soups for sauces and gravies as well as by combining two or even three different soups to make an unusual taste treat. Or you can go international with canned heat 'n' serve foods such as Chinese chow mein, Italian ravioli and south-of-the-border enchiladas" (74). If a cook found canned chow mein too insipid for her taste, she could wander farther afield.[15] Mexican casserole called for canned chili, ground beef, corn chips, and American cheese (Whitmore, 8). Curried chicken could be made with a can of cream-of-mushroom soup, a can of chicken, a can of mixed vegetable, and a quarter teaspoon of curry powder (Whitmore, 28). Or perhaps she might want to make "Dago dinner," a recipe containing two cans of Franco-American Spaghetti, olives, corn, cheese, and ground beef (Gillard, 5).

Canned foods and convenience foods promised cooks that they would spend less time in the kitchen, but they could still be creative. Imagination went hand in hand with convenience foods according to the decade's cooking literature. "A can opener plus a few things from the pantry shelf can produce a quick and tasty meal. Even the husband who like things cooked 'mother's way' will be pleased with what his wife can whip up with canned foods, a few spices and a large helping of imagination" (Morton, "Glamour Dishes," 16). The message here was that canned foods were useful, but needed to be fancied up by the creative woman, who recognized that she had an important role in the kitchen, no matter how many convenience foods she used. Excitement had to be added to the convenience foods she served. In an article entitled "120 Ways You Can Put Glamour into Just Plain Food" (1956), Edalene Stohr discussed "quick tricks to give your food a touch of genius" (102). Quick vichyssoise could be made with a package of onion soup mix, instant mashed potatoes, milk, and seasonings. Processed American cheese was transformed into a dessert cheese by being soaked in sherry. A recipe called spaghetti special was created by adding half a teaspoon of oregano to a can of spaghetti in tomato sauce, topping the dish with Parmesan, and cooking it as an oven casserole (102). Even lowly instant potatoes or a can of Spam could be made more intriguing by a creative cook. One article in *Sunset* enthusiastically described the joys of instant mashed potatoes, which, when piped through a pastry bag, became "much more attractive than the usual potato mound" ("Fancy Touches," 107). An article entitled "Take a Can of Luncheon Meat" (1952) suggested all kinds of ways to make Spam more elegant. The ambitious cook could prepare cucumber canoes stuffed with luncheon meat, make kaboblets—skewers of luncheon meat cubes, boiled onions, cucumber pieces, and pineapple pieces—or even make TV fingers—luncheon meat strips dipped in waffle mix and then deep fried (n. pag.). Whether preparing a mashed potato border or making TV fingers with Spam, the housewife expressed her creativity, becoming an artist.

Spam and instant mashed potatoes, two of the convenience foods that flourished in the fifties, could be used in countless ways to show the cook's creativity. But this demand for creativity ensured that women would stay in the kitchen and not invade the workplace outside the home. Housewives could never feel satisfied with their cooking since it would never be as aesthetically pleasing as the recipes pictured in the pages of glossy women's magazines.

Cooking Lessons

Cooking literature played an important role in the domestic re-entrenchment of the fifties. Cookbooks and cooking articles made cooking seem exciting, challenging, and technologically up-to-date. No wonder many women returned to their homes and kitchens after World War II. Cooking literature alone was not responsible for the vast shift, but it did make cooking more appealing to millions of women. Fifties women were promised that cooking would be enjoyable and creative; cooking was still women's "natural" responsibility.

Cooking also appeared modern when housewives were encouraged to use dozens of new kitchen appliances that filled the pages of cookbooks and cooking articles. The housewife was promised that technology would make her kitchen as technologically sophisticated as her husband's workplace. But even though the kitchen might have been filled with modern inventions, the gender stereotype that women were the ones responsible for the kitchen and its technology was not challenged.

In a similar fashion, the fifties craze for convenience foods also did not challenge the idea that the kitchen was woman's responsibility. Convenience foods were promoted as offering women new freedom because they could perform their cooking tasks and still have time for a trip to the movies with their friends or some other leisure-time activity. Instant foods no doubt saved some time for many busy homemakers; but cooking literature frequently suggested that this meant that they should aspire to grander cooking exploits that they would not have attempted without the aid of convenience foods. By the end of the fifties, women were still the ones in the kitchen performing the majority of the cooking. Despite the tremendous social changes of this postwar decade, women had little choice when it came to their kitchen tasks—they were still supposed to be Armour's Happy Housewives because domesticity and kitchen-related tasks were perceived as "naturally" satisfying to women.

Notes

Introduction

1. My earlier research on food and gender sparked my interest in writing this book. My previous book *Intimate Communities: Representation and Social Transformation in Women's College Fiction, 1895–1910* (1995) focuses on (among other issues) how women's college students at the turn of the century transgressed the social expectations of food reformers, who assumed that food was supposed to be scientific and hygienic, by using food in nonscientific ways, such as in elaborate midnight feasts. I discuss how such festive spreads were understood by administrators as a way to teach students domestic skills but also how students transgressed social expectations about the desirable relationship between women and food (34–44).

2. Similarly, Susan J. Leonardi speculates: "Do I erode my credibility with male academics by this feminine interest in cooking, cookbooks, and recipes?" ("Recipes for Reading," 347). She expresses a common concern that work in food-related areas might weaken a woman's academic credibility.

3. Many authors have discussed the problematic personal relationship between women and food. See Joan Jacobs Brumberg, *Fasting Girls*; Kim Chernin, *The Obsession*; Catherine Manton, *Fed Up*; and Lesléa Newman, *Eating Our Hearts Out*.

4. For other works on the cultural and social significance of food, see Arlene Voski Avakian, ed., *Through the Kitchen Window*; Amy Bentley, *Eating for Victory*; Linda Keller Brown and Kay Mussell, eds., *Ethnic and Regional Foodways in the United States*; Carole M. Counihan, *The Anthropology of Food and Body*; Carole Counihan and Penny Van Esterik, eds., *Food and Culture*; Deane W. Curtin and Lisa M. Heldke, eds., *Cooking, Eating, Thinking*; Mary Douglas, "Deciphering a Meal"; Gary Alan Fine, *Kitchens*; Joanne Finkelstein, *Dining Out*; Anne Goldman, "'I Yam What I Yam'"; Jack Goody, *Cooking, Cuisine and Class*; Leslie Howsam, ed., *Food, Cookery and Culture*;

Theodore C. Humphrey and Lin T. Humphrey, eds., *"We Gather Together"*; Lucy M. Long, "Culinary Tourism"; Sherrie A. Inness, ed., *Kitchen Culture*; Anne Murcott, ed., *The Sociology of Food and Eating*; Ron Scapp and Brian Seitz, eds., *Eating Culture*; Mary Anne Schofield, ed., *Cooking by the Book*; Barbara G. Shortridge and James R. Shortridge, eds., *The Taste of American Place*; and Doris Witt, *Black Hunger*.

5. See, for instance, Leslie Brenner, *American Appetite*; M. F. K. Fisher, *The Gastronomical Me*; Ruth Reichl, *Tender at the Bone*; Michael Stern and Jane Stern, *American Gourmet, Eat Your Way across the U.S.A., Roadfood,* and *Square Meals*; Calvin Trillin, *Alice, Let's Eat, American Fried,* and *Third Helpings*; James Villas, *American Taste,* and *Villas at Table*; and Michael Lee West, *Consuming Passions.*

6. For additional historical accounts about American food habits, see Nelson Algren, *America Eats*; Warren Belasco, *Appetite for Change*; Richard Osborn Cummings, *The American and His Food*; Cindy J. Dorfman, "The Garden of Eating"; Donna R. Gabaccia, *We Are What We Eat*; John L. Hess and Karen Hess, *The Taste of America*; Evan Jones, *American Food*; John Mariani, *America Eats Out*; Elaine N. McIntosh, *American Food Habits in Historical Perspective*; Gerry Schremp, *Kitchen Culture*; Laura Shapiro, "Do Women Like to Cook?"; Raymond Sokolov, *Fading Feast*; Michelle Stacey, *Consumed*; Betty Wason, *Cooks, Gluttons, and Gourmets*; and Peter W. Williams, "Foodways."

7. For a similar book, see Susan Williams, *Savory Suppers and Fashionable Feasts* (1985), a carefully researched study of the Victorian period and the complex dynamics of food preparation and food serving.

8. For examples of broad food studies that give little attention to women and gender, see Mariani's history of restaurants in the United States; and Richard Pillsbury, *No Foreign Food.*

9. Another important study about women and cooking rituals is Anne L. Bower, ed., *Recipes for Reading* (1997). This volume, which focuses primarily on community cookbooks, contains a number of thoughtful essays about the connections between women and cookbooks.

10. For a similar study, see Anne Murcott's essay "Women's Place."

11. For more information on the mixed academic reactions to food studies, see Jennifer K. Ruark, "A Place at the Table."

12. In "Relationship between Gender and Food Roles in the Family" (1989), Robert B. Schafer and Elizabeth Schafer also argue that there is little equality in the kitchen, despite changing job conditions. Women continue to take care of food-related work in domestic households. The Schafers claim that families rarely have an egalitarian sharing of domestic responsibilities, even when both husband and wife work (124).

13. As Sarah Fenstermaker Berk observes, "household members 'do' gender, as they 'do' housework and child care" (*The Gender Factory*, 201).

14. Works that have focused on the complex relationship between women and cookbooks include Evelyn Birkby, *Neighboring on the Air*; Lynne Ireland, "The Compiled Cookbook as Foodways Autobiography"; and Karal Ann Marling, "Betty Crocker's Picture Cook Book."

15. Like Wheaton, Eleanor T. Fordyce emphasizes the importance of cookbooks as cultural documents that reveal a great deal about domestic life; as she observes, "cookbooks are more than guides to food preparation; they provide evidence of the many changes occurring in family life throughout the United States" ("Cookbooks of the 1800s," 85).

16. Among the women's magazines I examine are *American Cookery*, *American Home*, *Better Homes and Gardens*, *Good Housekeeping*, *House and Garden*, *House Beautiful*, *Ladies' Home Journal*, and *Woman's Home Companion*.

17. For more of my research on the role that popular representation plays in constituting gender identities for American women, see Inness, *Tough Girls*.

1. *"Bachelor Bait": Men's Cookbooks and the Male Cooking Mystique*

1. The assumption that women are the primary individuals who shop and prepare food is so widespread today that it remains a common experience to find a contemporary cookbook or food-related article that explicitly addresses an audience of women or assumes that women are the typical cooks. For example, Cici Williamson and John A. Kelly, in their cookbook *For Men Only* (1986), refer to women as the chief cooks: "Since women usually do most of the cooking, it is a special treat to have a man take over and prepare something delicious" (n. pag.). The assumption that women will perform most of the day-to-day cooking remains unquestioned and unchallenged in millions of American households.

2. Adler describes a different relationship between men and cooking: "Dad can certainly mix drinks for a cocktail party, or carve the roast or Thanksgiving turkey, but he only takes complete charge of cooking operations when they are outdoors: on the campground or at the backyard barbecue. Amateur male cookery thus seems to be stereotyped as inept at the worst, limited at best, and rare in any case. . . . Professionalism puts the male in a different light; his capabilities are assumed to be great, especially if he works under the name 'chef.'" (46). As Adler points out, men often have the luxury of choosing their cooking experiences, while women, whether they like it or not, are typically responsible for the daily cooking rituals that are nearly impossible to escape in any family.

3. If you doubt that this belief is still alive and thriving, browse through your local newspaper. What is the section most commonly associated with women? The food section, produced mainly by and for women. What is the men's section? The sports section, written largely by and for men. Although this situation is changing as more men need to or decide to cook, the cooking section of the local newspaper is still considered women's territory. Popular magazines also highlight the connection between women and cooking. It comes as no surprise that *Woman's Day, Ladies' Home Journal,* and other women's lifestyle magazines are chock-full of recipes and food-related articles, while men's magazines contain relatively few, although an occasional magazine might sneak in a recipe on a properly "manly" topic—how to barbecue an ox or roast a wild duck.

4. I do not wish to suggest that the male cooking mystique began only in the last century. Its roots go far back in human history. In this chapter, however, I am primarily interested in exploring how the male cooking mystique has operated in the twentieth century.

5. A widespread assumption exists in American society that when a man *does* cook, his cooking is far better than a woman's. This common stereotype was embodied in Bozeman Bulger's article "What to Cook When the Wife Is Away" (1921), in which the author discussed what he cooked when his wife went on a trip. Whether he was eating cabbage and corned beef or bacon and eggs, everything he made proved to be delicious, far better than anything his wife ever prepared. Even the coffee that he brewed proved to be superior to the coffee she made.

6. Too many cookbooks addressed to a male audience exist to list them all. A few men's cookbooks not discussed in this chapter include Linda Ross Aldy and Carol Taff, eds., *"Down Here, Men Don't Cook"*; David Bowers and Sharon Bowers, *Bake It Like a Man*; *Dishes Men Like*; Michele Evans, *Fearless Cooking for Men*; Malcolm LaPrade, *That Man in the Kitchen*; Wilson Midgley, *Cookery for Men Only*; Glenn Quilty, *Food for Men*; George Rector, *Dine at Home with Rector*; and Scott Redman, *Real Men Don't Cook Quiche.*

7. Additional popular articles on men who enjoy cooking and their recipes include Harry Botsford, "Just a Man with a Frying Pan"; Katharine Fisher, "Men at Home at the Range"; Jean Guthrie, "Mere Men . . . But Can They Cook!"; and Demetria M. Taylor, "There's a Man in My Kitchen."

8. Another approach that men's cookbooks adopted was to suggest that cooking was a simple task that any man could master with ease: "[Cooking] demands no more magic or talent, and is no more difficult, than the driving of a car, the selling of a policy, the writing of an ad, or any activity practiced successfully by you and by us

and by the man in the next apartment" (Achmed Abdullah and John Kenny, *For Men Only*, 193).

9. Other studies of the construction of modern masculinity include Gail Bederman, *Manliness and Civilization*; R. W. Connell, *Masculinities*; and Michael Kimmel, *Manhood in America*.

10. Similarly, Caroline Kriz's *Cooking for Men Only* (1984) contains recipes for Bud Nardecchia's cornbread dressing (50), Stuart Brown's black turkey (50–51), Alvin Ray's braised lamb with red cabbage (79), and Ronnie Bull's braised pinto beans (82).

11. Additional men's cookbooks from the first half of the twentieth century that feature hearty, heavy cooking include J. H. Meyer's *A Man's Cook Book for Outdoors and Kitchen* (1950), which contains recipes for creamed dried beef, bacon and eggs, roast turkey, fried fish and hushpuppies, fish chowder, roast beef, pork chops and cream gravy, beef stew, and barbecue for three hundred people. Paul K. Tibbens's *Cookin' for the Helluvit* (1950) includes recipes for fried fish, broiled smelt, fried chicken, steak, hamburgers, broiled pork chops, hot roast beef sandwich, roast beef, lamb stew, baked cured ham, "he-man" salad, and bully boy soup.

12. "Meat remains a graphic vehicle through which notions of natural human power are widely conveyed" (Nick Fiddes, *Meat*, 70).

13. As Fiddes suggests, "The macho steak is perhaps the most visible manifestation of an idea that permeates the entire western food system: that meat (and especially red meat) is a quintessentially masculine food" (146). See also Carol J. Adams, *The Sexual Politics of Meat*.

14. For recent articles on the "natural" connection between men and outdoor cookery, see Digby Anderson, "Imperative Cooking"; Ted Hatch, "For the Male Cook in All His Glory!"; and Jeff Leen, "Pleasures of the Flesh."

15. Similarly, Frank Shay in his book *The Best Men Are Cooks* (1941) observed: "No one ever expects the women to do the cooking at a barbecue" (261). Another cookbook commented: "Playing with fire is a man's job. Even in this day of subtle matriarchal pressures, the man is usually permitted full control of the outdoor grill" (Frederic A. Birmingham, *The Complete Cook Book for Men*, 211). In a *New York Times* article in 1959, John Willig wrote about the craze for outdoor cooking by men: "In backyards from Scarsdale to Sacramento, . . . American men are busy with grills and skewers, sending up palls of smoke" ("Outdoor Cookery," 42). He queried: "Why is it that the most indolent, undomesticated men, seeing a grill, some charcoal and a piece of raw meat, turn to it as inevitably as they would turn to Marilyn Monroe in a bikini?" (46).

16. For an article that discussed men becoming cooks only when their wives left for a week or a whole summer, see Victor Bergeron, "The Summer Bachelor."

17. For an article that addressed whether women or men were superior cooks, see Harry Botsford, "Are Men Better Cooks?"

18. The *Century* commentator was not alone in his condemnation of women as having no "real taste for food." A writer in the popular magazine *American Home* was equally harsh: "I have wondered why women's cook books are so generally lousy. Why employ only women to write about food, instead of calling in a good male cook from a restaurant or hotel and adding a little practicality to your pages?" ("And We Learned about Cooking from Men!" 241). Similarly, Joseph Wechsberg, writing for the *New York Times* in 1959, declared: "Face it, ladies: very nearly all of the great cooks have been men. . . . The refinement of taste and the philosophy of eating are male achievements. . . . Most women lack the objectivity, detachment and discipline to be true epicures" ("Male Cooks," 17). In an article titled "Give Me a Man Cook Every Time!" (1935), Frazier Hunt observed: "I revel in man-cooks. I like 'em no matter whether they're professional or amateur, so long as the food is good. Now I don't mean to insinuate that there are not millions of fine woman-cooks—but woman's place is in the front part of the home, playing bridge and tuning in the radio. Man's place is in the kitchen" (24). Shay observed: "Men should be good cooks, for they have a greater feeling for food than women have; they taste as they go along; they are adventurous and are willing to take chances. . . . Women have reduced cooking to a science while men cooks are working to restore it to its former high estate as one of the finer arts" (vii). A male writer from the 1950s commented that "men *are* good cooks. I honestly think they have a greater feeling for food than women" ("Why Can't a Woman Cook Like a Man?" 58).

19. Hotcakes and salads were two of the many dishes that women supposedly could not prepare. Men's cookbooks harped on the many recipes that women ruined. *Esquire's Handbook for Hosts* proclaimed: "While there are many women cooks who can prepare a fairly presentable bouillabaisse the dish reaches the heights only in the hands of a man" (29). The same book also commented: "The average woman . . . can't make a good cup of coffee. It must be that, basically, coffee is a man's drink" (81). The *Handbook* contained the following description of women making salads: "[Women] marry pineapple to cream cheese, nuts to marshmallow, mayonnaise to onions, and so on. American women go berserk when it comes to salads; they try so hard to be unique that in their zeal they really confuse things" (71).

20. Some cookbooks took the opposite approach, emphasizing meals that required the most primitive of cooking skills. In *Tough Guys Don't Dice* (1989), James A. Thorson included culinary tips such as serving meat loaf with Rice-A-Roni

or Stove Top stuffing (143). He suggested serving frozen green pea with pearl onions, pouring melted Cheez Whiz over the top of cooked broccoli, and using Hamburger Helper (126, 144). Such "recipes" allow a man to eat while simultaneously proclaiming his complete ignorance about cooking, distancing himself from the forbidden feminine realm: the kitchen.

21. Some women were so terrified of having husbands in the kitchen that they pleaded with them to stay out. One 1930s *Better Homes and Gardens* author observed: "I think most women will agree with me that if it were put to a vote husbands would definitely be put out of the kitchen, but allowed in occasionally—to adjust the gas burners" (Helen Agin Gordon, "Never Ask Your Husband to Help, *Unless* . . . ," 24). Another writer from the 1950s declared: "Husband, please stay away from my kitchen door! You're just not welcome there, except when bid to remove stubborn jar tops, stop leaking faucets, unstop clogged drains and provide quests with liquid refreshments" (Lucille Britt, "Husband, Stay Away from My (Kitchen) Door!" 88). A "husband in a kitchen can be a terribly exasperating thing," she lamented (89).

22. Articles that stressed the importance of cooking meals that men would enjoy include "Dishes for Husbands" and Edna Sibley Tipton, "When Men Entertain."

2. "The Enchantment of Mixing-Spoons": Cooking Lessons for Girls and Boys

1. For example, General Mills promoted its products to young readers in *Betty Crocker's New Boys and Girls Cook Book* and Crocker's *Cook Book for Boys and Girls*. For other juvenile cookbooks that promoted brand-name foods, see Mary Blake, *Fun to Cook Book*; and *My First Cookbook*.

2. Additional juvenile cookbooks include Garel Clark, *The Cook-a-Meal Cookbook*; Helen Jill Fletcher, *The See and Do Book of Cooking*; Philip Harben, *The Teen-Age Cook*; Constance Johnson, *When Mother Lets Us Cook*; Alma S. Lach, *Let's Cook*; Betty Miles, *The Cooking Book*; Elizabeth Robins and Octavia Wilberforce, *Prudence and Peter and Their Adventures with Pots and Pans*; Esther Rudomin, *Let's Cook without Cooking*; Ezekial Schloss, *Junior Jewish Cook Book*; Charles M. Schulz, *Peanuts Cook Book*; Ursula Sedgwick, *My Learn-to-Cook Book*; and Jane Werner Watson, *Susie's New Stove: The Little Chef's Cookbook*.

3. For anyone curious about cooking culture, toys are a particularly fascinating area because of the prevalence of food-related toys (tea party sets, toy ovens, toy kitchen utensils, to name a few) and their long-lasting popularity across generations. As cultural critic Ellen Seiter observes in her book *Sold Separately* (1993), "The product categories of girls' toys have remained remarkably stable since the twenties: vacuum cleaners, ovens, strollers or shopping carts, kitchen sets, doll houses" (74).

Why have such toys remained so consistent through generations? More research needs to be done on toys and the entire material culture of cooking for girls and boys.

4. Studies of girls' material culture include Miriam Formanek-Brunell, *Made to Play House*; Seiter; and a number of the essays in Elliott West and Paula Petrik, eds., *Small World*. Mary Lynn Stevens Heininger et al., *A Century of Childhood, 1820–1920*, contains references to girls' material culture in the nineteenth century.

5. The practice of directing juvenile cookbooks at an audience composed primarily of girls was not limited to the twentieth century. In earlier eras, this was even more likely to be true. For example, Harriet J. Willard addressed *Familiar Lessons for Little Girls* (1886) specifically to "young girls selected from the poorer districts in a large city" (n. pag.). Her book did not discuss the possibilities of boys performing any cooking-related tasks.

6. Another example of a book that had an implied audience of girls is Clara Ingram Judson's *Cooking without Mother's Help* (1920), in which the two children learning how to cook from their mother are both girls. Louise Price Bell's *Kitchen Fun* (1932) was identified on the cover as "a cook book for children." Despite this claim, the book was directed solely at girls. A small girl was portrayed on the cover, and a girl was shown reading a cookbook on the title page; boys did not appear anywhere in Bell's work. In Mary Blake's *Fun to Cook Book* (1955), new cooks were urged to put aprons over their dresses before they began to cook (6).

7. In addition, both Freeman's *Fun with Cooking* and Hoffmann's *Miss B's First Cookbook* included pictures of girls cooking, not boys. *Let's Have Fun Cooking* (1953) also included pictures only of girls.

8. Similarly, Louise Price Bell's *Jane-Louise's Cook Book* contained recipes for creamed chicken, salmon, crabmeat, asparagus, creamed beets, celery, onions, peas, spinach, and string beans.

9. A 1940s children's cookbook also suggested a number of sweet sandwich fillings, such as cream cheese and dates, cream cheese and currant jelly, orange marmalade, grape conserve and thin slices of banana, grated sweet chocolate and preserved ginger, chopped prunes with walnuts and lemon juice, and lady fingers filled with chopped figs and whipped cream (Florence LaGanke Harris, *Patty Pans*, 256–57).

10. Similarly, *Patty Pans*, started off with a picture of a girl in a kitchen reading a cookbook, with the caption: "It is fun to work in a kitchen" (Harris, n. pag.). Fay Lange wrote in "Cooking Can Be Play" (1955): "Cooking is fun for the pigtail set. It is important play for my daughter, Carol, when she makes her famous chocolate stacks, company butterscotch pie, or other dishes for the family" (80).

11. A number of popular articles advocated cooking for girls and boys. See Jane

Burbank Bonneville, "Our Children Can Manage Meals"; Alice Bradley, "When the Children Get Supper"; "Children Can Cook"; Myrtle Cook Gillespie, "Let Them Cook!"; "In this Kitchen, Cooking Is Child's Play"; Margaret Moore Jacobs, "Let 'Em Can and Cook"; Betty Gregory LaRoche, "Mothers Share Tips on How to Bring Up a Good Cook"; Helen Dickinson Lange, "Our Young Cooks"; Marion LeBron, "Invite Them into the Kitchen"; Shirley Moore, "I Want to Cook"; Dorothy E. Rose, "Junior Chefs"; Louella G. Shouer, "Never Too Young to Bake"; "Small-Fry Cooks"; and "Why Don't You Cook Dinner?"

12. For instance, a cookbook from the 1940s observed: "Both boys and girls should learn to cook, and everybody—boy or girl, young or old—should know something about food values and balanced meals" (Irma S. Rombauer, *A Cookbook for Girls and Boys*, 13).

13. Articles that specifically addressed boys and encouraged them to cook included "Cub Chefs"; "Kid Kapers"; Byron MacFadyen, "Teach Your Boy to Cook"; Sterling Patterson, "Shall We Join the Ladies?"; Patty Patton, "Make Your Child Welcome in the Kitchen"; Sarah Shields Pfeiffer, "He Might Like Cooking!"; and Roy R. Silver, "L.I. High School Boys Excel as Chefs."

3. Paradise Pudding, Peach Fluff, and Prune Perfection: Dainty Dishes and the Construction of Femininity

1. Other articles and cookbooks from the early decades of the twentieth century that stressed the importance of daintiness in food include Auto Vacuum Freezer Company, *Dainty Frozen Delicacies Made the Auto Vacuum Freezer Way*; Rachel F. Dahlgren, "Some Beehive Dainties"; *Dainty Dishes for Slender Incomes*; Edgewater Catholic Woman's Club, *Table Dainties for Dainty Matrons*; Rosamund Lampman, "Frozen Dainties"; Mrs. Nelson B. Oliphant, *A Dainty Cook Book*; Louise Rice, *Dainty Dishes from Foreign Lands*; and Sargent and Company, *Gem Chopper Cook Book*.

2. One nineteenth-century cookbook that focused on dainty recipes was Sarah Tyson Rorer's *Dainty Dishes for All the Year Round* (1898).

3. For more information about early-twentieth-century attitudes toward women, eating, and food, see Inness, *Kitchen Culture*, 34–44.

4. For additional accounts of women's roles in this period, see Winifred D. Wandersee, *Women's Work and Family Values, 1920–1940*.

5. Articles that focused on the popularity of tea parties include Lucy G. Allen, "The Small Afternoon Tea"; Alice Bradley, "Five O'Clock Tea"; Katherine Campion, "The Return of the High Tea"; Jessamine Chapman, "Afternoon Tea"; "Entertaining in the Spirit of Olden Times"; Nathalie Schenck Laimbeer, "Teas You Will Like to Give";

Gabrielle Rosiere, "Tea and Friends: Their Etiquette"; and Florence Spring, "Around the Tea-Tray."

6. Articles that discussed starting a tearoom as a good business proposition for women include C. H. Claudy, "Organizing the Wayside Tea House"; Herminie Dudley and Sarah Leyburn Coe, "Taverns and Tea Rooms as a Business for Women"; Winnifred Fales and Mary Northend, "At the Sign of the Tea-Room"; Una Nixson Hopkins, "What Three Women Did with Their Home"; Gladys Beckett Jones and Jenoise Brown Short, "A Mother-Daughter Tea-House"; Carrie Pickett Moore, "'Step-Inn'—A Successful Tea Room"; and Amy Lyman Phillips, "Polly's Place—and How It Grew."

7. For articles that described the pleasures of bringing the dainty edible delights served at tearooms into the private home, see Helena Judson, "Popular Tea-Room Novelties," and "Try These Tea-Room Touches."

8. Another author wrote in 1920 that she thought timbales made one of the daintiest food items to serve at a tea, remarking that they were "very popular among fashionable hostesses" (King, "The Tasty Timbale," 185). For the daintiest of party foods, she suggested making timbales in a wide choice of varieties: vegetable, green pea, cheese, chicken, cold asparagus, and cold lobster or salmon (185).

9. Flowers represented the ultimate sign of delicacy and daintiness and appeared in more than just sandwiches. For instance, one article from 1925 suggested that a nasturtium canapé could be both "artistic and tasty" and that a gelatin salad could be made more glamorous by garnishing it with rose petals (Edna Sibley Tipton, "Gay Flower Garnishes and Food Fancies," 41).

10. Other dainty tea-time sandwiches in Neil's book included tutti-frutti sandwiches, filled with a mixture of figs, raisins, dates, and nuts spread on wafers and then decorated with "whipped cream, candied violets, and strips of angelica" (131). The nasturtium sandwiches contained blossoms atop lightly buttered bread cut in fancy shapes (111). Mint sandwiches were composed of mint, gelatin, and two cups of whipped cream mixed together and spread on bread (108–9).

11. Other accounts of Jell-O's social and symbolic significance include Rosemarie Dorothy Bria, "How Jell-O Molds Society and Society Molds Jell-O"; and Marjorie Garber, "Jell-O."

12. Earlier in the century, Jell-O came in seven flavors: strawberry, raspberry, lemon, orange, cherry, peach, and chocolate (*Jell-O and the Kewpies*, 2). Peach was dropped in 1918, and chocolate in 1927. Lime was added in 1930.

13. Cookbooks written later in the twentieth century continued to emphasize the delicacy and daintiness of Jell-O dishes. *Knox® On-Camera Recipes: A Completely New Guide to Gel-Cookery* (1960) contained recipes for dainty dishes such as "delec-

table" fruit nectar salad (10), "delicate" pineapple coconut delight (41), and Knox dainties (46).

14. *The Greater Jell-O Recipe Book* (1931) included similar exotic recipes: golden glow salad (lemon Jell-O, pineapple, carrots, and pecans), sea dream salad (lime Jell-O and grated cucumbers), beauty salad (raspberry Jell-O with bananas and walnuts), crimson crystal dessert (Strawberry Jell-O and maraschino cherries), and paradise pudding (cherry Jell-O, one cup of cream, almonds, marshmallows, maraschino cherries, and macaroons) (18, 22, 23, 30, 37).

15. Throughout the twentieth century, cooking literature continued to emphasize creative ways with Jell-O, reaching new heights of elaborateness, it seemed, with each new decade. For example, one Jell-O cookbook from the 1960s informed readers that a delightful new way to serve Jell-O was disguised as a "Frosty Melon," a whole melon filled with fruited gelatin and frosted with softened cream cheese (General Foods Corporation, *Joys of Jell-O® Gelatin*, 39).

16. It is not surprising that marshmallows cropped up in many a Jell-O recipe since they were considered to be one of the daintiest foods, as mentioned frequently in advertising. For instance, the brochure *Dainty Desserts Made with Campfire, the Original Food Marshmallows* (1920s?) included recipes for Campfire cake icing (thirty marshmallows, walnuts, a cup of sugar, and a dozen maraschino cherries [n. pag.]) and Campfire Marshmallow splendo (dates, bananas, nuts, and marshmallows served with cream [n. pag.]). Similarly, an advertisement for Campfire Marshmallows assured readers: "Because of the manner in which these soft, fluffy marshmallows lend themselves to the preparation of dainty, delicious food dishes, they are no longer thought of merely as a confection. They have become established as a staple food product in thousands of progressive homes" (Campfire Marshmallows, 177). Another advertisement described a frozen fruit salad composed of apricot halves, a banana, maraschino cherries, Campfire Marshmallows, pineapple juice, chunks of pineapple, heavy cream, and mayonnaise (Campfire White Marshmallows, 622). Because marshmallows tasted and looked sweet and delicate, they were one of the most popular additions to Jell-O concoctions. Jell-O was even daintier if the cook tossed in a handful of marshmallows.

4. *Waffle Irons and Banana Mashers:*
Selling Mrs. Consumer on Electric Kitchen Gadgets

1. Studies that address technology, the kitchen, and women's roles include Ruth Schwartz Cowan, *More Work for Mother*; Wendy Faulkner and Erik Arnold, *Smoth-*

ered by Invention; Siegfried Giedion, *Mechanisation Takes Command*; and Doreen Yarwood, *Five Hundred Years of Technology in the Home*.

2. For further information on domestic service in the early twentieth century, see David M. Katzman, *Seven Days a Week*; Susan Strasser, *Never Done*; Daniel Sutherland, *Americans and Their Servants*; and Doris Weatherford, *Foreign and Female*.

3. For an account that persuaded early-twentieth-century women to have electrical appliances of all kinds in their homes, see Mary Ormsbee Whitton, "Running Your House on Greased Wheels."

4. Articles that discussed how electrical equipment could replace servants include Jones and Short, John R. McMahon, "Making Housekeeping Automatic"; and Anne Walker, "Three of Us and—Electricity."

5. A *Sunset* article in 1926 described the advantages of owning an electric mixer: "This mechanical servant, this household robot, will do for you uncomplainingly all the hard work, will do it better than you would be able to and will give a sure and exact result" ("Your Obedient Servant," 76).

6. Even after a woman replaced many of her servants with electric devices, people assumed that she would continue to have problems with her hired help since they would be ill-prepared to handle electrical appliances: "Although householders may find difficulty in inducing servants to use modern equipment, the householder herself should miss no opportunity to investigate these new devices. Once convinced of their value, she may be able, by subtle diplomacy, to introduce them into her kitchen" (Peter Dunham, "To Lessen Kitchen Labor," 72).

7. Other popular articles about the joys of electrical kitchen appliances include "Aladdin's Newest Magic Is the Touch-a-Button Kitchen"; Alice Bradley, "Do You Cook Electrically?" and "Push-Button Cookery"; Ethel Wan-Ressel Chantler, "Getting the Most Out of Your Electric Table Devices"; Dorothy Marsh, "Refrigerators Work Overtime in Summer"; and Demetria M. Taylor, "Your Electric Beater."

8. Articles that focused particularly on electric refrigerators include Florence R. Clauss, "To Get the Most from the Refrigerator"; Mabel Jewett Crosby, "Refrigeration Cookery by Electricity"; Marsh, "Refrigerators"; and Ethel R. Peyser, "The Passing of the Ice Man."

9. Everywhere a woman looked, she was barraged with messages about how practical it was to own an electric refrigerator. One example appeared in the advertising booklet *Your Electric Refrigerator and Knox Sparkling Gelatin* (1929). Mrs. Charles B. Knox began the booklet with a letter to her readers: "I have written you many letters in the past, giving recipes for good dishes to serve on your table—but this time I am writing to tell you of the merits of Electric Refrigerators; you know we once thought

they were a luxury in the household, but we now know they are an everyday necessity" (1). An author wrote enthusiastically about the many benefits of the automatic refrigerator in *Woman's Home Companion* in 1931: "When you first enlist the aid of this appliance in preparing foods, surprises greet you on every turn. Grocery bills descend. The time spent in the kitchen is shortened. Meals are better than ever before. And all the time you are enjoying the discoveries you are making" (Nell B. Nichols, "Let the Automatic Refrigerator Help," 66). The message sent by such advertisements and articles was that a refrigerator belonged in every middle-class household.

10. Yet another article trumpeted the modern pleasures of the electric cooker: "The biggest modern aid to the household as we find it is the electric cooker. . . . [which] transforms the old order of 'woman's work never being done' to the new and magical one of 'touch the button and we'll do the rest'" (Mary Pattison, "Abolition of Household Slavery," 125).

11. For further information about table stove cookery, see Mabel J. Stegner, "Informal Meals"; and Helen Morse Whitson, "Table Stove Cookery."

12. One advertisement for the KitchenAid electrical food preparer made kitchen tasks sound more like play than work: "In the many thousands of homes where KitchenAid is employed, women no longer associate meal-time with the thought of work. For this wonderful electric servant performs *all* the irksome tasks so often responsible for tired arms, aching backs, and 'kitchen nerves'" (KitchenAid, 239). It is no wonder that women bought such gadgets.

13. The belief that electrical household devices would beautify life for the housewife was apparent in the title of Mary Ormsbee Whitton's *House Beautiful* article, "The Mechanics of Living Beautifully" (1920).

14. Other articles that discussed the joys of cooking with an electric range include Katharine Fisher, "If You Have an Electric Range, Let the Institute Help You Use It to Advantage"; Helen E. Ridley and Truman L. Henderson, "The New Electric Range Brings the Whole Family to the Kitchen"; Mabel Stearns, "My Electric Range"; and Clara H. Zillissen, "Electricity in the Home."

15. A similar advertisement for a Westinghouse Electric range depicted two stylish ladies looking at a stove. One remarked to the other, "Sounds queer but it's an absolute fact. You know, my dear, it's simply uncanny the way that range works. . . . I just put dinner in the oven, set the clock and off I go to the movies or anywhere I wish. I know everything will be ready when I return" (Westinghouse Electric Range, 130).

5. *"Fearsome Dishes": International Cooking*
and Orientalism between the Wars

1. For international cookbooks from this period, see Frances P. Belle, comp., *California Cook Book*; Julia Lovejoy Cuniberti, *Practical Italian Recipes for American Kitchens*; Josie Millsaps Fitzhugh, *The International Cook Book*; Good Housekeeping, *Around the World Cook Book*; Lowell International Institute, *As the World Cooks*; Madeline May, *The International Cook Book*; and Eleanor F. Wells, *Nationality Recipes*.

2. For more research on the role of foreign foods in twentieth-century America, see Warren Belasco, "Ethnic Fast Foods"; Amy Bentley, "From Culinary Other to Mainstream American"; Susan Kalcik,"Ethnic Foodways in America"; and Lucy M. Long, "Culinary Tourism."

3. The educational aspect of international meals was often stressed by authors of cookbooks that included foods from around the globe. One such cookbook in 1939 informed its readers that "with recipes handed to us here from countries of the world, there is no reason why the planning of the food for the family should not be interesting and educational. With these international recipes it should be an easy and enjoyable task to plan for the family meals that are nutritious, interesting, palatable, and colorful" (Margaret Weimer Heywood, comp., *The International Cook Book*, xiv).

4. Another cookbook writer wrote in 1933: "The appetizing blend of flavors to which we are unaccustomed. The appeal of the truly good things to eat, that knows no boundary of race, creed, or country. These are the universal pleasures of the epicure" (May, n. pag.).

5. Cookbooks with recipes from many countries include L. L. McLaren's *Pan-Pacific Cook Book* (1915; Algeria, Armenia, Bolivia, Guatemala, India, Panama, Persia, Uruguay, and Venezuela), *Foreign Cookery* (1932; Albania, Armenia, Austria, Bulgaria, China, Croatia, Denmark, the Philippines, Finland, France, Germany, Greece, Hungary, India, Italy, Japan, Korea, Mexico, Norway, Poland, Russia, Spain, Sweden, Switzerland, Syria, and Turkey); and Countess Marcelle Morphy's *Recipes of All Nations* (1935; Austria, Belgium, China, Denmark, England, France, Germany, Holland, Hungary, India, Italy, Japan, Norway, Poland, Portugal, Russia, Spain, and Sweden).

6. Studies by nutritionists and dietitians between the wars that addressed the nutritional needs of foreign-born Americans include Alberta B. Childs, "Some Dietary Studies of Poles, Mexicans, Italians, and Negroes"; and Bertha M. Wood, *Foods of the Foreign-Born in Relation to Health*.

7. For more information on the popularity of Italian food during the Progressive

Era, see Harvey A. Levenstein, "The American Response to Italian Food, 1880–1930."

8. For other articles between the wars on the appeal of Italian food, see Alice Bradley, "Italian Dinner Party"; Florence Brady, "A Taste of Old Italy"; Katharine Fisher, "Dining in Italy at Your Own Table"; Marie Jacques, "Straight from Italy"; Byron MacFadyen, "Let's Have Spaghetti"; and Mrs. J. Riordan, "Americans Getting Macaroni Appetite."

9. Not all American cooks were equally enthusiastic about Italian pasta. Many still viewed macaroni as too foreign and not very appetizing. For instance, in 1925, Freda Winn wrote for *Delineator* magazine: "Macaroni and the other members of that old Italian family—spaghetti and vermicelli, are foods that have not been duly appreciated in this country. They are generally considered, both by the average housewife and the general public, as dishes peculiarly suited and adapted to Italy" ("When America Eats Macaroni," 62). Winn expressed the sentiment of many Americans who thought pasta too unusual to add to their meals. Americans often overcooked pasta (cooking spaghetti for half an hour or longer), which did not help to make it more palatable.

10. Other popular magazine articles that demonstrate the popularity of Mexican food between the wars with at least some adventuresome American eaters include Constance D. Borrowe, "A Mexican Dinner"; Ruth Moore Morris, "Hot Stuff"; Mildred O. Tidwell, "Dining at the End of the Trail"; and Florence A. Utting, "Four Mexican Recipes."

11. For another Mexican cookbook published in the United States between World War I and World War II, see Blanche McNeil and Edna V. McNeil, *First Foods of America*.

12. Writing in 1913, Sara Bossé mentioned the popularity of Chinese food at the turn of the century: "Chinese cooking has become very popular of recent years in America. The restaurants are no longer merely the resort of curious idlers intent upon studying types peculiar to Chinatown, for the Chinese restaurants have pushed their way out of Chinatown, and are now found in all parts of the large cities of America" ("Cooking and Serving a Chinese Dinner in America," 27). These restaurants, however, frequently served food that bore hardly any resemblance to real Chinese food.

13. Articles that discuss Asian foods between the two world wars include Roberta Allen, "Be Your Own Chinese Chef"; Alice Bradley, "Mah Jung Refreshments"; Jean Caroline Evans, "As the Chinese Cook"; Harriet Acheson Koch, "Food with a Foreign Accent"; Louise Leung, "Foreign Cookery"; "Prize-Winning Oriental Recipes"; "Quaint Chinese Dishes"; and Nellie Choy Wong, "As We Cook in China."

14. For a contemporary article about the anti-Chinese sentiments in the United States between the wars, see William C. Smith, "Born American, But—."

15. This supposedly authentic Chinese cookbook contained recipes for tofu soup, fried tofu, fried duck feet, bird's nest soup, and homemade crisp noodles. But this same book contained Americanized recipes such as planked steak garnished "with mashed potatoes, peas, carrots and two cups of bean sprouts" (32), cabbage with corned beef, Oriental coleslaw made with bean sprouts, Chinese tuna salad, and roast beef.

6. "It's Fun Being Thrifty!" Gendered Cooking Lessons during the Depression

1. Some Depression-era cooking literature went to great lengths to suggest ways to economize. For instance, Cora Brown's *Most for Your Money Cookbook* (1938) contained a full chapter on what it called "queer fish": octopus, squid, skate, and eel. The book also included a chapter on polenta, including a number of economical recipes, among them one for pig's liver polenta.

2. For general accounts of women's lives during the Depression, see Robert S. Lynd and Helen Merrell Lynd, *Middletown in Transition*; Susan Ware, *Holding Their Own*; and Jeane Westin, *Making Do*.

3. Other Depression-era articles that discuss the benefits and problems of both a husband and wife working include Rita S. Halle, "Do You Need Your Job?"; Frank L. Hopkins, "Should Wives Work?"; Judith Lambert, "I Quit My Job"; Rose Wilder Lane, "Woman's Place Is in the Home"; Lois Scharf, *To Work and to Wed*; "Should I Take a Job When My Husband Has One Too?"; Lois Hayden Meek, "The Problem of a Working Mother"; Frances Perkins, "Should Women Take Men's Jobs?"; and "Working Wives."

4. For a similar study of married women who worked outside the home, see Cecile T. La Follette, *A Study of the Problems of 652 Gainfully Employed Married Women Homemakers*.

5. A number of articles discuss the pleasures of housekeeping as a vocation for a woman. See Gwenivere Lamoreaux, "Housekeeping."

6. For other Depression-era articles on the importance of serving tasty, nutritious food and staying within a budget, see Dorothy Marsh's "Keep Tabs on Your Food Bills" and "More Food for the Same Money"; Gove Hambridge, "Make the Diet Fit the Pocketbook"; Dorothy Kirk, "Pocketbook Meals"; Mrs. Penrose Lyly, "Delicious Thrift"; and Louella G. Shouer, "Biscuits, Bonnets and Budgets."

7. Women's cooking literature during the Depression did not always mention the

difficult economic times, as Harvey A. Levenstein points out: "The most striking fact about this outpouring of information about food is the dearth of material on economizing. Yes, there were 'economical' or 'budget' recipes, along with advice on how to cut corners, but in no greater proportion than in other, more prosperous, times. To a certain extent, of course, this reflects editors' and marketers' perceptions that those most in need of advice on low-cost cooking could not afford the magazines. . . . However, it also reflected a perception that in hard times Americans wanted reassuring food, that they yearned for the stability and wholesomeness traditionally associated with mother's home cooking" (*Paradox*, 34). Levenstein is correct in noting that Depression-era cooking literature did not always emphasize economizing, but the focus on thrift and economizing was stronger than it was in other periods. Eleanor Roosevelt's interest in writing about the importance of being a thrifty cook was one of the most prominent examples of a larger cultural discourse about the importance of domestic thriftiness for housewives.

8. Additional Depression cookbooks that describe how to eat for less include George E. Cornforth, *Better Meals for Less*; and Hazel Young, *Better Meals for Less Money*.

9. The expensive meat course was an easy way to economize. Many cooking articles emphasized the importance of reducing the meat bill. See Julia Bliss Joyner, "How to Save Money on Meat"; Imogene Powell, "Down Goes the Meat Bill"; and "Stretching the Meat Dollar."

7. "Wear This Uniform Proudly, Mrs. America!" Rosie the Riveter in the Kitchen

1. For additional information on the conditions for women during World War II, see Karen Anderson, *Wartime Women*; D'Ann Campbell, *Women at War with America*; Sherna Berger Gluck, *Rosie the Riveter Revisited*; Susan M. Hartmann, *The Home Front and Beyond*; Maureen Honey, *Creating Rosie the Riveter*; Mark H. Leff, "The Politics of Sacrifice on the American Home Front in World War II"; Leila Rupp, *Mobilizing Women for War*; and Doris Weatherford, *American Women and World War II*.

2. The media emphasized the similarities between these new wartime jobs in male-dominated areas and women's traditional domestic responsibilities: "The techniques used in wielding the egg beater, the can opener, and the laundry mangle are apparently transferable to the activities of manipulating drills, testing primers for shells and other mechanical devices" (Stella B. Applebaum, "War Jobs for Mothers?" 17).

3. World War II sources that focus on the importance of women working outside

their homes include Susan B. Anthony II, *Out of the Kitchen—Into the War*; Laura Nelson Baker, *Wanted*; Eva Lapin, *Mothers in Overalls*; and Mary Elizabeth Pidgeon, *Women's Work and the War*.

4. The U.S. government played a direct role in promoting the dissemination of a glorified vision of women workers, especially those who worked in traditional male pursuits, such as riveting or flying (Campbell, 8). For the course of the war at least, Washington, D.C., accepted the image of Rosie the Riveter; after the war, that acceptance would wear thin.

5. Amy Bentley also discusses the anxiety that society felt about women's changing roles: "Social scientists, journalists, and others warned that women in the public sphere led to distortion of values, irregular family routines, promiscuity, lack of respect by men [for women], and a rejection of feminine roles" ("Islands of Serenity," 134).

6. During the war, many women never left behind their domestic responsibilities, so their roles did not shift as greatly as might appear to be the case. Women often held double jobs, both inside the home and outside it. Little evidence exists that families were eager to help mothers perform their domestic duties, even if mom was building ships for ten hours a day. She was expected to do her wartime job without allowing it to interfere with her domestic duties (Weatherford, *American Women*, 164).

7. Additional World War II cookbooks include Alice Bradley, *The Wartime Cook Book*; Delineator Home Institute, *The Victory Binding of the American Woman's Cook Book*; Marion Gregg, ed., *The American Women's Voluntary Services Cook Book*; Harriet H. Hester, *300 Sugar Saving Recipes*; Margot Murphy, *Wartime Meals*; Barbara Rae, *Cooking without Meat*; and Elizabeth Fuller Whiteman, *Wartime Fish Cookery*.

8. Similarly, Sophie Kerr wrote for the magazine *Woman's Home Companion*: "The American housewife has often been called wasteful and careless. In this land of overflowing plenty she might be excused for this fault. But now, with our young men on the fighting front and the war raging, if I know the American housewife she will go into the kitchen with her sleeves rolled up and put on a magnificent performance of economical good living, and enjoy doing it" ("Good Eating in Wartime," 35).

9. The author of one wartime preparedness guide wrote in 1942 to women on the home front: "We consumers have a big job to do in this war. . . . We can and must keep our civilian population strong and fit" (Caroline F. Ware, *The Consumer Goes to War*, 1).

10. For wartime articles that counsel the housewife about how to use her points, see Katharine Fisher, "What You Should Know about the New Point System of Rationing"; Louise Andrews Kent, "Mrs. Appleyard Rescues a Girl Who Has Run Out of

Points"; Dorothy Kirk, "Patterns for Points"; and Florence Paine, "Good Eating on a Ration Card."

11. For additional information on how women shopped during World War II, see Jerome Beatty, "Cooking for a Defense Worker"; Robert Heide and John Gilman, *Home Front America*, 54–55; and "The Way to Market in Wartime."

12. Articles on ways to conserve sugar include Margaret Ball, "Little Sugar— Much Dessert"; Julia Hoover, "Easy Ways to Save Sugar"; Doris McCray, "Short on Sugar? Try Syrups!"; Edwin Neff, "Life Is Sweet, Anyway"; and Charlotte Scripture, "Saving Sugar in Making Pies."

13. Basically, women were wartime strategists whose responsibility was to ensure that their families ate a healthy diet. *Good Housekeeping* encouraged its readers to take their cooking responsibilities seriously: "As top strategists on the food front, we must get out of some of our food ruts and ways from old patterns in planning our meals. We even may find it necessary to persuade our families to acquire new food tastes" (Katharine Fisher, "Main Dishes for These Times," 89).

14. See also Jean Prescott Adams's *Meatless Meals* (1943), which contained recipes for soy bean roast, nut loaf, polenta with cheese, Chinese cabbage salad, and black bean soup. Natalie K. Fitch and Mary Agnes Davis's *Meat Saving Recipes* (1943) included recipes such as baked brown rice and cheese (27), soybean and cheese casserole (30), soybean stew (31), and peanut loaf (34).

15. Advertisements emphasized a similar message. For instance, one entitled "Join Up—But Don't Let Your Family Down" counseled women that numerous food markets were available to help them with their "double job." The ad was quick to point out that women should not forget their domestic duties: "Nobody expects you to be on the side lines—with so many wartime tasks begging to be done. But don't forget, part of your job in winning the war is to keep your family's health at Grade A level" ("Join Up," 124).

16. Similarly, another wartime author wrote: "Every homemaker who knows and understands food values is a soldier on the winning side" (Demetria M. Taylor, *Ration Cook Book*, 3).

17. An article from the American Meat Institute also mentioned the importance of keeping good health for everyone. It urged women to pay special attention to protein-rich meat: "In the trim uniform or the simple house dress, women today are called upon to do more . . . to give more . . . to endure more. Never have the springy step, the abundant spirit, the bright eye, the good body been more vital . . . which is another way of saying 'All the girls of Uncle Sam must eat right'" (American Meat Institute, 17).

18. In *Good Housekeeping*, Margaret Cousins was already writing about the im-

portance of conservation in the kitchen in 1941: "Home is the place where every American—man, woman, child—will find his first duty, a duty for which he is responsible—to conserve every resource, to make an end of extravagance and profligate ways of living, to understand and put a stop to waste, to realize that thrift is not a word or a joke but an essential" ("Home Is the Place . . . ," 115). Before the war, kitchen and other domestic responsibilities were considered relatively unimportant; during the war, these activities were raised to a level of utmost importance.

19. Many other advertisements touted the dream kitchen overflowing with appliances and gadgets. An advertisement for Gibson refrigerators and ranges raved about what the homemaker of tomorrow was going to receive: "Lady, we're positively itching to tell you—and the whole world—about the NEW Gibson Freez'r Shelf Refrigerators and Kookall Automatic Electric Ranges that will gladden your heart when the days of peace return. . . . Entirely NEW features will amaze you with the automatic, almost-human way they'll save you time and trouble and money!" (Gibson Refrigerator Company, 183). An advertisement for Westinghouse Appliances featured the postwar dreams of a new bride caught up with the splendor of the kitchen appliances she would own: "We'll have a new Westinghouse Electric Range so completely automatic that I can put a meal in the oven and then forget all about it!" (Westinghouse Appliances, 80). The bride was even more excited about her future refrigerator: "Boy, it'll be fun marketing when we can buy all we want. And in our Westinghouse Refrigerator there will be a special place for everything—including the grand new frozen foods" (80). The advertisement promised: "When the war is over, and you and that man of yours set up a dream home of your own, Westinghouse will make all those new time-and-work saving appliances you've set your heart on" (80). See also the Crosley Corporation advertisement.

8. Of Casseroles and Canned Foods:
Building the Happy Housewife in the Fifties

1. Richard Armour, "Portrait of a Happy Housewife," 157.

2. For additional cookbooks from this period, see Betty Crocker, *Good and Easy Cook Book*; *House and Garden's Cook Book*; Agnes Murphy, *American Hostess Library Book of Cooking*; June Platt and Sophie Kerr, *The Best I Ever Ate*; and *Today's Woman Cookie Cook Book*.

3. This chapter primarily explores the positive portrayal of food and cooking in women's magazines. It is important to recognize that not all women were happy housewives in this period, and popular literature did not always portray domesticity in a trouble-free fashion. The domestic imperative was not the sole ideology of the

1950s, as Joanne Meyerowitz suggests in her study of popular magazines: "The popular literature . . . did not simply glorify domesticity or demand that women return to or stay at home. . . . In this literature, domestic ideals coexisted in ongoing tension with an ethos of individual achievement that celebrated nondomestic activity, individual striving, public service, and public success" (*Not June Cleaver*, 231). She writes further: "The postwar mass culture embraced the same central contradiction—the tension between domestic ideals and individual achievement—that Betty Friedan addressed in *The Feminine Mystique*" (232). Domesticity was portrayed in an ambivalent fashion in the 1950s, according to Meyerowitz: "Despite the support for marriage and motherhood, the role of the housewife and mother was problematic in the postwar popular discourse. On the one hand, all the magazines assumed that women wanted to marry, that women found being wives and mothers rewarding, and that women would and should be the primary parents and housekeepers. . . . On the other hand, throughout the postwar era, numerous articles portrayed domesticity itself as exhausting and isolating, and frustrated mothers as overdoting and smothering" (242). Despite this societal ambivalence about women's roles, 1950s cooking literature painted an often deliriously happy vision of the delights of cookery.

4. For other historical accounts of the 1950s and women's roles in this decade, see Wini Breines, *Young, White, and Miserable*; Benita Eisler, *Private Lives*; Joel Foreman, ed., *The Other Fifties*; Eugenia Kaledin, *Mothers and More*; and Elaine Tyler May, *Homeward Bound*.

5. Additional information on food habits in the 1950s can be found in Gerry Schremp, *Kitchen Culture*, 35–65.

6. Hostess books were popular in the 1950s. See works such as Maureen Daly, *The Perfect Hostess*; and Elizabeth Stuart Hedgecock, *The Successful Hostess*.

7. Of course, casseroles did not begin in the 1950s. For an earlier popular article about casseroles, see Henrietta Jessup, "Out of the Casserole."

8. For 1950s articles on casserole cooking, see "Casseroles, Hot and Hearty"; "Casseroles with a Foreign Accent"; Ethel W. Cordner, "Our Best Cook Makes You a Summer Casserole"; "Easygoing Casseroles"; "For Your Casserole"; "Hearty Casseroles"; Sara Hervey, "Champion Casseroles"; "Holiday Casseroles"; Dorothy Kirk, "The Obliging Casserole"; "Shelf Magic for Short-Order Cooks"; "Soup Seasons These Casseroles"; "Tasty Casserole Bargains"; "Topics of the Times"; and Elizabeth Wood, "Casseroles for Casual Suppers."

9. For similar 1950s casserole cookbooks, see Jim Beard, *The Casserole Cookbook*; Edna Beilenson, comp., *Holiday Party Casseroles*; Florence Brobeck, *The New Cook It in a Casserole*; and Marian Tracy, *Casserole Cookery Complete* and *More Casserole Cookery*.

10. Canned foods were not a new invention in the 1950s. They had existed for over a century. As early as 1812, Brian Donkin owned a canning factory (Reay Tannahill, *Food in History*, 310). By 1868, the invention of machine-cut cans allowed the cost of canned foods to plummet. Over the decades, canned foods went from being an expensive luxury to an inexpensive necessity for many, especially city dwellers who lived far from the farms where the canned foods originally grew. This long historical past for canned foods did not stop 1950s advertisers and cookbook writers from promoting canned foods as distinctly modern and up-to-date.

11. In the 1950s, every cookbook seemed to include recipes for ethnic casseroles. A section of *Good Housekeeping's Casserole Cook Book* (1958) labeled "casseroles from other countries" included recipes for lasagna, stuffed cabbage, coq au vin, and arroz con pollo (23). Lousene Rousseau Brunner's *Casserole Magic* (1953) contained recipes for Algerian cassoulet, Basque chicken dinner, Flemish stew, Polish hunter's stew, Hungarian chicken paprika, Chinese chicken curry, East Indian curry, and Norwegian herring pudding. Casseroles were a cheap and easy way to experience the foreign and unknown without leaving the comfort of your own home.

12. Popular articles on blender recipes include "Blender Magic"; Frances French, "Make These Favorites with a Blender"; and "How to 'Cook' with Your Blender."

13. Out of the thousands of convenience foods available to the housewife of the 1950s, frozen TV dinners seemed to be one of the most alluring. Article after article praised them. At the Association of Frozen Food Packers convention held in New York City in 1954, it seemed as though the TV dinner could provide any gustatory delight to its consumers. The convention's guests "were served such items as turkey-dinners from New Jersey, Normandy trout in champagne from Maxim's in Paris, chow mein, chicken pot pie, breaded shrimp and fried rice, all taken from the freezing cabinets and heated . . . on electric plates and ovens that would fit in any dinette" ("Pre-Cooked Meals Raise Sales Hope," L33). For more on the spread of frozen foods in the 1950s, see "Gains Foreseen in Frozen Foods."

14. A fifties article that emphasized the pleasures of canned foods was "Four Family Dinners Featuring Canned Food."

15. Cookbooks in the 1950s encouraged women to explore international dishes but not grow too adventuresome. For example, *Betty Crocker's Dinner for Two Cook Book* (1958) invited readers to try preparing a French meal. The aspiring French cook was told to make chocolate éclairs by following the recipe on the box of a package of Betty Crocker Cream Puff Mix and to make croissants with Bisquick (169). The same cookbook also provided recipes for an "authentic" Mexican meal. Speedy tortillas were made with Bisquick, and "Even Quicker Tortillas" with a can of Betty Crocker Bisquick Biscuits rolled thin (188).

Works Cited

The ABC of Casseroles. Mount Vernon: Peter Pauper P, 1954.

Abdullah, Achmed, and John Kenny. *For Men Only: A Cook Book.* New York: Putnam's, 1937.

Adams, Carol J. *The Sexual Politics of Meat: A Feminist-Vegetarian Critical Theory.* New York: Continuum, 1990.

Adams, Charles Magee. "The Best Electric Refrigerator for You." *American Cookery* Apr. 1934: 533–35.

Adams, Jean Prescott. *Meatless Meals.* Chicago: Whitman, 1943.

Adler, Thomas A. "Making Pancakes on Sunday: The Male Cook in Family Tradition." *Western Folklore* 40.1 (1981): 45–54.

"Advice to Brides . . . by Experts." *Better Homes and Gardens* June 1933: 24+.

"Aladdin's Newest Magic Is the Touch-a-Button Kitchen." *Ladies' Home Journal* Feb. 1924: 102+.

Aldy, Linda Ross, and Carol Taff, eds. *"Down Here, Men Don't Cook": A Cookbook by Mississippi Men.* Jackson: Southern Images, 1984.

Algren, Nelson. *America Eats.* Iowa City: U of Iowa P, 1992.

Allen, Ida Bailey. *Double-Quick Cooking for Part-Time Homemakers.* New York: Barrows, 1943.

Allen, Ida Cogswell Bailey. *The Budget Cook Book.* New York: Best Foods, 1935.

Allen, Lucy G. "The Small Afternoon Tea." *Good Housekeeping* May 1925: 79+.

Allen, Roberta. "Be Your Own Chinese Chef." *Ladies' Home Journal* Nov. 1927: 143.

Alsop, Gulielma Fell, and Mary F. McBride. *Arms and the Girl: A Guide to Personal Adjustment in War Work and War Marriage.* New York: Vanguard P, 1943.

American Can Company. Advertisement. *Good Housekeeping* Aug. 1954: 46–47.

American Meat Institute. Advertisement. *Good Housekeeping* Oct. 1943: 17.

Anders, Nedda C. *Casserole Specialties.* New York: Gramercy, 1955.

Anderson, Digby. "Imperative Cooking: The Moral of the Barbecue." *Spectator* 7 May 1994: 42.

Anderson, Karen. *Wartime Women: Sex Roles, Family Relations, and the Status of Women during World War II.* Westport: Greenwood, 1981.

Anderson, Kate Peel. "A Mexican Kitchen." *House Beautiful* Dec. 1923: 628+.

"And We Learned about Cooking from Men!" *American Home* Oct. 1933: 241+.

Anthony, Susan B., II. *Out of the Kitchen—Into the War: Woman's Winning Role in the Nation's Drama.* New York: Stephen Daye, 1943.

Applebaum, Stella B. "War Jobs for Mothers?" *Parents' Magazine* Feb. 1943: 17+.

Armour, Richard. "Portrait of a Happy Housewife." *Better Homes and Gardens* Feb. 1954: 157.

Armstrong Table Stove. Advertisement. *Good Housekeeping* July 1924: 131.

The Art and Secrets of Chinese Cookery. Detroit: La Choy Food Products, 1937.

Au, M. Sing. *The Chinese Cook Book: Covering the Entire Field of Chinese Cookery in the Chinese Order of Serving, from Nuts to Soup.* Reading: Culinary Arts, 1936.

Auto Vacuum Freezer Company. *Dainty Frozen Delicacies Made the Auto Vacuum Freezer Way.* New York: Auto Vacuum Freezer Co., 1923.

Avakian, Arlene Voski, ed. *Through the Kitchen Window: Women Explore the Intimate Meanings of Food and Cooking.* Boston: Beacon, 1997.

Bailey-Allen, Ida Cogswell. "The Right Way to Give a Tea." *Ladies' Home Journal* Mar. 1915: 37.

Baker, Laura Nelson. *Wanted: Women in War Industry.* New York: Dutton, 1943.

Baker, Russell. "Grilled Macho." *New York Times Magazine* 27 July 1986: 10.

Ball, Margaret. "Little Sugar—Much Dessert." *Good Housekeeping* Feb. 1943: 88–89.

Barber, Edith. "Mexican Dishes for American Meals." *Good Housekeeping* Oct. 1939: 176+.

Barclay, Tekla. "Pinch-Penny Privates." *American Home* June 1943: 68.

Barthes, Roland. *Mythologies.* 1957. New York: Hill and Wang, 1972.

———. "Toward a Psychosociology of Contemporary Food Consumption." In *Food and Drink in History,* ed. Robert Forster and Orest Ranum, 166–73. Baltimore: Johns Hopkins UP, 1979.

Batchelder, Ann. "For the Bridge Party." *Delineator* Oct. 1929: 43+.

———. "Those Important First Meals." *Delineator* June 1932: 26+.

Bates, Helen K. "Feeding Five on $14 a Week." *Good Housekeeping* Jan. 1940: 109+.

Bauer, Steven. "A Man Who Cooks." *Glamour* June 1995: 236.

Bavicchi, Sarah. "Macaroni: As the Italians Really Cook It." *Ladies' Home Journal* Oct. 1928: 118.

Beard, Belle Boone. *Electricity in the Home*. New York: Workers Education Bureau P, 1927.

Beard, James. *Cook It Outdoors*. New York: M. Barrows, 1941.

Beard, Jim. *The Casserole Cookbook*. Indianapolis: Bobbs-Merrill, 1955.

Beardsworth, Alan, and Teresa Keil. *Sociology on the Menu: An Invitation to the Study of Food and Society*. London: Routledge, 1997.

Beatty, Jerome. "Cooking for a Defense Worker." *Parents' Magazine* Jan. 1942: 24+.

Bederman, Gail. *Manliness and Civilization: A Cultural History of Gender and Race in the United States, 1880–1917*. Chicago: U of Chicago P, 1995.

Beilenson, Edna, comp. *Holiday Party Casseroles*. Mount Vernon: Peter Pauper P, 1956.

Beim, Jerrold. *The First Book of Boys' Cooking*. New York: Watts, 1957.

Belasco, Warren. *Appetite for Change: How the Counterculture Took on the Food Industry, 1966–1988*. New York: Pantheon Books, 1989.

———. "Ethnic Fast Foods: The Corporate Melting Pot." *Food and Foodways* 2 (1989): 1–30.

Belden, Louise Conway. *The Festive Tradition: Table Decoration and Desserts in America, 1650–1900*. New York: Norton, 1983.

Bell, David, and Gill Valentine. *Consuming Geographies: We Are Where We Eat*. New York: Routledge, 1997.

Bell, Louise Price. "Children Like to Cook." *Parents' Magazine* May 1941: 54+.

———. *Jane Louise's Cook Book: A Cook Book for Children*. New York: Coward-McCann, 1930.

———. *Kitchen Fun: Teaches Children to Cook Successfully*. Cleveland: Harter, 1932.

———. "Some Rainy Afternoon." *American Home* Dec. 1943: 80–82.

Belle, Frances P., comp. *California Cook Book: An Unusual Collection of Spanish Dishes and Typical California Foods for Luncheons and Dinners Which May Be Quickly and Easily Prepared*. Chicago: Regan, 1925.

Bentley, Amy. *Eating for Victory: Food Rationing and the Politics of Domesticity*. Urbana: U of Illinois P, 1998.

———. "From Culinary Other to Mainstream American: Meanings and Uses of Southwestern Cuisine." *Southern Folklore* 55.3 (1998): 238–52.

———. "Islands of Serenity: Gender, Race, and Ordered Meals During World War II." *Food and Foodways* 6.2 (1996): 131–56.

Benton, Caroline French. *The Fun of Cooking: A Story for Boys and Girls*. New York: Century, 1915.

———. *A Little Cook Book for a Little Girl*. Boston: Estes, 1905.

Bereano, Philip, Christine Bose, and Erik Arnold. "Kitchen Technology and the Liberation of Women from Housework." In *Smothered by Invention: Technology in Women's Lives*, ed. Wendy Faulkner and Erik Arnold, 162–81. London: Pluto, 1985.

Bergeron, Victor. "The Summer Bachelor." *House Beautiful* Aug. 1952: 98+.

Berk, Sarah Fenstermaker. *The Gender Factory: The Apportionment of Work in American Households*. New York: Plenum, 1985.

Berolzheimer, Ruth, ed. *250 Ways to Save Sugar Cook Book*. Chicago: Consolidated Book Publishers, 1942.

———. *How to Feed a Family of Five on $15 a Week Cook Book*. Chicago: Consolidated Book Publishers, 1942.

———. *Military Meals at Home Cook Book*. Chicago: Consolidated Book Publishers, 1943.

———. *The Wartime Cook Book: 500 Recipes, Victory Substitutes and Economical Suggestions for Wartime Needs*. Chicago: Consolidated Book Publishers, 1942.

Better Homes and Gardens. *Holiday Cook Book: Special Foods for All Special Occasions*. Des Moines: Meredith, 1959.

Better Homes and Gardens Cook Book. Des Moines: Meredith, 1943.

Better Homes and Gardens Junior Cook Book for the Hostess and Host of Tomorrow. New York: Meredith, 1963.

Betz, Betty. *The Betty Betz Teen-Age Cookbook*. New York: Holt, 1953.

Birkby, Evelyn. *Neighboring on the Air: Cooking with the KMA Radio Homemakers*. Iowa City: U of Iowa P, 1991.

Birmingham, Frederic A. *The Complete Cook Book for Men*. New York: Harper, 1961.

Blake, Mary. *Fun to Cook Book*. Los Angeles: Carnation, 1955.

Blake, Richard. "Pop's in the Kitchen!" *Parents' Magazine* June 1947: 51+.

"Blender Magic." *Good Housekeeping* Sept. 1951: 113–14.

Boileau, Helen Houston. "Casserole Cover-alls." *American Home* Sept. 1956: 82.

Bonneville, Jane Burbank. "Our Children Can Manage Meals." *Parents' Magazine* Sept. 1996: 48–49.

Borrowe, Constance D. "A Mexican Dinner." *Good Housekeeping* Feb. 1910: 271.

Bossé, Sara. "Cooking and Serving a Chinese Dinner in America." *Harper's Bazaar* Jan. 1913: 27+.

———. "Giving a Chinese Luncheon Party." *Harper's Bazaar* Mar. 1913: 135+.

Botsford, Harry. "Are Men Better Cooks?" *Rotarian* Mar. 1954: 30–32.

———. *Elsie's Cook Book: Tested Recipes of Every Variety by Elsie the Cow*. New York: Bond Wheelwright, 1952.

———. "Just a Man With a Frying Pan." *Woman's Home Companion* Nov. 1941: 82–83.

———. *What's Cookin' Men? A Handy Cook Book for Men Who Enjoy Outdoor Cooking.* Portland: A. T. Spring and F. L. Tower Companies, 1957.

Bourdieu, Pierre. *Distinction: A Social Critique of the Judgement of Taste.* Trans. Richard Nice. Cambridge: Harvard UP, 1984.

Bower, Anne L., ed. *Recipes for Reading: Community Cookbooks, Stories, Histories.* Amherst: U of Massachusetts P, 1997.

Bowers, David, and Sharon Bowers. *Bake It Like a Man: A Real Man's Cookbook.* New York: Morrow, 1999.

Bradley, Alice. "Do You Cook Electrically?" *Woman's Home Companion* Feb. 1921: 39+.

———. *Electric Refrigerator Menus and Recipes: Prepared Especially for General Electric Refrigerator.* 5th ed. Cleveland: General Electric, 1929.

———. "Five O'Clock Tea." *Woman's Home Companion* Jan. 1920: 32+.

———. "For a Club Hostess." *Woman's Home Companion* Feb. 1923: 41+.

———. "For Your Bridge Party." *Woman's Home Companion* Nov. 1923: 104–5.

———. "Italian Dinner Party." *Woman's Home Companion* May 1926: 167–68.

———. "Mah Jung Refreshments." *Woman's Home Companion* Jan. 1924: 89–90.

———. "Push-Button Cookery." *Woman's Home Companion* Feb. 1924: 86–88.

———. *The Wartime Cook Book.* Cleveland: World, 1943.

———. "When the Children Cook." *Woman's Home Companion* Aug. 1926: 98+.

———. "When the Children Get Supper." *Woman's Home Companion* Apr. 1923: 100+.

Brady, Florence. "A Taste of Old Italy." *American Cookery* June–July 1932: 53–54.

Brandom, Loie E. "Dainty Accessories in Which to Serve Ice Cream." *American Cookery* Apr. 1930: 683–85.

Breines, Wini. *Young, White, and Miserable: Growing Up Female in the Fifties.* Boston: Beacon P, 1992.

Brenner, Leslie. *American Appetite: The Coming of Age of a Cuisine.* New York: Avon/Bard, 1999.

Brewer, Lucile. "'Eats' for the Sweet Girl Graduate." *Delineator* June 1935: 50+.

Bria, Rosemarie Dorothy. "How Jell-O Molds Society and Society Molds Jell-O: A Case Study of an American Food Industry Creation." Dissertation. Columbia University Teachers College, 1991.

Britt, Lucille. "Husband, Stay Away from My (Kitchen) Door!" *American Mercury* Dec. 1958: 88–91.

Brobeck, Florence. "Casseroles by the Lady-of-the-House." *House and Garden* Feb. 1952: 60+.

———. *The New Cook It in a Casserole.* New York: Barrows, 1955.

Brody, Meredith. "Refriger-Dating: Putting Guy Food in the Fridge." *Mademoiselle* June 1990: 74.

Brown, Cora. *Most for Your Money Cookbook*. New York: Modern Age Books, 1938.

Brown, Helen Evans, and Philip S. Brown. *The Boys' Cook Book*. Garden City: Doubleday, 1959.

Brown, Linda Keller, and Kay Mussell, eds. *Ethnic and Regional Foodways in the United States: The Performance of Group Identity*. Knoxville: U of Tennessee P, 1984.

Brown, Will C. "Men, Meet the Kitchen! Women, Please Stay Out!" *American Home* May 1933: 288+.

Brumberg, Joan Jacobs. *Fasting Girls: The Emergence of Anorexia Nervosa as a Modern Disease*. Cambridge: Harvard UP, 1988.

Brunner, Lousene Rousseau. *Casserole Magic*. New York: Harper, 1953.

Buckler, Helen. "Shall Married Women Be Fired?" *Scribner's Magazine* Mar. 1932: 166–68.

Bulger, Bozeman. "What to Cook When the Wife Is Away." *Ladies' Home Journal* July 1921: 75.

California Limas. Advertisement. *Good Housekeeping* Dec. 1931: 212.

Callahan, Genevieve. "Casserole Dishes Men Like." *Good Housekeeping* Feb. 1950: 140+.

Camp, Charles. *American Foodways: What, When, Why and How We Eat in America*. Little Rock: August House, 1989.

Campbell, D'Ann. *Women at War with America: Private Lives in a Patriotic Era*. Cambridge: Harvard UP, 1984.

Campfire Marshmallows. Advertisement. *Good Housekeeping* Sept. 1920: 177.

Campfire White Marshmallows. Advertisement. *American Cookery* Mar. 1922: 622.

Campion, Katherine. "The Return of the High Tea." *Good Housekeeping* June 1921: 76+.

"Canned Food Picture Book." *Woman's Home Companion* May 1954: 105–17.

"Caring for the Summer Bachelor." *Sunset* June 1957: 154+.

Cassady, Constance. *Kitchen Magic*. New York: Farrar and Rinehart, 1932.

"Casserole Combinations." *Good Housekeeping* Apr. 1951: 298–99.

"Casseroles, Hot and Hearty." *Woman's Home Companion* Dec. 1953: 117+.

"Casseroles with a Foreign Accent." *Sunset* June 1954: 162.

Cecil, G. "Chinese Dainties." *Catholic World* May 1927: 176–78.

Celehar, Jane H. *Kitchens and Gadgets 1920 to 1950*. Des Moines: Wallace-Homestead, 1982.

Chafe, William H. *The Paradox of Change: American Women in the Twentieth Century*. New York: Oxford UP, 1991.

Chan, Shiu Wong. *The Chinese Cook Book: Containing More Than One Hundred Recipes for Everyday Food Prepared in the Wholesome Chinese Way, and Many Recipes of*

Unique Dishes Peculiar to the Chinese, Including Chinese Pastry, "Stove Parties," and Chinese Candies. New York: Stokes, 1917.

Channing, Andrea. "Stretch the Budget by Using Onions." *American Home* Sept. 1936: 55–56.

Chantler, Ethel Wan-Ressel. "Getting the Most Out of Your Electric Table Devices." *Ladies' Home Journal* May 1926: 157+.

Chapman, Jessamine. "Afternoon Tea." *Good Housekeeping* Nov. 1915: 688–89.

Charles, Nickie, and Marion Kerr. *Women, Food and Families.* Manchester: Manchester UP, 1988.

Chef Boy-ar-dee. Advertisement. *Good Housekeeping* Oct. 1943: 174.

Chernin, Kim. *The Obsession: Reflections on the Tyranny of Slenderness.* New York: Harper and Row, 1981.

"Children Can Cook." *Parents' Magazine* Jan. 1954: 56–59.

Childs, Alberta B. "Some Dietary Studies of Poles, Mexicans, Italians, and Negroes." *Child Health Bulletin* 9 (1933): 84–91.

Clark, Francis E. *Our Italian Fellow Citizens: In Their Old Homes and Their New.* Boston: Small, Maynard, 1919.

Clark, Garel. *The Cook-a-Meal Cook Book.* New York: Scott, 1953.

Claudy, C. H. "Organizing the Wayside Tea House." *Country Life* June 1916: 54–55.

Clauss, Florence R. "To Get the Most from the Refrigerator." *Electrical Merchandising* Aug. 1929: 82+.

Cleveland Electrical League. *Electrical Homemaking with 101 Recipes.* Cleveland: Electrical League, 1928.

Coe, Sarah Leyburn. "The Temporary Tea Room." *Good Housekeeping* June 1911: 698–99.

Coffin, Caroline Cook. "Mexican Cookery." *Ladies' Home Journal* Oct. 1920: 111–12.

Connell, R. W. *Masculinities.* Berkeley: U of California P, 1995.

"Convenience by Wire." *Sunset* June 1923: 84+.

Cook, Edith V. *The Married Woman and Her Job.* Washington, D.C.: National League of Women Voters, 1936.

"Cooking at the Table." *Sunset* Feb. 1924: 70–74.

"Cooking with a Blender." *House and Garden* May 1958: 102+.

"Cook Your Way into His Heart." *McCall's* Jan. 1960: 74+.

"Cook Your Way into a Man's Heart." *Look* 19 Mar. 1957: 70–71.

Cordner, Ethel W. "Our Best Cook Makes You a Summer Casserole." *McCall's* Aug. 1953: 58–59.

Cornforth, George E. *Better Meals for Less.* Washington, D.C.: Review and Herald Publishing Association, 1930.

Counihan, Carole M. *The Anthropology of Food and Body: Gender, Meaning, and Power*. New York: Routledge, 1999.

Counihan, Carole, and Penny Van Esterik, eds. *Food and Culture: A Reader*. New York: Routledge, 1997.

Cousins, Margaret. "Home Is the Place. . . ." *Good Housekeeping* Oct. 1941: 115.

Cowan, Ruth Schwartz. *More Work for Mother: The Ironies of Household Technology from the Open Hearth to the Microwave*. New York: Basic Books, 1983.

Craig, Nancy. "Introduction to the Womanly Arts." *House Beautiful* Dec. 1956: 166+.

Crocker, Betty. *Betty Crocker's Dinner for Two Cook Book*. New York: Golden P, 1958.

———. *Betty Crocker's New Boys and Girls Cook Book*. New York: Golden P, 1965.

———. *Betty Crocker's Picture Cook Book*. New York: McGraw-Hill, 1950.

———. *Cook Book for Boys and Girls*. New York: General Mills, 1957.

———. *Good and Easy Cook Book*. New York: Simon and Schuster, 1954.

Crosby, Mabel Jewett. "Refrigeration Cookery by Electricity." *Ladies' Home Journal* June 1927: 129+.

Crosley Corporation. Advertisement. *Good Housekeeping* Dec. 1944: 97.

Crowell, Elsinore R. "Peppers and Garlic." *Good Housekeeping* Sept. 1918: 63+.

"Cub Chefs." *Woman's Home Companion* July 1949: 120–22.

Culinary Arts Institute. *The Casserole Cookbook*. Chicago: Culinary Arts Institute, 1956.

Cummings, Richard Osborn. *The American and His Food: A History of Food Habits in the United States*. Chicago: U of Chicago P, 1940.

Cuniberti, Julia Lovejoy. *Practical Italian Recipes for American Kitchens*. Janesville, Wis.: Gazette Printing, 1918.

Curtin, Deane W., and Lisa M. Heldke, eds. *Cooking, Eating, Thinking: Transformative Philosophies of Food*. Bloomington: Indiana UP, 1992.

Cutting, E. B. "Roadside Tea Rooms: A New Industry." *Harper's Bazar* May 1909: 494–97.

Dahlgren, Rachel F. "Some Beehive Dainties." *Ladies' Home Journal* Oct. 1925: 124.

Dainty Desserts Made with Campfire, the Original Food Marshmallows. Milwaukee: Campfire Co., [1920s?].

Dainty Dishes for Slender Incomes. New York: New Amsterdam Book Co., 1902.

Daly, Maureen. *The Perfect Hostess: Complete Etiquette and Entertainment for the Home*. New York: Dodd, Mead, 1950.

Davis, Bob. "Come into the Kitchen, Boys." *Delineator* July 1936: 20–21.

De Both, Jessie. *It's Easy to Be a Good Cook*. Garden City: Doubleday, 1951.

Delineator Home Institute. *The Victory Binding of the American Woman's Cook Book.* Chicago: Consolidated Book Publishers, 1942.

Dempsey, Jack. "He-Men Wear Aprons." *American Magazine* July 1935: 16+.

Deute, Arthur H. *200 Dishes for Men to Cook.* New York: Barrows, 1944.

DeVault, Marjorie L. *Feeding the Family: The Social Organization of Caring as Gendered Work.* Chicago: U of Chicago P, 1991.

"Dishes for Husbands." *Delineator* Mar. 1917: 35.

Dishes Men Like. New York: Lea and Perrins, 1952.

"Dishes to Tempt the Hard-to-Please Husband." *Delineator* May 1928: 49.

Dorfman, Cindy J. "The Garden of Eating: The Carnal Kitchen in Contemporary American Culture." *Feminist Issues* 12 (1992): 21–38.

Douglas, Mary. "Deciphering a Meal." *Daedalus* 101 (1972): 61–81.

Dudley, Herminie, and Sarah Leyburn Coe. "Taverns and Tea Rooms as a Business for Women." *Good Housekeeping* June 1911: 689–97.

Dunbar, Ruth. "Push-Button Mary." *Country Gentleman* 26 May 1923: 10+.

Dunham, Mary. "Men Can't Cook." *Collier's* 13 Mar. 1939: 17+.

Dunham, Peter. "To Lessen Kitchen Labor." *House and Garden* Sept. 1922: 72+.

DuSablon, Mary Anna. *America's Collectible Cookbooks: The History, the Politics, the Recipes.* Athens: Ohio UP, 1994.

"Easygoing Casseroles." *Better Homes and Gardens* Sept. 1951: 86+.

Edgewater Catholic Woman's Club. *Table Dainties for Dainty Matrons.* Chicago: n.p., 1923.

Egan, Maurice Francis. "Sex in Cookery: Why Men Are Better Cooks Than Women." *Century* June 1924: 196–203.

Eisler, Benita. *Private Lives: Men and Women of the Fifties.* New York: Franklin Watts, 1986.

Electrical Merchandising Feb. 1935: cover.

"Electrical Servants." *Edison Monthly* Jan. 1923: 11–12.

Electric Cooking at Its Best: Instructions and Recipes for Electromaster Ranges. Detroit: Electromaster, 1939.

"Electricity in the Home." *Electrical Merchandising* Aug. 1921: 68–70.

Electric Refrigeration Bureau. Advertisement. *Good Housekeeping* Oct. 1931: 187.

Ellsworth, Mary Grosvenor. "Pietro Calls it Pasta." *House Beautiful* Feb. 1939: 32+.

"Encounter." *Newsweek* 3 Aug. 1959: 15–19.

"Entertaining in the Spirit of Olden Times." *Good Housekeeping* Feb. 1927: 72+.

Esquire's Handbook for Hosts. New York: Grosset and Dunlap, 1949.

Estate Electric Ranges. Advertisement. *Good Housekeeping* Apr. 1920: 246.

Evans, Jean Caroline. "As the Chinese Cook." *Good Housekeeping* Mar. 1923: 67.

Evans, Michele. *Fearless Cooking for Men.* New York: Mason/Charter, 1977.

Fales, Winnifred, and Mary Northend. "At the Sign of the Tea-Room." *Good House-keeping* July 1917: 56+.

"Fancy Touches with 'Instant' Foods." *Sunset* Mar. 1953: 107.

Farb, Peter, and George Armelagos. *Consuming Passions: The Anthropology of Eating.* Boston: Houghton Mifflin, 1980.

Farrar, Addie. "Oriental Recipes That Are Worth the Making." *American Cookery* Feb. 1919: 518–20.

Faulkner, Wendy, and Erik Arnold. *Smothered by Invention: Technology in Women's Lives.* London: Pluto, 1985.

Federal Writers' Project. *The Italians of New York.* New York: Random House, 1938.

Felder, Deborah G. *A Century of Women: The Most Influential Events in Twentieth-Century Women's History.* Secaucus: Carol Publishing, 1999.

Fenderson, Mark. "Delectable Dinners." *Woman's Home Companion* Apr. 1918: 42.

Fiddes, Nick. *Meat: A Natural Symbol.* London: Routledge, 1991.

Filippini, Alexander. *The International Cook Book: Over 3,300 Recipes Gathered from All Over the World, Including Many Never Before Published in English.* 1906. Garden City: Doubleday, 1911.

Fine, Gary Alan. *Kitchens: The Culture of Restaurant Work.* Berkeley: U of California P, 1996.

Finkelstein, Joanne. *Dining Out: A Sociology of Modern Manners.* New York: New York UP, 1989.

Fisher, Katharine. "Dining in Italy at Your Own Table." *Good Housekeeping* Oct. 1931: 84+.

———. "If You Have an Electric Range, Let the Institute Help You Use It to Advantage." *Good Housekeeping* Jan. 1927: 72+.

———. "It's Harder to Plan Meals These Times." *Good Housekeeping* Nov. 1943: 92–93.

———. "Main Dishes for These Times." *Good Housekeeping* Sept. 1943: 89–91.

———. "March Meals That Fortify the Home Front." *Good Housekeeping* Mar. 1942: 104+.

———. "Men at Home at the Range." *Good Housekeeping* Apr. 1936: 86+.

———. "What You Should Know about the New Point System of Rationing." *Good Housekeeping* Feb. 1943: 156–57.

Fisher, Katharine A., and Demetria M. Taylor. "What Should We Spend for Food?" *Good Housekeeping* Jan. 1929: 80–81.

Fisher, M. F. K. *The Gastronomical Me*. San Francisco: North Point, 1988.

Fitch, Natalie K., and Mary Agnes Davis. *Meat Saving Recipes*. New York: Teachers College, 1943.

Fitzhugh, Josie Millsaps. *The International Cook Book*. Memphis: American Printing Co., 1941.

Fleck, Henrietta Christina. *A First Cook Book for Boys and Girls*. New York: Alumni Offset, 1953.

Fletcher, Helen Jill. *The See and Do Book of Cooking*. New York: Stuttman, 1959.

"The Flexible Casserole." *Sunset* Oct. 1954: 127.

Fontaine, Robert. "Lady, You Can Cook, But . . . You Just Haven't Enough Imagination." *Better Homes and Gardens* Feb. 1946: 8.

"Food for Husbands." *Delineator* Oct. 1935: 53.

Fordyce, Eleanor T. "Cookbooks of the 1800s." In *Dining in America 1850–1900*, ed. Kathryn Grover, 85–113. Amherst: U of Massachusetts P, 1987.

Foreign Cookery. St. Louis: International Institute, 1932.

Foreman, Joel, ed. *The Other Fifties: Interrogating Midcentury American Icons*. Urbana: U of Illinois P, 1997.

Formanek-Brunell, Miriam. *Made to Play House: Dolls and the Commercialization of American Girlhood, 1830–1930*. New Haven: Yale UP, 1993.

"For Your Casserole." *House and Garden* May 1951: 202–3.

Foster, Olive Hyde. *Housekeeping, Cookery and Sewing for Little Girls*. New York: Duffield, 1925.

"Four Family Dinners Featuring Canned Food." *Parents' Magazine* Oct. 1952: 66–67.

Frederick, J. George. *Cooking as Men Like It*. New York: Business Bourse, 1930.

Freeman, Mae Blacker. *Fun with Cooking*. New York: Random House, 1947.

French, Frances. "Make These Favorites with a Blender." *Better Homes and Gardens* Oct. 1953: 90+.

Friedan, Betty. *The Feminine Mystique*. New York: Norton, 1963.

Frigidaire. Advertisement. *Good Housekeeping* July 1941: 62.

Frigidaire Corporation. Advertisement. *Good Housekeeping* June 1927: 161.

Frigidaire Electric Refrigeration. Advertisement. *Good Housekeeping* Aug. 1926: 127.

Fryer, Jane Eayre. *Easy Steps in Cooking for Big and Little Girls; or Mary Frances among the Kitchen People*. Philadelphia: Winston, 1912.

Furness, Betty, and Julia Kiene. *The Betty Furness Westinghouse Cook Book*. New York: Simon and Schuster, 1954.

Gabaccia, Donna R. *We Are What We Eat: Ethnic Food and the Making of Americans*. Cambridge: Harvard UP, 1998.

Gagos, Bertha. "Children Love to Cook." *Parents' Magazine* Jan. 1949: 43+.

Gaige, Crosby. *Food at the Fair: A Gastronomic Tour of the World*. New York: New York World's Fair Exposition Publications, 1939.

"Gains Foreseen in Frozen Foods." *New York Times* 24 Feb. 1954: L40.

Garber, Marjorie. "Jell-O." In *Secret Agents: The Rosenberg Case, McCarthyism, and Fifties America*, ed. Marjorie Garber and Rebecca L. Walkowitz, 11–22. New York: Routledge, 1995.

Gayer Mealtimes with the New Jell-O. Battle Creek: General Foods, 1934.

General Foods Corporation. *Joys of Jell-O® Gelatin*. White Plains: General Foods, 1962.

Gentile, Maria, comp. *The Italian Cook Book*. New York: Italian Book Co., 1919.

Gibson Refrigerator Company. Advertisement. *Good Housekeeping* Feb. 1944: 183.

Giedion, Siegfried. *Mechanisation Takes Command*. New York: Oxford UP, 1948.

Gillard, Barbara. *Pot Luck: Casserole Entertaining*. San Francisco: Letter Shop, 1952.

Gillespie, Myrtle Cook. "Let Them Cook!" *Parents' Magazine* Mar. 1948: 52+.

Gillett, Lucy H. "Factors Influencing Nutrition Work among Italians." *Journal of Home Economics* 14 (Jan. 1922): 14–19.

Girl Scouts of the United States of America. *Kettles and Campfires: The Girl Scout Camp and Trail Cook Book*. New York: Girl Scouts, 1928.

Gitelson, Joshua. "Populox: The Suburban Cuisine of the 1950s." *Journal of American Culture* 15.3 (1992): 73–78.

Gluck, Sherna Berger. *Rosie the Riveter Revisited: Women, the War, and Social Change*. Boston: Twayne, 1987.

Goldman, Anne. "'I Yam What I Yam': Cooking, Culture, and Colonialism." In *De/Colonizing the Subject: The Politics of Gender in Women's Autobiography*, ed. Sidonie Smith and Julia Watson, 169–95. Minneapolis: U of Minnesota P, 1992.

Good Housekeeping. *Around the World Cook Book*. Chicago: Consolidated Book Publishers, 1936.

Good Housekeeping's Casserole Cook Book. Chicago: Hearst, 1958.

Goody, Jack. *Cooking, Cuisine and Class: A Study in Comparative Sociology*. Cambridge: Cambridge UP, 1982.

Gordon, Brick. *The Groom Boils and Stews: A Man's Cook Book for Men*. San Antonio: Naylor, 1947.

Gordon, Helen Agin. "Never Ask Your Husband to Help, *Unless*. . . ." *Better Homes and Gardens* Feb. 1933: 24+.

Gossett, Margaret, and Mary Elting. *Now We're Cookin': The Book for Teen-Age Chefs*. 1948. Irvington-on-Hudson: Harvey House, 1968.

Grandma's Cook Book: Designed to Meet Present Day Conditions. South Bend: American Trade Council, 1932.

The Greater Jell-O Recipe Book. Battle Creek: General Foods, 1931.

Gregg, Marion, ed. *The American Women's Voluntary Services Cook Book: A Book for Wartime Living.* San Francisco: Recorder-Sunset P, 1942.

Gregory, Chester W. *Women in Defense Work during World War II: An Analysis of the Labor Problem and Women's Rights.* New York: Exposition P, 1974.

Grinde, Frederick. "Electricity—the Reliable Servant." *Illustrated World* Sept. 1921: 64–66.

Grover, Kathryn, ed. *Dining in America, 1850–1900.* Amherst: U of Massachusetts P, 1987.

Guthrie, Jean. "Mere Men . . . But Can They Cook!" *Better Homes and Gardens* June 1937: 36+.

Haber, Barbara. "Follow the Food." *Through the Kitchen Window: Women Explore the Intimate Meanings of Food and Cooking,* ed. Arlene Voski Avakian, 65–74. Boston: Beacon, 1997.

———. "Food, Sex, and Gender." In *Food, Cookery and Culture,* ed. Leslie Howsam, 27–43. Windsor: Humanities Research Group, U of Windsor, 1998.

Hagemeyer, Virginia. "Casserole Favorites." *Good Housekeeping* May 1951: 178.

Halle, Rita S. "Do You Need Your Job?" *Good Housekeeping* Sept. 1932: 24+.

Hambridge, Gove. "Make the Diet Fit the Pocketbook." *Ladies' Home Journal* May 1934: 44+.

Harben, Philip. *The Teen-Age Cook.* New York: Arco, 1957.

Hardyment, Christina. *From Mangle to Microwave: The Mechanization of Household Work.* Cambridge: Polity P, 1988.

Hargrove, Mrs. Raymond. "He's an Outdoor Chef." *Parents' Magazine* Aug. 1956: 63+.

Harris, Florence LaGanke. *Patty Pans: A Cook Book for Beginners.* 1929. Boston: Little, Brown, 1941.

———. *Victory Vitamin Cook Book for Wartime Meals.* New York: Penn Publishing, 1943.

Hartmann, Susan M. *The Home Front and Beyond: American Women in the 1940s.* Boston: Twayne, 1982.

Harvey, Brett. *The Fifties: A Women's Oral History.* New York: HarperCollins, 1993.

Hatch, Ted. "For the Male Cook in All His Glory!" *American Home* June 1940: 32+.

Hausman, A. F. A. "Electric Equipment in the Home." *American Cookery* Dec. 1932: 340–41.

Hayes, Jim. *How to Cook a Deer—and Other Critters: A Game Cookbook for Men.* Berryville: Country Publishers, 1991.

Head, Ethel McCall. "Do You Cook for Men?" *American Home* Feb. 1941: 88–90.

"Hearty Casseroles." *Better Homes and Gardens* Apr. 1954: 103–6.

Hedgecock, Elizabeth Stuart. *The Successful Hostess*. Minneapolis: Burgess, 1953.

Heffington, Virginia. "Quick and Good with a Canned Food Start." *Better Homes and Gardens* Sept. 1958: 72+.

Heide, Robert, and John Gilman. *Home Front America: Popular Culture of the World War II Era*. San Francisco: Chronicle Books, 1995.

Heineman, Esther. "Meat Substitutes." *Hygeia* Apr. 1944: 284+.

Heininger, Mary Lynn Stevens, Karin Calvert, Barbara Finkelstein, Kathy Vandell, Anne Scott MacLeod, and Harvey Green. *A Century of Childhood, 1820–1920*. Rochester: Strong Museum, 1984.

Hervey, Sara. "Champion Casseroles." *Country Gentleman* Sept. 1953: 128–30.

Hess, John L., and Karen Hess. *The Taste of America*. 1977. Columbia: U of South Carolina P, 1989.

Hester, Harriet H. *300 Sugar Saving Recipes*. New York: Barrows, 1942.

Hewes, Amy. "Electrical Appliances in the Home." *Social Forces* 2 (Dec. 1930): 235–42.

Heywood, Margaret Weimer, comp. *The International Cook Book*. Boston: Humphries, 1939.

Hill, Janet McKenzie. *Salads, Sandwiches and Chafing-Dish Dainties*. 1899. Boston: Little, Brown, 1922.

Hill, Janet M., and Mary D. Chambers. "Seasonable and Tested Recipes." *American Cookery* Mar. 1930: 608–17.

Hill, Marie P., and Frances H. Gaines, eds. *Fun in the Kitchen: A Record Cook Book of Easy Recipes for Little Girls*. Chicago: Reilly and Lee, 1927.

Hodgson, Madge. "Dainty Fillings for Small Tarts." *Good Housekeeping* Mar. 1912: 388.

Hoffmann, Peggy. *Miss B.'s First Cookbook: Twenty Family-Sized Recipes for the Youngest Cook*. Indianapolis: Bobbs-Merrill, 1950.

"Holiday Casseroles." *Better Homes and Gardens* Dec. 1956: 95–98.

Honey, Maureen. *Creating Rosie the Riveter: Class, Gender, and Propaganda during World War II*. Amherst: U of Massachusetts P, 1984.

Hooker, Richard J. *Food and Drink in America: A History*. Indianapolis: Bobbs-Merrill, 1981.

Hooper, Jessie. "According to Taste." *American Home* Sept. 1943: 73–75.

Hoover, Julia. "Easy Ways to Save Sugar." *Good Housekeeping* Apr. 1942: 98+.

Hopkins, Frank L. "Should Wives Work?" *American Mercury* Dec. 1936: 409–16.

Hopkins, Una Nixson. "What Three Women Did with Their Home." *Ladies' Home Journal* Mar. 1913: 29.

Hotpoint Appliances. Advertisement. *Good Housekeeping* June 1927: 191.

Hotpoint Electric Range. Advertisement. *Good Housekeeping* July 1927: 154.

Hotpoint Servants. Advertisement. *Good Housekeeping* Sept. 1927: 142.

House and Garden's Cook Book. New York: Bonanza Books, 1958.

Howsam, Leslie, ed. *Food, Cookery and Culture.* Windsor: Humanities Research Group, U of Windsor, 1998.

"How to 'Cook' with Your Blender." *Better Homes and Gardens* May 1956: 293–94.

Hughes Electric Range. Advertisement. *Good Housekeeping* May 1920: 117.

Humphrey, Theodore C., and Lin T. Humphrey, eds. *"We Gather Together": Food and Festival in American Life.* Ann Arbor: UMI Research P, 1988.

Humphreys, Evelyn. "Whose Kitchen Is It Anyway?" *House Beautiful* Apr. 1952: 189–91.

Hunt, Frazier. "Give Me a Man Cook Every Time!" *Better Homes and Gardens* Feb. 1935: 24+.

Hussong, Mary E. "Dressing Up Familiar Foods." *American Home* Apr. 1935: 357+.

Inness, Sherrie A. *Intimate Communities: Representation and Social Transformation in Women's College Fiction, 1895–1910.* Bowling Green: Bowling Green State U Popular P, 1995.

———. ed. *Kitchen Culture: Women, Gender, and Cooking.* Philadelphia: U of Pennsylvania P, 2000.

———. *Tough Girls: Women Warriors and Wonder Women in Popular Culture.* Philadelphia: U of Pennsylvania P, 1999.

"In This Kitchen, Cooking Is Child's Play." *House and Garden* Feb. 1955: 58–59.

Ireland, Lynne. "The Compiled Cookbook as Foodways Autobiography." *Western Folklore* 40 (1981): 107–14.

Jacobs, Margaret Moore. "Let 'Em Can and Cook." *American Home* July 1937: 47+.

Jacques, Marie. "Straight from Italy." *Woman's Home Companion* Apr. 1924: 64+.

Jell-O. Advertisement. *Good Housekeeping* Sept. 1927: 150.

Jell-O and the Kewpies. Le Roy: Genesee Pure Food Co., 1915.

Jervey, Phyllis Pulliam. "Gay Garden-Parties and Porch-Teas." *Pictorial Review* Aug. 1928: 29.

———. "Novel Bridge Teas and Suppers." *Pictorial Review* June 1928: 32.

Jessup, Henrietta. "Out of the Casserole." *Good Housekeeping* Feb. 1924: 68+.

Johnson, Constance. *When Mother Lets Us Cook.* New York: Moffat, 1908.

Johnston, Myrna. "Let's Make It a Casserole Super." *Better Homes and Gardens* Feb. 1954: 72+.

"Join Up—But Don't Let Your Family Down." Advertisement. *Good Housekeeping* June 1942: 124.

Jones, Evan. *American Food: The Gastronomic Story.* 2nd ed. New York: Random House, 1981.

Jones, Gladys Beckett, and Jenoise Brown Short. "A Mother-Daughter Tea-House." *Pictorial Review* June 1924: 30.

———. "New Electrical Apparatus." *House Beautiful* Sept. 1924: 248+.

Joyner, Julia Bliss. "How to Save Money on Meat." *Pictorial Review* Nov. 1935: 56–57.

Judson, Clara Ingram. *Child Life Cookbook.* New York: Rand McNally, 1926.

———. *Cooking without Mother's Help: A Story Cook Book for Beginners.* New York: Nourse, 1920.

Judson, Helena, ed. *Light Entertaining: A Book of Dainty Recipes for Special Occasions.* New York: Butterick, 1910.

———. "Popular Tea-Room Novelties." *Delineator* May 1916: 33.

———. "Try These Tea-Room Touches." *Pictorial Review* Mar. 1926: 49.

Kalcik, Susan. "Ethnic Foodways in America: Symbol and the Performance of Identity." In *Ethnic and Regional Foodways in the United States: The Performance of Group Identity*, ed. Linda Keller Brown and Kay Mussell, 37–65. Knoxville: U of Tennessee P, 1984.

Kaledin, Eugenia. *Mothers and More: American Women in the 1950s.* Boston: Twayne, 1984.

Katzman, David M. *Seven Days a Week: Women and Domestic Service in Industrializing America.* New York: Oxford UP, 1978.

Keating, Lawrence A. *Men in Aprons: "If He Could Only Cook."* New York: Mill, 1944.

Kelvinator. Advertisement. *Good Housekeeping* Nov. 1944: 111.

Kendall, Helen W. "How to Eat Out of a Refrigerator." *Good Housekeeping* June 1940: 146–47.

Kent, Louise Andrews. "Mrs. Appleyard Rescues a Girl Who Has Run Out of Points." *House Beautiful* Aug. 1943: 28+.

Kerr, Sophie. "Good Eating in Wartime." *Woman's Home Companion* July 1942: 21+.

"Kid Kapers." *American Magazine* Mar. 1954: 57.

Kiene, Julia. *The Step-by-Step Cook Book for Girls and Boys.* New York: Simon and Schuster, 1956.

Kilbourn, Donald. *Pots and Pants: Man's Answer to Women's Lib: A Cook Book for Men.* London: Luscombe, 1974.

Kimmel, Michael. *Manhood in America: A Cultural History.* New York: Free P, 1996.

King, Caroline B. "Hostess Dishes from the Tea Rooms." *Ladies' Home Journal* Oct. 1923: 129+.

———. "The Tasty Timbale." *Ladies' Home Journal* Mar. 1920: 185.

Kirk, Dorothy. "The Obliging Casserole." *Woman's Home Companion* Oct. 1950: 94+.

———. "Patterns for Points." *Woman's Home Companion* Oct. 1943: 92–93.

Kirk, Dorothy, and Helen S. Cahill. "No Time for Failures." *Woman's Home Companion* Mar. 1943: 1–9.

———. "Pocketbook Meals." *Woman's Home Companion* Oct. 1936: 117–18.

Kirkland, E. S. [Elizabeth Stansbury]. *Six Little Cooks, or, Aunt Jane's Cooking Class.* Chicago: Jansen, 1877.

KitchenAid. Advertisement. *American Cookery* Oct. 1929: 239.

Knopf, Mildred O. *The Perfect Hostess Cook Book.* New York: Knopf, 1950.

Knox® On-Camera Recipes: A Completely New Guide to Gel-Cookery. Johnstown: Knox Gelatine, 1960.

Koch, Harriet Acheson. "Food with a Foreign Accent." *Hygeia* Mar. 1938: 234–37.

Kriz, Caroline. *Cooking for Men Only.* San Francisco: 101 Productions, 1984.

Lach, Alma S. *A Child's First Cook Book.* New York: Hart, 1950.

———. *Let's Cook.* Chicago: Child Training Assn., 1956.

La Choy Chow Mein. Advertisement. *Good Housekeeping* Nov. 1936: 198.

La Follette, Cecile T. *A Study of the Problems of 652 Gainfully Employed Married Women Homemakers.* New York: Teachers College, 1934.

Laimbeer, Nathalie Schenck. "Teas You Will Like to Give." *Ladies' Home Journal* Oct. 1920: 38+.

Lambert, Judith. "I Quit My Job." *Forum* July 1937: 9–15.

Lamborn, Merle. "An Oriental Dinner to Please the Most Fastidious Occidental Taste." *American Home* Apr. 1940: 49+.

Lamoreaux, Gwenivere. "Housekeeping: A Vocation." *American Home* Feb. 1939: 45+.

Lampman, Rosamund. "Frozen Dainties." *Harper's Bazar* Aug. 1910: 497.

Lane, Rose Wilder. "Woman's Place Is in the Home." *Ladies' Home Journal* Oct. 1936: 18+.

Lange, Fay. "Cooking Can Be Play." *American Home* Mar. 1955: 80.

Lange, Helen Dickinson. "Our Young Cooks." *American Cookery* Jan. 1942: 275+.

Lapin, Eva. *Mothers in Overalls.* New York: Workers Library Publishers, 1943.

LaPrade, Malcolm. *That Man in the Kitchen: How to Teach a Woman to Cook.* Boston: Houghton Mifflin, 1946.

LaRoche, Betty Gregory. "Mothers Share Tips on How to Bring Up a Good Cook." *Farm Journal* Jan. 1962: 56–57.

LeBron, Marion. "Invite Them into the Kitchen." *Parents' Magazine* Apr. 1944: 32+.

Leen, Jeff. "Pleasures of the Flesh." *Gentlemen's Quarterly* May 1995: 110.

Leff, Mark H. "The Politics of Sacrifice on the American Home Front in World War II." *Journal of American History* 77.4 (1991): 1296–318.

Lehr, Lewis C. *Cookbook for Men.* New York: Didier, 1949.

Leonardi, Susan J. "Recipes for Reading: Pasta Salad, Lobster à la Riseholme, and Key Lime Pie." *PMLA* 104 (1989): 340–47.

Let's Have Fun Cooking: The Children's Cook Book. Chicago: Moody, 1953.

Leung, Louise. "A Chinese Luncheon." *American Cookery* Oct. 1933: 154–56.

———. "Foreign Cookery: Chinese Recipes for American Tables." *Ladies' Home Journal* July 1931: 31.

Levenstein, Harvey A. "The American Response to Italian Food, 1880–1930." *Food and Foodways* 1.1 (1985): 1–23.

———. *Paradox of Plenty: A Social History of Eating in Modern America.* New York: Oxford UP, 1993.

———. *Revolution at the Table: The Transformation of the American Diet.* New York: Oxford UP, 1988.

The Life Picture Cook Book. New York: Time Incorporated, 1958.

"A Little Summer Cook Book for the Man with No Woman in the House." *Good Housekeeping* Aug. 1958: 94–100.

Loeb, Robert H., Jr. *Date Bait: The Younger Set's Picture Cookbook.* Chicago: Wilcox and Follett, 1952.

———. *Wolf in Chef's Clothing: The Picture Cook and Drink Book for Men.* Chicago: Wilcox and Follett, 1950.

Long, Lucy M. "Culinary Tourism: A Folkloristic Perspective on Eating and Otherness." *Southern Folklore* 55.3 (1998): 181–204.

Lovegren, Sylvia. *Fashionable Food: Seven Decades of Food Fads.* New York: Macmillan, 1995.

Lowell International Institute. *As the World Cooks: Recipes from Many Lands.* Lowell: Lowell International Institute, 1938.

Lupton, Deborah. *Food, the Body and the Self.* London: Sage, 1996.

Lupton, Ellen. *Mechanical Brides: Women and Machines from Home to Office.* New York: Princeton Architectural P, 1993.

Lyly, Mrs. Penrose. "Delicious Thrift." *Pictorial Review* Feb. 1933: 30.

Lynd, Robert S., and Helen Merrell Lynd. *Middletown in Transition: A Study in Cultural Conflicts.* New York: Harcourt Brace Jovanovich, 1937.

MacFadyen, [R.] Byron. "Give a Man Man's Food." *Good Housekeeping* Mar. 1941: 106+.

———. "Let's Have Spaghetti." *Good Housekeeping* Mar. 1935: 88+.

———. "Teach Your Boy to Cook." *Good Housekeeping* Aug. 1929: 100+.

Magic Chef. Advertisement. *Good Housekeeping* Oct. 1944: 234.

"Making a Cook Out of Butch." *House Beautiful* Oct. 1948: 225–26.

Malmberg, Carl. "Dad and Daughter Cook." *Parents' Magazine* Feb. 1941: 44+.

Maltby, Lucy Mary. *It's Fun to Cook.* Philadelphia: Winston, 1938.

Manning, Murray. "From Antipasto to Gorgonzola." *American Home* Feb. 1940: 47+.

Manning-Bowman Quality Ware. Advertisement. *Good Housekeeping* Oct. 1924: 245.

Manton, Catherine. *Fed Up: Women and Food in America.* London: Bergin and Garvey, 1999.

Mariani, John. *America Eats Out: An Illustrated History of Restaurants, Taverns, Coffee Shops, Speakeasies, and Other Establishments That Have Fed Us for 350 Years.* New York: Morrow, 1991.

———. *The Dictionary of American Food and Drink.* New York: Hearst Books, 1994.

Marling, Karal Ann. "Betty Crocker's Picture Cook Book: The Aesthetics of Food in the 1950s." In *As Seen on TV: The Visual Culture of Everyday Life in the 1950s,* 203–40. Cambridge: Harvard UP, 1994.

Marsh, Dorothy. "Don't Let Your Family Down." *Good Housekeeping* June 1942: 107+.

———. "Keep Tabs on Your Food Bills." *Good Housekeeping* Jan. 1936: 78+.

———. "More Food for the Same Money." *Good Housekeeping* Sept. 1940: 82+.

———. "Refrigerators Work Overtime in Summer." *Good Housekeeping* July 1940: 100–101.

———. "Tips Busy Women Have Given Us on Managing Their Meals." *Good Housekeeping* Dec. 1943: 85–87.

Marshall, Peggy. "Try This on Your Chopsticks." *Collier's* 4 Dec. 1937: 38–40.

Martensen, Mary. "Spaghetti Universally Popular." *Macaroni Journal* 15 Mar. 1933: 7.

Matthews, Glenna. *"Just a Housewife": The Rise and Fall of Domesticity in America.* New York: Oxford UP, 1987.

May, Elaine Tyler. *Homeward Bound: American Families in the Cold War Era.* New York: Basic Books, 1988.

May, Madeline. *The International Cook Book: A Selection of the Most Celebrated Foreign Recipes, Dedicated to Those Who Appreciate Good Things to Eat.* Boston: Josephs, 1933.

McCarthy, Josephine. *Josie McCarthy's Favorite TV Recipes.* Englewood Cliffs: Prentice-Hall, 1958.

McCray, Doris. "Short on Sugar? Try Syrups!" *Hygeia* June 1942: 436+.

McCully, Helen. "Short-Cut Foods Revolutionize American Cooking." *McCall's* Jan. 1955: 42–51.

McFee, Inez N. *Young People's Cook Book.* New York: Crowell, 1925.

McIntosh, Elaine N. *American Food Habits in Historical Perspective.* Westport: Praeger, 1995.

McKelvey, Thelma. *Women in War Production.* New York: Oxford UP, 1942.

McLaren, L. L., comp. *Pan-Pacific Cook Book: Savory Bits from the World's Fare.* San Francisco: Blair-Murdock, 1915.

McMahon, John R. "Making Housekeeping Automatic." *Ladies' Home Journal* Sept. 1920: 3+.

McNeil, Blanche, and Edna V. McNeil. *First Foods of America.* Los Angeles: Suttonhouse, 1936.

McNutt, Paul V. "Why You Must Take a War Job." *American Magazine* Dec. 1943: 24+.

McQuillan, Susan. "Macho Meals." *Family Circle* 14 May 1991: 141–44.

Meals Go Modern Electrically. New York: National Kitchen Modernizing Bureau, 1937.

Meats for Men: Eighteen Favorite Meat Dishes for Men. Long Island City: Tested Recipe Institute, 1954.

Meek, Lois Hayden. "The Problem of a Working Mother." *Woman's Home Companion* Sept. 1937: 17+.

Men Cooking. Menlo Park: Lane, 1963.

Mennell, Stephen, Anne Murcott, and Anneke H. van Otterloo. *The Sociology of Food: Eating, Diet and Culture.* London: Sage, 1992.

Metz, Harold W. *Is There Enough Manpower?* Washington, D.C.: Brookings Institution, 1942.

Metzelthin, Pearl V. *World Wide Cook Book: Menus and Recipes of Seventy-five Nations.* New York: Julian Messner, 1940.

Meyer, J. H. *A Man's Cook Book for Outdoors and Kitchen.* Coral Glades: Glade House, 1950.

Meyerowitz, Joanne, ed. *Not June Cleaver: Women and Gender in Postwar America, 1945–1960.* Philadelphia: Temple UP, 1994.

Midgley, Wilson. *Cookery for Men Only.* London: Chaterson, 1948.

"Midsummer Dainties." *Good Housekeeping* Aug. 1911: 267.

Miles, Betty. *The Cooking Book.* New York: Knopf, 1959.

Mills, Marjorie. *Cooking on a Ration: Food Is Still Fun.* New York: Houghton Mifflin, 1943.

Mintz, Sidney W. *Tasting Food, Tasting Freedom: Excursions into Eating, Culture, and the Past.* Boston: Beacon, 1996.

Mintz, Steven, and Susan Kellogg. *Domestic Revolutions: A Social History of American Family Life.* New York: Free P, 1988.

Mitchell, Lilliace M. "Children Enjoy It!" *American Home* July 1944: 66–67.

Moats, Leone B. "Meals for Men." *House and Garden* Feb. 1934: 33+.

Moore, Alice. *Chinese Recipes: Letters from Alice Moore to Ethel Moore Rook.* Garden City: Doubleday, 1923.

Moore, Carrie Pickett. "'Step-Inn'—A Successful Tea Room." *Woman's Home Companion* Nov. 1913: 26.

Moore, Shirley. "I Want to Cook." *American Home* Feb. 1954: 75–76.

"More Short Cuts to Dinner." *Good Housekeeping* Mar. 1954: 112.

Morphy, Marcelle, Countess, ed. *Recipes of All Nations*. New York: Wise, 1935.

Morris, Ruth Moore. "Hot Stuff." *Collier's* 1 Feb. 1936: 22+.

Morton, Alice D. *Cooking Is Fun*. New York: Hart, 1962.

Morton, Carol. "Glamour Dishes—Quick!" *Coronet* Aug. 1952: 16.

Mosse, George L. *The Image of Man: The Creation of Modern Masculinity*. New York: Oxford UP, 1996.

Mudge, Gertrude Gates. "Italian Dietary Adjustments." *Journal of Home Economics* 15 (Apr. 1923): 181–85.

Murcott, Anne, ed. *The Sociology of Food and Eating: Essays on the Sociological Significance of Food*. Aldershots, Hants, England: Gower Publishing, 1983.

———. "Women's Place: Cookbooks' Images of Technique and Technology in the British Kitchen." *Women's Studies International Forum* 6.2 (1983): 33–39.

Murdoch, Maud. *The Girls' Book of Cooking*. New York: Roy Publishers, 1961.

Murphy, Agnes. *American Hostess Library Book of Cooking*. New York: Educational Book Guild, 1955.

Murphy, Margot. *Wartime Meals*. New York: Greenberg, 1942.

My First Cookbook. Sugar Land, Tex.: Imperial Sugar, 1959.

Nash, Gerald D. *The Crucial Era: The Great Depression and World War II, 1929–1945*. 2nd ed. New York: St. Martin's, 1992.

Neff, Edwin. "Life Is Sweet, Anyway." *Science News Life* 11 Apr. 1942: 234–35.

Neil, Marion H. *Salads, Sandwiches and Chafing Dish Recipes*. Philadelphia: McKay, 1916.

Nejelski, Leo. "Come on in, Men—Cooking's Fine!" *Good Housekeeping* May 1939: 120+.

Newman, Lesléa. *Eating Our Hearts Out*. Freedom: Crossing P, 1993.

Newton, Sarah E. "'The Jell-O Syndrome': Investigating Popular Culture/Foodways." *Western Folklore* 51 (July 1992): 249–67.

New Ways to Gracious Living: Waring Blendor [sic] *Cook Book*. New York: Waring Products, 1957.

Nichols, Nell B. "Let the Automatic Refrigerator Help." *Woman's Home Companion* Dec. 1931: 66+.

———. "My Adventures with Electricity." *Woman's Home Companion* Oct. 1922: 50+.

Oliphant, Mrs. Nelson B. *A Dainty Cook Book*. New York: Abbey, 1902.

O'Malley, Suzanne. "Help! There's a Man in My Kitchen." *Cosmopolitan* Jan. 1992: 166–68.

"On Leave!" *American Home* Apr. 1942: 82–84.

Paine, Florence. "Good Eating on a Ration Card." *House Beautiful* Mar. 1943: 77+.

Palmer, Elisabeth G. "All Ready, Let's Go!" *Woman's Home Companion* Sept. 1935: 60–63.

"Pantry and Kitchen." *Countryside Magazine* Mar. 1916: 150.

Parry, Albert. *What Women Can Do to Win the War.* Chicago: Consolidated Book Publishers, 1942.

Patterson, Sterling. "Shall We Join the Ladies?" *Better Homes and Gardens* Oct. 1936: 107+.

Pattison, Mary. "Abolition of Household Slavery." *Annals of the American Academy of Political and Social Science* Mar. 1925: 124–27.

Patton, Patty. "Make Your Child Welcome in the Kitchen." *Parents' Magazine* Oct. 1956: 104–5.

Peet, Louise J., and Lenore E. Sater. *Household Equipment.* New York: John Wiley, 1934.

Penny, Prudence [pseud.]. *Coupon Cookery: A Guide to Good Meals under Wartime Conditions of Rationing and Food Shortages.* Hollywood: Murray and Gee, 1943.

Perkins, Frances. "Should Women Take Men's Jobs?" *Woman's Journal* Apr. 1930: 7+.

Peyser, Ethel R. "The Facts about Electric Ranges." *House and Garden* July 1921: 54+.

———. "The Passing of the Ice Man." *House and Garden* May 1921: 64+.

———. "Some Aspects of Electric Cookery." *House and Garden* June 1924: 82+.

Pfeiffer, Sarah Shields. "He Might Like Cooking!" *Parents' Magazine* Feb. 1946: 47.

Phillips, Amy Lyman. "Polly's Place—and How It Grew." *Woman's Home Companion* Jan. 1922: 30+.

Phillips, Velma, and Laura Howell. "Racial and Other Differences in Dietary Customs." *Journal of Home Economics* 41 (1920): 396–411.

Pidgeon, Mary Elizabeth. *Women' s Work and the War.* Chicago: Science Research Associates, 1943.

Pilcher, Jefferey M. *Que Vivan los Tamales! Food and the Making of Mexican Identity.* Albuquerque: U of New Mexico P, 1998.

Pillsbury, Richard. *No Foreign Food: The American Diet in Time and Place.* Boulder: Westview P, 1998.

Pillsbury Mills. *Ann Pillsbury's New Cook Book.* Greenwich: Fawcett Books, 1954.

Platt, June, and Sophie Kerr. *The Best I Ever Ate: A Practical Home Cook Book.* New York: Rinehart, 1953.

Plumley, Ladd. "Boys and Cookery." *American Cookery* Oct. 1917: 177–79.

Pollock, Eleanor. "Men Are Dopes as Cooks." *Good Housekeeping* Feb. 1949: 38+.

Powell, Imogene. "Down Goes the Meat Bill." *Better Homes and Gardens* Mar. 1936: 70+.

"Pre-Cooked Meals Raise Sales Hope." *New York Times* 3 Feb. 1954: L33.

"Prize-Winning Oriental Recipes." *Sunset* Apr. 1930: 62.

"Quaint Chinese Dishes." *Delineator* May 1920: 44.

Quayle, Eric. *Old Cook Books: An Illustrated History.* New York: Dutton, 1978.

Quilty, Glenn. *Food for Men: A Treasury of Hearty and Tasty Cookery.* New York: Sheridan House, 1954.

Rae, Barbara. *Cooking without Meat: A Supplementary Kitchen Guide for War-Time Cookery.* New York: M. S. Mill, 1943.

Rector, George. *Dine at Home with Rector: A Book on What Men Like, Why They Like It, and How to Cook It.* New York: Dutton, 1937.

Redman, Scott. *Real Men Don't Cook Quiche: The Real Man's Cookbook.* New York: Pocket Books, 1982.

Redmann, Gail R. "Electrifying Cleveland." *Timeline* 14.2 (Mar./Apr. 1997): 32–49.

Reichl, Ruth. *Tender at the Bone: Growing Up at the Table.* New York: Random House, 1998.

Rice, Louise. *Dainty Dishes from Foreign Lands.* Chicago: McClurg, 1911.

"Rich and Subtle Casseroles." *Sunset* Feb. 1953: 91.

Rider, Dorothy, and Betty Taylor. *The Teenage Cook Book.* Boston: Meador, 1958.

Ridley, Helen E., and Truman L. Henderson. "The New Electric Range Brings the Whole Family to the Kitchen." *Good Housekeeping* May 1938: 76+.

Riordan, Mrs. J. "Americans Getting Macaroni Appetite." *Macaroni Journal* 15 June 1928: 16.

Roberson, John, and Marie Roberson. *The Casserole Cook Book.* New York: Castle Books, 1952.

———. *Complete Small Appliance Cookbook.* New York: Wyn, 1953.

Robins, Elizabeth, and Octavia Wilberforce. *Prudence and Peter and Their Adventures with Pots and Pans.* New York: Morrow, 1928.

Rombauer, Irma S. *A Cookbook for Girls and Boys.* Indianapolis: Bobbs-Merrill, 1946.

———. *The Joy of Cooking: A Compilation of Reliable Recipes with a Casual Culinary Chat.* 1931. Indianapolis: Bobbs-Merrill, 1936.

Roosevelt, Mrs. Franklin D. *It's Up to the Women.* New York: Frederick A. Stokes, 1933.

Root, Waverley, and Richard de Rochemont. *Eating in America: A History.* New York: Morrow, 1976.

Rorer, Mrs. S. T. "Cakes and Candies Children Can Make." *Ladies' Home Journal* 15 Dec. 1910: 40.

Rorer, Sarah Tyson. *Dainty Dishes for All the Year Round: Recipes for Ice Creams, Water Ices, Sherbets and Other Frozen Desserts.* Philadelphia: North Brothers, 1898.

Rose, Dorothy E. "Junior Chefs." *Parents' Magazine* June 1951: 53+.

Rose, Mark H. *Cities of Light and Heat: Domesticating Gas and Electricity in Urban America*. University Park: Pennsylvania State UP, 1995.

Rosiere, Gabrielle. "Tea and Friends: Their Etiquette." *Good Housekeeping* June 1920: 78–79.

Ruark, Jennifer K. "A Place at the Table." *Chronicle of Higher Education* 9 July 1999: A17–A19.

Rudomin, Esther. *Let's Cook without Cooking*. New York: Crowell, 1955.

Rupp, Leila. *Mobilizing Women for War: German and American Propaganda, 1939–1945*. Princeton: Princeton UP, 1978.

Said, Edward W. *Orientalism*. New York: Pantheon Books, 1978.

Salvail, Rose Amiot. "From Foreign Lands." *Woman's Home Companion* Feb. 1936: 117.

Sargent and Company. *Gem Chopper Cook Book: Valuable Recipes for Substantial Dishes and Dainty Desserts*. New York: Sargent, 1902.

Scapp, Ron, and Brian Seitz, eds. *Eating Culture*. Albany: State U of New York P, 1998.

Schafer, Robert B., and Elisabeth Schafer. "Relationship between Gender and Food Roles in the Family." *Journal of Nutrition Education* 21.3 (1989): 119–26.

Scharf, Lois. *To Work and to Wed: Female Employment, Feminism, and the Great Depression*. Westport: Greenwood P, 1980.

Schauffler, Helen Powell. "The Five-Year-Old Cook." *Good Housekeeping* Dec. 1926: 78+.

———. "Oriental Cookery Makes for Economy." *Good Housekeeping* Jan. 1928: 72+.

Schloss, Ezekial. *Junior Jewish Cook Book*. New York: Ktav Publishing House, 1956.

Schofield, Mary Anne, ed. *Cooking by the Book: Food in Literature and Culture*. Bowling Green: Bowling Green State U Popular P, 1989.

Schremp, Gerry. *Kitchen Culture: Fifty Years of Food Fads*. New York: Pharos Books, 1991.

Schulz, Charles M. *Peanuts Cook Book*. New York: Scholastic Book Services, 1969.

Scott, Natalie V. *Your Mexican Kitchen: A Compilation of Mexican Recipes Practicable in the United States*. New York: Putnam's, 1935.

Scripture, Charlotte. "Saving Sugar in Making Pies." *Good Housekeeping* June 1942: 118+.

Sea Foam's Collection of Dainty Receipts. New York: Sea Foam Baking Powder Co., 1907.

Seder, Blanche. "A Modern Hostess Serves Simple Food with Variations." *Better Homes and Gardens* May 1933: 14+.

Sedgwick, Ursula. *My Learn-to-Cook Book*. New York: Golden P, 1967.

Seiter, Ellen. *Sold Separately: Children and Parents in Consumer Culture*. New Brunswick: Rutgers UP, 1993.

Servel Electric Refrigeration. Advertisement. *Good Housekeeping* Sept. 1926: 102.

The Seventeen Cookbook. New York: Macmillan, 1964.

Shallcross, Ruth. *Should Married Women Work?* New York: National Federation of Business and Professional Women's Clubs, 1940.

Shapiro, Laura. "Do Women Like to Cook?" *Granta* 52 (Winter 1995): 153–62.

———. *Perfection Salad: Women and Cooking at the Turn of the Century*. New York: Farrar, Straus, and Giroux, 1986.

Shay, Frank. *The Best Men Are Cooks*. New York: Coward-McCann, 1941.

"Shelf Magic for Short-Order Cooks." *Ladies' Home Journal* Mar. 1955: 146–48.

Sheridan, C. Mac, ed. *The Stag Cook Book, Written for Men, by Men*. New York: Doran, 1922.

Sherman, Maybel. "Digesting the Immigrant." *Sunset* Sept. 1924: 38–39.

Shortridge, Barbara G., and James R. Shortridge, eds. *The Taste of American Place: A Reader on Regional and Ethnic Foods*. Lanham: Rowman and Littlefield, 1998.

Shouer, Louella G. "Biscuits, Bonnets and Budgets." *Ladies' Home Journal* Apr. 1936: 42+.

———. "Casserole Collection." *Ladies' Home Journal* Apr. 1951: 226–28.

———. "Never Too Young to Bake." *Ladies' Home Journal* Oct. 1949: 204–5.

"Should I Take a Job When My Husband Has One Too?" *American Magazine* Feb. 1933: 134.

Silver, Roy R. "L.I. High School Boys Excel as Chefs: Cook Dinner as Culmination of Course." *New York Times* 25 May 1958: L57.

"Small-Fry Cooks." *Look* 26 Jan. 1954: 56–57.

"Smart Cook!" *Better Homes and Gardens* June 1952: 100–101.

Smith, Helen Treyz. "We Help You Plan Thrifty Meals." *Better Homes and Gardens* Oct. 1932: 16+.

Smith, William C. "Born American, But—." *Survey* 1 May 1926: 167–68.

Sokolov, Raymond. *Fading Feast: A Compendium of Disappearing American Regional Foods*. New York: Farrar, Straus, Giroux, 1981.

"Soup Seasons These Casseroles." *Sunset* Apr. 1954: 216.

Spring, Florence. "The Afternoon-Tea Sandwich." *Good Housekeeping* Jan. 1923: 64.

———. "Around the Tea-Tray." *Good Housekeeping* June 1917: 75+.

———. "When You Serve Five O'Clock Tea." *Good Housekeeping* June 1922: 66–67.

Stacey, Michelle. *Consumed: Why Americans Love, Hate, and Fear Food*. New York: Simon and Schuster, 1994.

Standish, Betsy. "Two Dainty February Festivals." *Delineator* Feb. 1915: 24.

STAR-Rite Reversible Electric Toaster. Advertisement. *Good Housekeeping* Apr. 1924: 301.

Stearns, Mabel. "My Electric Range." *Delineator* Nov. 1926: 30+.

Stegner, Mabel J. "Informal Meals." *Better Homes and Gardens* Feb. 1933: 22+.

Stein, Toby. *How to Appeal to a Man's Appetites.* New York: Stein and Day, 1962.

Stemple, Antonia J. "Eating in Other Lands Than Ours." *American Cookery* Nov. 1929: 278–81.

Stern, Michael, and Jane Stern. *American Gourmet.* New York: HarperCollins, 1991.

———. *Eat Your Way across the U.S.A.* New York: Broadway Books, 1997.

———. *Roadfood: The All-New, Updated, and Expanded Edition.* New York: Harper-Perennial, 1992.

———. *Square Meals.* New York: Knopf, 1984.

Stewart, Marion. *One Hundred Favorite Foreign Recipes.* Los Angeles: Saturday Night Pub. Co., 1933 [?].

Stewart, Martha. *Holidays: Recipes, Gifts and Decorations, Thanksgiving and Christmas.* New York: Clarkson Potter, 1993.

———. *Martha Stewart's Menus for Entertaining.* New York: Clarkson Potter, 1994.

Stiers, Louise. "Dump-In Casserole." *Farm Journal* June 1958: 80.

Stohr, Edalene, et al. "120 Ways You Can Put Glamour into Just Plain Food." *Woman's Home Companion* Mar. 1956: 92+.

Stokely's Finest Foods. Advertisement. *Good Housekeeping* May 1943: 126.

Stover, Blanche. "Canned Foods for Better Family Meals." *Parents' Magazine* Feb. 1955: 51–54.

Strasser, Susan. *Never Done: A History of American Housework.* New York: Pantheon Books, 1982.

"Stretching the Meat Dollar." *Delineator* Mar. 1935: 22+.

Sunset Magazine. Cooking with Casseroles. Menlo Park: Lane, 1958.

"Susan Serves Canned Vegetables." *Good Housekeeping* Jan. 1950: 128+.

Sutherland, Daniel. *Americans and Their Servants: Domestic Service in the United States from 1800 to 1920.* Baton Rouge: Louisiana State UP, 1981.

Swann, Ada Bessie. "Electrical Aids to Good Cooking." *Pictorial Review* July 1932: 30.

Symons, Michael. *One Continuous Picnic: A History of Eating in Australia.* Adelaide, Australia: Duck P, 1982.

"Take a Can of Luncheon Meat." *American Home* July 1952: 58+.

"Take-It-Easy Meals with Electric Helpers." *Better Homes and Gardens* Aug. 1954: 72+.

Tannahill, Reay. *Food in History.* 1973. New York: Crown Publishers, 1988.

"Tasty Casserole Bargains." *Better Homes and Gardens* Oct. 1952: 84+.

Taylor, Demetria M. *Ration Cook Book*. New York: Reklam, 1943.

———. "There's a Man in My Kitchen." *Ladies' Home Journal* Oct. 1957: 96–97.

———. "Why Not Buy the Cheaper Cuts of Meat?" *Good Housekeeping* Mar. 1930: 90+.

———. "Your Electric Beater." *Good Housekeeping* May 1933: 88+.

Thorson, James A. *Tough Guys Don't Dice: A Cookbook for Men Who Can't Cook*. New York: Morrow, 1989.

Thrifty Jell-O Recipes to Brighten Your Menus. Le Roy: Jell-O Company, 1931.

Through the Menu with Jell-O. Le Roy: Jell-O Company, 1927.

Tibbens, Paul K. *Cookin' for the Helluvit*. Tulsa: Vickers, 1950.

Tidwell, Mildred O. "Dining at the End of the Trail." *Better Homes and Gardens* Oct. 1940: 44+.

Tipton, Edna Sibley. "Gay Flower Garnishes and Food Fancies." *Pictorial Review* Aug. 1925: 41.

———. "When Men Entertain." *Better Homes and Gardens* Mar. 1931: 25+.

Toastmaster. Advertisement. *Good Housekeeping* Dec. 1931: 227.

"A Toast to the Toaster." *Electrical Merchandising* Sept. 1923: n.p.

Today's Woman Cook Book. New York: Arco, 1953.

Today's Woman Cookie Cook Book. Greenwich: Fawcett, 1952.

"Topics of the Times." *New York Times* 30 Oct. 1952: L30.

Towne, June. "Take a Package of Marshmallows." *American Home* Sept. 1956: 88+.

Tracy, Marian. *Casserole Cookery Complete*. New York: Viking, 1956.

———. *More Casserole Cookery*. New York: Viking, 1951.

"Treat Yourself to Mixes and Pre-Prepared Foods." *Parents' Magazine* Oct. 1955: 62+.

Trillin, Calvin. *Alice, Let's Eat: Further Adventures of a Happy Eater*. New York: Vintage Books, 1979.

———. *American Fried: Adventures of a Happy Eater*. New York: Vintage Books, 1979.

———. *Third Helpings*. New Haven: Ticknor and Fields, 1983.

Trueblood, Ted. "Man Dishes." *Field and Stream* Aug. 1961: 12+.

Turnbull, Ray W. "Teaching the Housewife to Cook Electrically." *Journal of Electricity and Western Industry* 1 Mar. 1923: 171–74.

Universal Appliances. Advertisement. *Good Housekeeping* Oct. 1944: 141.

Utting, Florence A. "Four Mexican Recipes." *Sunset* Jan. 1922: 64–65.

Van Arsdale, May B. *Tested International Recipes*. New York: Teachers College, 1917.

Veblen, Thorstein. *The Theory of the Leisure Class*. 1899. Boston: Houghton Mifflin, 1973.

Villas, James. *American Taste: A Celebration of Gastronomy Coast-to-Coast.* New York: Arbor House, 1982.

———. *Villas at Table: A Passion for Food and Drink.* New York: Harper and Row, 1988.

Voellmig, Gertrude. *Wartime Cooking Guide: Stretching the Points.* Chicago: Reilly and Lee, 1943.

Walker, Anne. "Three of Us and—Electricity." *Woman's Home Companion* Dec. 1919: 76.

Wallace, Lily. *The American Family Cook Book.* New York: Books Inc., 1950.

Wandersee, Winifred D. *Women's Work and Family Values, 1920–1940.* Cambridge: Harvard UP, 1981.

Ware, Caroline F. *The Consumer Goes to War: A Guide to Victory on the Home Front.* New York: Funk and Wagnalls, 1942.

Ware, Susan. *Holding Their Own: American Women in the 1930s.* Boston: Twayne, 1982.

Wason, Betty. *Cooks, Gluttons, and Gourmets: A History of Cookery.* Garden City: Doubleday, 1962.

Watson, Jane Werner. *Susie's New Stove: The Little Chef's Cookbook.* New York: Simon and Schuster, 1950.

"The Way to Market in Wartime." *Woman's Home Companion* July 1942: 66–67.

Weatherford, Doris. *American Women and World War II.* New York: Facts on File, 1990.

———. *Foreign and Female: Immigrant Women in America: 1840–1930.* New York: Schocken, 1986.

Weaver, Louise Bennett, and Helen Cowles LeCron. *A Thousand Ways to Please a Husband with Bettina's Best Recipes: The Romance of Cookery and Housekeeping.* New York: Burt, 1917.

Wechsberg, Joseph. "Male Cooks: The Best and the Worst." *New York Times Magazine* 27 Dec. 1959: 17–18.

Wells, Eleanor F. *Nationality Recipes.* Providence: YWCA, 1935.

West, Elliott, and Paula Petrik, eds. *Small World: Children and Adolescents in America, 1850–1950.* Lawrence: UP of Kansas, 1992.

West, Michael Lee. *Consuming Passions: A Food-Obsessed Life.* New York: Harper-Collins, 1999.

Westin, Jeane. *Making Do: How Women Survived the '30s.* Chicago: Follett Publishing, 1976.

Westinghouse Appliances. Advertisement. *Good Housekeeping* July 1944: 80.

Westinghouse Electric Range. Advertisement. *Good Housekeeping* Mar. 1924: 130.

Westinghouse Streamline Refrigerators. Advertisement. *Electrical Merchandising* Mar 1935: 41.

Wheaton, Barbara. "Finding Real Life in Cookbooks: The Adventures of a Culinary Historian." In *Food, Cookery and Culture*, ed. Leslie Howsam, 1–11. Windsor: Humanities Research Group, University of Windsor, 1998.

Whelan, Jean MacGregor. "Soup in the Can Is Sauce for the Casserole." *Parents' Magazine* Mar. 1951: 64–65.

Whitehorne, Earl E. "Should We Cook Electrically Now?" *House Beautiful* Aug. 1921: 128+.

Whiteman, Elizabeth Fuller. *Wartime Fish Cookery*. Washington, D.C.: U.S. Department of the Interior, Fish and Wildlife Service, 1943.

Whitmore, Lois. *Career Girls' Cook Book*. Chicago: Dartnell, 1955.

Whitson, Helen Morse. "Table Stove Cookery." *Good Housekeeping* Mar. 1923: 74.

Whitton, Mary Ormsbee. "The Mechanics of Living Beautifully." *House Beautiful* Mar. 1920: 208+.

———. "Running Your House on Greased Wheels." *Woman's Home Companion* June 1925: 136+.

"Why Can't a Woman Cook Like a Man?" *American Home* Mar. 1958: 58–60.

"Why Don't You Cook Dinner?" *Sunset* Feb. 1956: 131+.

"Why Not Beans-Rice-Macaroni Sometimes in Place of Meat and Potatoes Everyday?" *Delineator* Mar. 1929: 43.

Wiggin, Kate Douglas. "A Little Talk to Girls on Cookery." *Good Housekeeping* May 1912: 689–92.

Wiley-Kleemann, Pauline, ed. *Ramona's Spanish-Mexican Cookery: The First Complete and Authentic Spanish-Mexican Cook Book in English*. Los Angeles: West Coast Publishing, 1929.

Willard, Harriet J. *Familiar Lessons for Little Girls: A First Book of the Art of Cookery*. Chicago: Sherwood, 1886.

Williams, Peter W. "Foodways." In *Encyclopedia of American Social History*, ed. Mary Kupiec Cayton, Elliott J. Gorn, and Peter W. Williams, 1331–44. New York: Scribner, 1993.

Williams, Susan. *Savory Suppers and Fashionable Feasts: Dining in Victorian America*. New York: Pantheon, 1985.

Williams-Heller, Ann. *The Busy Woman's Cook Book*. New York: Stephen Daye P, 1951.

Williamson, Cici, and John A. Kelly. *For Men Only: Mastering the Microwave*. Woodbury: Barron's, 1986.

Willig, John. "Outdoor Cookery: The Inside Story." *New York Times* 16 Aug. 1959: sec. VI, 42+.

Willson, Inez Searles. "Sandwiches That Are Confections." *Ladies' Home Journal* May 1927: 173.

Winn, Freda. "When America Eats Macaroni." *Delineator* Feb. 1925: 62.

Winn-Smith, Alice B. *Thrifty Cooking for Wartime*. New York: Macmillan, 1942.

"With a Little Blender Magic." *Sunset* Apr. 1959: 178+.

Witt, Doris. *Black Hunger: Food and the Politics of U.S. Identity*. New York: Oxford UP, 1999.

Wong, Nellie Choy. "As We Cook in China." *Good Housekeeping* May 1930: 85+.

Wood, Bertha M. *Foods of the Foreign-Born in Relation to Health*. Boston: Whitcomb and Barrows, 1922.

Wood, Elizabeth. "Casseroles for Casual Suppers." *Better Homes and Gardens* Nov. 1958: 76+.

Wood, Leonard. "Who's Buying the Cookbooks?" *Publishers Weekly* 26 Aug. 1988: 29.

Wood, Nancy Crawford. "Papa Does the Cooking." *Ladies' Home Journal* Feb. 1956: 166–67.

Woolf, Virginia. *A Room of One's Own*. 1929. New York: Harcourt Brace, 1957.

"Working Wives." *Woman's Home Companion* Oct. 1939: 1.

Wright, Mary M. *Dainty Desserts: A Large Collection of Recipes for Delicious Sweets and Dainties*. Philadelphia: Penn Publishing, 1922.

Wyman, Carolyn. *I'm a Spam® Fan: America's Best-Loved Foods*. Stamford: Longmeadow P, 1993.

Yarwood, Doreen. *Five Hundred Years of Technology in the Home*. London: Batsford, 1983.

"You and Your Automatic Refrigerator." *Delineator* July 1929: 36+.

Young, Hazel. *Better Meals for Less Money*. Boston: Little, Brown, 1940.

Young America's Cook Book: A Cook Book for Boys and Girls Who Like Good Food. New York: Scribner, 1938.

Youngstown Kitchens. Advertisement. *Parents' Magazine* Dec. 1943: 50.

Youngstown Pressed Steel. Advertisement. *Good Housekeeping* Aug. 1943: 15.

Your Electric Refrigerator and Knox Sparkling Gelatin. Johnstown: Charles B. Knox Gelatin, 1929.

"Your Obedient Servant." *Sunset* Jan. 1926: 76.

Zillissen, Clara H. "Electricity in the Home." *House Beautiful* Aug. 1919: 102+.

Index